Sexual Pleasure

This book is dedicated to my clients.

Ordering

Trade bookstores in the U.S. and Canada please contact:

Publishers Group West
1700 Fourth Street, Berkeley CA 94710
Phone: (800) 788-3123   Fax: (510) 528-3444

Hunter House books are available at bulk discounts for textbook course adoptions; to qualifying community, health-care, and government organizations; and for special promotions and fund-raising. For details please contact:

Special Sales Department
Hunter House Inc., PO Box 2914, Alameda CA 94501-0914
Phone: (510) 865-5282   Fax: (510) 865-4295
E-mail: sales@hunterhouse.com

Individuals can order our books from most bookstores, by calling **(800) 266-5592,** or from our website at **www.hunterhouse.com**

Sexual
Pleasure

Reaching New Heights of
Sexual Arousal and Intimacy

second edition

Barbara Keesling, Ph.D.

Hunter House PUBLISHERS

Hunter House Inc., Publishers
PO Box 2914
Alameda CA 94501-0914

Library of Congress Cataloging-in-Publication Data
Keesling, Barbara.
     Sexual pleasure : reaching new heights of sexual arousal and intimacy /
     Barbara Keesling.— 2nd ed.
          p. cm.
     Includes bibliographical references and index.
     ISBN 0-89793-435-0
          1. Sex instruction. 2. Sex (Psychology) I. Title.
     HQ31.K393 2004
     613.9'6—dc22   2004015225

Project Credits
Cover Design and Book Production: Brian Dittmar Graphic Design
Illustrator: Eric Venuto, Berkeley
Copy Editor: Kelley Blewster
Proofreader: John David Marion
Indexers: Robert and Cynthia Swanson
Acquisitions Editor: Jeanne Brondino
Editor: Alexandra Mummery
Publishing Assistant: Antonia T. Lee
Publicist: Jillian Steinberger
Foreign Rights Coordinator: Elisabeth Wohofsky
Customer Service Manager: Christina Sverdrup
Order Fulfillment: Washul Lakdhon
Administrator: Theresa Nelson
Computer Support: Peter Eichelberger
Publisher: Kiran S. Rana

Printed and Bound by Bang Printing, Brainerd, Minnesota

Manufactured in the United States of America

9 8 7 6 5 4 3 2 1   Second Edition   05 06 07 08 09

Contents

List of Exercises
by Chapter

Chapter 9: **Making the Pleasure Last and Last**

Chapter 10: **Getting Better and Better (Erections)**

Acknowledgments

Thanks to all the people at Hunter House who were involved in bringing this edition to publication, including publisher Kiran Rana, acquisitions editor Jeanne Brondino, editors Alex Mummery and Kelley Blewster, and publicist Jillian Steinberger.

Important Note

The material in this book is intended to provide a review of information regarding how to enhance sexual and sensual pleasure. Every effort has been made to provide accurate and dependable information. The contents of the book have been compiled through professional research and in consultation with medical professionals and professional sex therapists. The sensuality advice given in this book should pose no risk to any healthy person. However, if you have any sexually transmitted disease, we recommend consulting with your doctor before using this book.

The publisher, authors, and editors, as well as the professionals quoted in the book, cannot be held responsible for any error, omission, or dated material in the book. The authors and publisher assume no responsibility for any outcome of applying the information in this book. If you have questions concerning the application of the information described in this book, consult a qualified professional.

Introduction

by Paul Dahlquist

*P*eople *seek pleasure. That's just the way we are; it's a fact of human existence. And one of the main ways we get pleasure is through our sexual interactions with other people.*

From an evolutionary standpoint, the primary reason for us humans to have sexual intercourse has been to reproduce so our species could survive. But evolutionary psychologists now believe that people would not reproduce unless it felt good to do so. So, in a sense, sexual pleasure is a primary motive for having sex, one that supercedes even the motive to reproduce. (In fact, studies suggest that sex wouldn't even have to feel as good as it does. People would still do it even if it only felt "pretty good.")

I've taught human sexuality at a major Southern California university for many years. None of the three main textbooks I've used has included the word *pleasure* in the index. If pleasure is the primary motive for having sex, why isn't the topic being addressed?

Sexual pleasure requires two things: stimulation of our erogenous zones and our interpretation of that stimulation. Some writers divide sexual pleasure into two types, fore-pleasure and orgasmic pleasure. I believe that sexual pleasure has eight foundations: relaxation, touch, self-awareness, desire, arousal, orgasm, intimacy, and mutuality. You'll find all of these addressed in this book. And, in addition to being a noun describing what we feel during sex, *pleasure* is a verb. By participating in the exercises presented in this book, you and your partner will learn to pleasure yourselves and pleasure each other.

The first edition of *Sexual Pleasure* was published in 1993 and has been one of my best-selling books over the years. I've revised it now because there is a lot of new information about sexual pleasure, and over the years my perspective on important issues like desire and female sexuality has changed and evolved. So, this second edition contains much new material. The basic progression of the book is the same as before: First, you will learn important information about your body, especially your sexual anatomy. Then we will move to basic exercises that introduce sensate-focus techniques, done alone and with a partner. Finally, you will learn more advanced exercises that will help you to increase desire, arousal, and pleasure.

Here is a chapter-by-chapter breakdown of how the new edition is laid out. In Chapter 1, you'll learn how to relax and set the stage for pleasure. Chapter 2 will teach you all about the sensate-focus process and techniques. This is a special way of touching—and of concentrating on the touch—that is basic to almost all of the techniques in the book. In Chapter 3, I describe the male and female sexual-pleasure cycles, which progress from desire to arousal to orgasm. What I've basically done in this chapter is to take William Masters and Virginia Johnson's groundbreaking work on sexual response and add to it so that it's more current and user-friendly.

From here we move into a more active phase. Chapter 4 includes basic solo exercises that will help you learn about your own sexual-pleasure cycle. Chapter 5 is an interlude in which I discuss what we know about sexual desire. Chapter 6 introduces you to basic sensate-focus exercises you can do with your partner. Chapters 7 and 8 are completely new and describe the sensate-focus approach to oral sex and intercourse—and how to get the maximum pleasure from both.

Next comes a series of chapters that are addressed more specifically to women *or* to men, though readers of both sexes will benefit from reading all five chapters. Chapters 9 and 10 are for men who would like to last longer during intercourse and who would like to improve their erections. Chapters 11 and 12 deal with female arousal and orgasm. There's a lot of in-depth information here, especially on female orgasm. Chapter 13 is for men who would like to improve their orgasms and ejaculations. There's a reason why I arranged these five chapters in this order. As a sex therapist,

I've found that the better a man functions sexually—that is, the better he can control his ejaculation and maintain an erection—the more likely it is that his female partner will be orgasmic. Note that the exercises in Chapters 9 through 13 rely largely on two processes, called *peaking* and *plateauing*. Peaking and plateauing allow you to modulate your arousal so that you can experience maximum sexual pleasure.

The closing chapters are about broader issues of relationships. Chapter 14 includes many exercises for strengthening the intimacy or emotional bond between you and your partner. Chapter 15 is a newly added chapter on love. You may be a little puzzled that I have placed the chapters on intimacy and love last. Shouldn't we try to become more intimate before we engage in sexual exercises? My experience with clients has shown that the opposite works better: Learning about your own body, learning basic exercises, and increasing desire and arousal provide the foundation for the mutuality and intimacy skills that the last two chapters will help you to develop.

Who Can Use This Book?

By learning the techniques and approaches given in this book, people of any age or experience level can get more out of sex than they currently do. With a little practice and a loving partner, the exercises described in *Sexual Pleasure* will help anyone increase their sexual desire, deepen their arousal, strengthen their orgasm, and enhance intimacy in their relationship.

While I have written this book with heterosexual couples in mind, most of the exercises can be used—in some cases with slight modifications—by same-sex couples, since the sensate-focus process is enriching for everybody. You can even start this program if you have no sexual experience at all. The exercises are not strenuous and can also be adapted for use by people who have physical limitations due to illness or age. If you have arthritis or knee problems, it may help to do the intercourse exercises in a side-to-side position rather than with one partner on top. If you have a heart condition, please check with your doctor before starting on this or any program of increased physical activity. For more information on how to keep having great sex as you get older, consult my book on the subject, *Making Love Better Than Ever: Reaching New Heights of Pleasure and Passion After 40.*

If you are a survivor of sexual abuse, male or female, you may find that reading this book brings back many painful memories. If you still want to work with this material, consider working through it with a therapist's guidance. Experiencing these exercises with a loving, supportive partner can bring real healing, but doing so will take time and will require you to develop enough trust so that you feel safe with your lover.

Whether or not you are an abuse survivor, you need to be aware that the intimate touch prescribed in these exercises will stir emotions. Sharing profound sensual and sexual pleasure awakens deeper aspects of ourselves. This can be wonderful and empowering, but if the intimate work raises issues that become too challenging for you, please stop the exercises and seek the help of a professional counselor.

Because of the emotional impact of these exercises, I recommend them most for couples who are willing to develop the patience, commitment, honesty, and openness that are the foundations of a strong relationship. Changing the way you make love can change you and your relationship. It is important for each partner to be aware of this.

How to Use This Book

First, read all the way through the book, reading the first few exercises fully and skimming the others, so you understand the nonperformance philosophy behind the exercises and get a feel for them. Then you and your partner can separately start doing the exercises in Chapter 4, "Self-Pleasure: Learning the Ways of Your Body." You can also do these exercises if you do not have a current sexual partner. Once you have a good feeling for the self-pleasuring exercises, start the basic partner exercises described in Chapter 6, "Partner Caresses That Kindle Desire."

Next, choose a progression of exercises you and your partner would like, based on your particular sexual interests. As a general sequence, I would suggest going through Chapter 9 on lasting longer for men and then Chapters 11 and 12 on arousal and orgasm for women. After these, you may wish to do the exercises in Chapter 10 on erection and Chapter 13 on male orgasm, and finally the exercises in Chapter 14 that build mutuality and intimacy. As mentioned above, in my experience this progression works best because couples often find it easier to do the female arousal exercises if the man has already developed a good level of ejaculation control.

Alternatively, you may have or could identify a goal, such as developing fuller, larger erections. After you understand the arousal process as described in Chapter 3, and after you do the self-exercises in Chapter 4 and the basic partner exercises in Chapter 6, you can target the exercises in the other chapters that address this goal.

You can repeat the exercises as many times as you like. Set aside about half an hour for a session of the self-exercises and about an hour to do a partner exercise. If you only plan to do each exercise once, you will learn most effectively if you schedule practice sessions one to three times a week. If you do the exercises irregularly, you will forget what you have learned. On the other hand, if you try to do them more than three times a week, you may get burned out.

If you do these exercises one to three times a week, you will certainly see a change in your sexual pleasure within a month. Most of the changes are gradual, so look for improvement after you do two or three exercises instead of after each one.

A Personal Note

The approach I advocate in *Sexual Pleasure* is the culmination of many years of study and clinical work. I have been a professional in the field of sex therapy since 1980, and I have a doctorate in health psychology from the University of California. Health psychologists study the relationship between physical health and mental health, or mind and body, if you will. Consequently, I take a mind-body approach to human sexuality.

Since receiving my doctorate, I have taught human sexuality at several universities. I have taught techniques similar to the ones described in this book to students who wish to become marriage and family counselors. I have also practiced as a sexual surrogate partner and a sex therapist. I know that the techniques described in this book work, because I have taught them to hundreds of clients and seen the effect.

It was out of this experience that I wrote my first book, *Sexual Healing: A Self-Help Program to Enhance Your Sensuality and Overcome Common Sexual Problems*. It was for people with specific sexual difficulties. *Sexual Pleasure* naturally followed. The sensate-focus approach and specific techniques outlined in the book can add richness to anyone's sex life, even if your sex life is already fulfilling. I'm really pleased to have had the opportunity to revise this book. Some exciting research on sexuality has taken place recently, especially in the areas of male erection and female desire, arousal, and orgasm.

I am pleased to share all of these techniques with you. I know that they can work for you and your lover. May the pleasure you take in each other deepen in the months and years ahead.

chapter 1

Relax—and Heighten Your Pleasure Response

by Paul Dahlquist

*R*elaxation is the first foundation of sexual pleasure. To learn
how to relax—or to activate what is often called the relaxation
response—you need to know a little bit about the nervous system.
I'll try not to make my explanation too technical, but bear with me;
this is important information.

The nervous system is the system in your body that allows all of the other
systems to communicate with each other. The nervous system has two
major divisions—the central nervous system and the peripheral nervous

system (see Figure 1 below). The *central nervous system* is composed of the brain and spinal cord. The *peripheral nervous system* includes all of the nerves that go from your spinal cord to your limbs and internal organs. The nerves in the sex organs and the nerves that travel from the spinal cord to the sex organs are part of the peripheral nervous system.

The peripheral nervous system has two divisions—the skeletal nervous system and the autonomic nervous system. (I've lost you, haven't I? I just saw your eyes glaze over.) The *skeletal nervous system* provides nerves to limbs like your arms and legs that you can control voluntarily. The *autonomic nervous system* provides nerves to internal organs like the diaphragm, heart, and intestines, which we don't normally think of as being under our voluntary control.

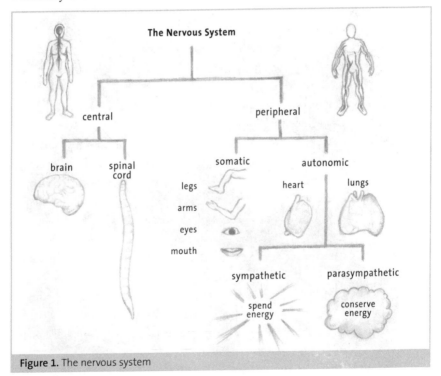

Figure 1. The nervous system

Still with me? The autonomic nervous system has two divisions—the sympathetic nervous system and the parasympathetic nervous system. The *sympathetic nervous system* is responsible for expending energy, and the *parasympathetic nervous system* is responsible for conserving energy. If you are faced with some immediate danger, the sympathetic nervous system springs into action and helps your body mobilize the energy you need to either fight or run away. When this happens, your eyes dilate, your heart rate speeds up, and your breathing and blood pressure increase dramatically. Another important effect is that blood flows immediately to your limbs. This complex response developed through evolution because certain parts of your body needed extra resources to deal with the danger. The sympathetic nervous system is activated very rapidly. It only takes seconds for the blood to flow away from the center of your body and out to your arms and legs.

If you think about the direction of the blood flow during this "fight or flight" response, it should become clear how anxiety can interfere with your sexual response. Essentially, when you are anxious, blood flows away from the center of your body, meaning it flows away from the genitals. For arousal, blood needs to flow into the genitals and other erogenous zones. So the quick-response sympathetic system is useful if you are in some kind of real danger. But for those times that are full of stress but not much real danger, most of our sympathetic nervous systems are a little too active. As a result, many of us experience that sympathetic nervous system adrenalin surge when we have to take a test, speak in public, or even have sex!

The parasympathetic nervous system, the other branch of the auto-nomic nervous system, is responsible for slowing your body down so that you can conserve energy for use at a later time. This system is active when your body is taking care of its life-sustaining processes like diges-tion. When the parasympathetic nervous system is "on," you feel deeply relaxed. The beginning stages of sexual arousal are a function of the parasympathetic nervous system. To put it simply, it's easier to start becoming aroused and feeling pleasure if you are in a relaxed state, which enhances the activity of the parasympathetic nervous system.

Although the sympathetic nervous system response happens almost instantaneously, the relaxation response is rather slow. These two systems do not normally operate simultaneously, except during orgasm. As we know, we cannot feel anxious and relaxed at the same time.

Because of how these two parts of the nervous system function, it is impossible to turn off the sympathetic nervous system by *trying* to turn it off. If you try to turn it off, you will become more anxious rather than less anxious. The only way to turn off the anxiety is to consciously activate the parasympathetic, or relaxation, system. The sensate-focus exercises that you will learn in this book will provide you with one way of doing this.

Activating Your Relaxation Response

With practice, you can learn to consciously activate your relaxation response within about five minutes. One great way to do this is to close your eyes, lie quietly without moving, and take several slow, deep breaths. Realize that it may take several minutes of doing this for your whole body to relax.

This deeply relaxed state has been described very well by Dr. Herbert Benson in his book *The Relaxation Response*. According to Dr. Benson, there are four things necessary to reach a relaxed state:

1. A quiet environment

2. A mental device (like a favorite prayer or phrase you repeat to yourself again and again, or a number you focus on)

3. A comfortable physical position

4. A receptive or passive attitude

I would like to add a fifth item to Dr. Benson's list: a predictable activity.

The sensate-focus exercises that you will learn in this book satisfy each of these conditions. You always do them in a quiet room. Focusing on your sensations and on the exact point of skin contact provides the mental device to keep your mind occupied, so that you are less likely to get caught up in anxious thoughts. As you do the exercises, you and your partner will take the steps needed to make yourselves physically comfortable. You will each take turns being passive during the exercises, during which time your only concern is to focus on sensations. Finally, if you do each exercise as described, you will know exactly what is going to happen (the predictable activity), which will further relax you.

The Brain, Relaxation, and Arousal

Your mind functions differently when you are relaxed than it does when you are anxious. Your brain constantly produces mild electrical activity, usually called *brain waves*. When you are in a state of alert wakefulness, your brain produces fast waves called *beta waves*. Waves characteristic of a more relaxed state are slower and are called *alpha waves*. The best way to induce alpha waves is to lie down, close your eyes, relax all of your muscles, slow your breathing, and let your mind drift without focusing on anything in particular.

During some of the exercises described in this book, you may find that you relax so much that you actually reach a very advanced state of relaxation called an *alpha state*. In this state you may feel as if you are floating or drifting. It is a wonderful feeling, but you do not need to be in this deeply relaxed state to do the exercises.

When you begin any exercise, you may relax right into an alpha state. At this phase the parasympathetic nervous system is activated. Then, if the exercise includes genital contact, chances are you will start to become aroused. As you reach higher and higher levels of arousal, the sympathetic nervous system starts to come into play, and more and more blood flows to your genitals and more and more tension accumulates in your muscles, especially in the pelvic area. At the point of orgasm, the sympathetic nervous system is fully activated, and all that energy that has accumulated in your pelvis is discharged. Other body changes at that point include heavy breathing and elevated heart-rate and blood-pressure levels, resulting in an intense feeling of release.

Sexual activity is one of the very few experiences a person can have in which the sympathetic nervous system and the parasympathetic nervous system work together. Sexual arousal and orgasm depend on a delicate interplay and balance between these two systems. But none of it will work unless you start out in a relaxed state. That is why so many of the exercises in this book emphasize the importance of relaxation.

There is another change that takes place in your body when you reach extremely high levels of sexual arousal and stay there for a while. The combination of controlled intense physical activity, heavy breathing, and sexual arousal produces the release of *endorphins* in the brain. You may have heard of endorphins in the context of sports like marathon running. They are produced during intense physical activity and can dull or even eliminate pain. The receptor sites in our brain that endorphins "latch on to" are the same sites that interact with opioid drugs such as heroin and others. That's why these drugs induce the feelings and euphoria they do. Endorphins are also responsible for the sensations of pleasure we experience when we are sexually aroused. In fact, the endorphin release during extreme sexual arousal and orgasm can bring about such intense feelings of pleasure that you may experience an altered or even a transcendent state of consciousness.

Relaxation and Touching

Certain types of touch activate the parasympathetic nervous system, and other types of touch activate the sympathetic nervous system. The type of touching you will learn to do in the sensate-focus exercises described in this book activates the parasympathetic nervous system—your relaxation response.

In the beginning stages, sensate-focus touching is slow, light, and soothing. It starts on the arms and legs and moves to the genitals. Touching or being touched in this caressing style will activate the relaxation response for you and your partner. As you become more aroused during some of the advanced sensate-focus exercises, it is okay to touch your partner more deeply.

On the other hand, being touched in a threatening, unpredictable, mechanical, or heavy way makes us anxious. Being touched in an intimate body area also makes us anxious if the touch is sudden or inappropriate. When you do the exercises in this book, take care to touch your partner in a way that will trigger relaxation rather than anxiety. If you are passive during an exercise and your partner's touch is so heavy that it triggers anxiety, tell your partner.

Anxious Thoughts

Your thoughts can also activate either the sympathetic nervous system or the parasympathetic nervous system. Fearful or worried thoughts are the mental component of anxiety, whereas slowing down your thoughts contributes to relaxation. There are several thought patterns that can contribute to anxiety during sex and thus short-circuit the relaxation response and your sexual pleasure. The most common of these thought patterns are spectatoring, racing thoughts, and performance thoughts.

Spectatoring is a term coined by Masters and Johnson. It refers to a habit of mentally watching yourself and evaluating or grading your performance during sexual activity. A person who is spectatoring is constantly monitoring and making mental notes about sexual arousal instead of experiencing sexual arousal. For example, a man might find himself thinking, "She's touching my penis. It's starting to feel a little hard. What if she—

oh, no, I'm losing my erection." Spectatoring often takes on an obsessive quality; that is, a person feels compelled to consciously monitor what is going on.

As you do the sensate-focus exercises, you will learn to focus on and *feel* what is happening sensually and sexually instead of worrying about it. You'll become more accustomed to *experiencing* what is happening instead of thinking about it. Gradually, spectatoring will cease to occur.

If you have *racing thoughts,* it means your mind is working very fast and jumping from thought to thought rather than staying on any one topic or idea. Many people have this tendency, but I see it most frequently in highly intelligent people who have cultivated the ability to switch quickly from topic to topic. Although this ability is advantageous in the work arena, it can get in the way of enjoying sex.

Fortunately, this is one of the easiest types of anxiety-related thoughts to deal with. As you start to do some of the caressing exercises described in this book, the pace at which you do the caress will actually slow your thoughts down. And when you are the passive partner in an exercise and are most susceptible to racing thoughts, your partner's slow touch will set the speed for your thoughts.

Performance thoughts, in which you think of sex as an achievement or as a performance, can also interfere with your sexual pleasure. Have you ever caught yourself thinking, "Darn, I was unable to perform," or, "Great—I achieved an orgasm"? Thinking of sex in these terms keeps you in your head rather than in your body. You become so focused on orgasm as a goal that you hardly pay attention to the sensuous feelings throughout your body and you lose track of pleasure.

Probably the most damaging type of anxious thoughts are the performance fears that lead to what sex therapists call "performance anxiety." These are thoughts that cause you to worry that someone is watching you or that something other than pleasure depends on the outcome of a sexual encounter. I have worked with people whose entire self-esteem was based on their sexual performance. If an encounter was not perfect, they were devastated. Others depended on sexual performance to build an image as a good lover or to keep a marriage together. You can imagine how much tension this can add to sex.

Performance thoughts also occur when you start to wonder if your partner is enjoying himself or herself, or wonder what he or she is thinking. Other typical performance thoughts include "Is he watching me?" "Am

I doing a good job?" "Why don't I have an erection yet?" "Why isn't she coming?" or "Was his previous lover better than I am?"

These kinds of thoughts have the power to shut down pleasure. Many sex therapists believe that performance anxiety is either directly or indirectly responsible for the majority of sexual problems.

If sex has been a work or performance activity all your life, do not expect to change those feelings overnight. It will take some practice to view sex as a pleasure activity rather than a situation in which you have to achieve. But try to remember that sex is for your pleasure. The rules that apply in achievement situations—"If I try hard, I will succeed," or, "If I move faster, I will succeed"—do not apply here. In fact, they're usually counterproductive.

To enjoy the exercises in this book, you need to go as slowly as you can. You need to stop "trying." *Working at* an exercise instead of *experiencing* it won't allow you to enjoy the exercise.

If you do the exercises regularly, you will find that they actually help you decrease your performance-oriented thoughts. They do this by teaching you how to focus on your own enjoyment before you have any activity with a partner. They also do this by having you focus on your sensations, which occupies your mind and forces out those intrusive thoughts. They also do this by showing you how to interpret your partner's responses so that you have no questions or doubts about your partner's enjoyment.

But What If the Pressure Is Real?

Not all causes of anxiety and performance pressure are "in your head." What if the reason you are feeling performance pressure is because the pressure is really there? What if your partner really is putting pressure on you, rather than you putting it on yourself?

People can pressure each other sexually in both subtle and not-so-subtle ways, not all of which are verbal. Verbal pressure is usually very easy to recognize. It can take the form of questions such as, "Do you have an erection yet?" or, "Are you going to come pretty soon?" or even, "Did you come?"

Nonverbal pressure is more subtle. Your sexual partner cannot read your mind. However, he or she can most likely tell if you are thinking about something else or wishing you were somewhere else. A facial expression or even a sigh can convey that you are bored with an activity or that you are somehow disappointed in your own response or your partner's response.

How can you deal with this situation? If the problem during a sexual encounter has been that you aren't feeling much sexual pleasure because you feel pressured to perform, and if you are giving and receiving nonverbal cues indicating this, try the exercises in this book. Learning to pay attention to your own sensations, not worrying about your partner, and improving your communication when you talk about sex will alleviate these performance issues. If you are under constant verbal pressure from your partner, however, you both should consider professional counseling.

I've mentioned "sensate focus" in this chapter as one of the methods you can use to help trigger your relaxation response in order to set the stage for enhanced sexual pleasure. Now let's take a closer look at the "whys" and "hows" of sensate focus. Then later, in Chapter 4, I'll introduce the first exercises incorporating sensate focus.

chapter 2

Sensate Focus:
The Touch That
Transforms Sex

by Paul Dahlquist

Sometimes the simplest ideas have the greatest power to change our experience. Here is one I would like you to consider: Your fingertips and skin are two of the most important elements in sexual pleasure. If you find this hard to believe, it may be because you have grown used to a way of touching that doesn't give you maximum pleasure. Sensate-focus exercises can change that.

Sensate-focus exercises, also simply called *caresses*, can be done on any part of the body, including the genitals. They range from the sensual to the highly sexual, depending on which part of the body is being touched. Sensuality is about touch and sensation, not necessarily arousal. Sensual touch, however, can enhance sexual arousal. I will ask you to experiment with sensate-focus touching techniques on yourself first, so that you can explore what pleases you and discover where you are most sensitive. Then you and your partner will take turns touching the other and being touched.

The Principles of Sensate-Focus Touching

There are seven principles of sensate-focus touching:

- Focus on sensations

- Touch for your own pleasure

- Stay in the here and now

- Eliminate expectations from your touch

- Use active and passive roles

- Take the pressure off yourself

- Take the pressure off your partner

Let's look at each of these in turn.

Focus on Sensations

The term *sensate focus* may sound somewhat technical, but it is actually self-explanatory. As you do the touching exercises described in this book, you focus your attention as closely as you can on the sensation, on what you are feeling at the point where you are touching. This is the essence of the technique. You draw your attention into your body and focus it on the places where your skin touches your partner's skin, or hair, or fingertips. As the point of contact shifts, your attention follows. Every time your mind wanders off, you consciously bring it back to the point of contact between your skin and your partner's skin.

Recent advances in both psychology and medicine have shown the importance of considering the body and the mind as a whole. Research in sexuality shows that we need to work with the body and the mind together to enhance our sexual awareness and pleasure. Sensate-focus exercises reinforce this mind-body connection.

During any sensate-focus exercise, both partners concentrate as much as they can on exactly where they are touching or being touched. If you find your mind drifting to something else, catch it and bring it back. If you are touching your partner's face with your fingertips, keep your attention on what your fingertips feel. Is the skin smooth or rough? Do you like how it feels? Are your partner's muscles under the skin tense or relaxed? What parts feel best?

If you are receiving a sensate-focus caress, you also keep your attention on the exact point of contact between your skin and your partner's skin. If your face is being touched, follow the sensations in your skin as your partner's fingertips move across it. Is the touch too heavy or too light? What sensations are created by the contact? What other feelings come up, positive or negative? Are you comfortable with them? If not, can you relax and let yourself become comfortable with them? By noticing all of the sensations you are feeling, you increase your awareness of the amount of sensation you will be able to feel in the future—and therefore the amount of potential pleasure available to you.

Realize that distractions always occur during a sensate-focus exercise. You might hear a noise in another part of the house, or you might find yourself wondering what to make for dinner or what you really should have said during negotiations at work. During any sensate-focus exercise, it doesn't matter if your mind drifts off fifty times—the important thing is that you recognize when you are thinking about something else and consciously bring your mind back to the touch. Don't criticize yourself for being unable to maintain perfect focus. Everybody gets distracted. You will become better at staying focused each time you practice an exercise. It is also a little easier to concentrate during a sensate-focus exercise than it is during usual sex, because most of the sensate-focus exercises are nonverbal. This leaves both you and your partner free to concentrate 100 percent on the touch without verbal distractions.

Another way to help yourself and your partner focus on sensations is to keep your touch steady and very slow. Being touched in a slow, sensuous way is comforting and relaxing, which is necessary if you are to reach optimal levels of pleasure. Bringing your mind and body to a single point of focus adds to the feeling of relaxation that we explained in the last chapter as being important.

Touch for Your Own Pleasure

When you touch your partner during a sensate-focus exercise, touch for your own pleasure; make it feel good for yourself. This attitude may sound selfish, but it actually frees up your partner to experience the exercise without pressure. As mentioned above, the touch used in a sensate-focus exercise is called a *caress*. In a caress, you touch the skin to get as much sensation for yourself as possible. It is not the same type of touch as massage. Massage is a heavy touch, often with manipulation of body muscles, usually done for the therapeutic benefit of the person being massaged. Caressing gives both you and your partner an acute awareness of touching and being touched.

Though there are principles underlying sensate-focus touching, there is no right or wrong way to do a sensate-focus exercise. In some ways, sensate focus is an almost a "technique-free" technique because everyone has his or her own style of touching. However, certain types of touch are easier to concentrate on. Your caress should be light and very slow. You can use either long, sweeping strokes or short ones—try them both and do whatever feels best to you. You and your partner will be able to concentrate best if you caress as slowly as possible. Even if you think you are touching slowly enough, try closing your eyes and cutting your touching speed in half to see if this helps you focus. As you touch, pay attention to temperatures, textures, and shapes on whatever part of the body you are caressing.

Touch your partner to make yourself feel good and to help your partner focus on your touch. Again, this emphasis might sound kind of selfish, but it really applies mostly to the first few exercises, when you are just starting to learn the sensate-focus technique. Many of the later exercises in this book show you how to pay attention to and interpret your partner's responses.

The best physical position for any caress is one that allows you to touch with the least amount of exertion. Part of any sensate-focus exercise is to keep your body as comfortable as possible. If you are caressing your partner's back, for example, try lying next to your partner and touching with one hand, rather than straddling your partner.

Stay in the Here and Now

Each time you successfully bring your mind back to the sensations you are experiencing, you bring it back to the present moment. When you are touching, this means that you are focusing on the body area you are touching right now, not the area you will be touching a minute from now or the area you just touched. If you are receiving during a sensate-focus exercise, staying in the here and now means focusing on the body area your partner is touching now, not the area that he or she touched five minutes ago or the area that you wish he or she would touch. If you have thoughts such as, "I wish she'd go back to touching my chin," or even, "When are we going to have sex?" then you are not concentrating fully and staying in the here and now. When you recognize this happening, consciously bring your attention back to the point of contact between your skin and your partner's fingertips.

Staying in the here and now also means that you are focusing on the sensual or sexual encounter that you are having right now, rather than one you may have had in the past or that you may have in the future. Sex, like life, happens in the here and now. Dwelling on thoughts of sexual encounters in the past will distract you. Speculating about what will happen in the future may make you anxious and unable to enjoy a caress. Staying in the here and now is the key to pleasure—it brings you back into your body so your mind can register all of the exquisite sensations of being touched in a loving way.

Eliminate Expectations from Your Touch

When you do sensate-focus exercises, there is no pressure to perform in a particular way. This is called a "nondemand" style of interaction, and it is the result of several conscious choices that help you to fully experience pleasure. One choice is to take turns using active and passive roles in the exercises. Another choice is to take the pressure off yourself to perform or respond sexually in any way. A third choice is to take the pressure off your partner to perform.

Use Active and Passive Roles

As we mentioned earlier, most sensate-focus exercises for couples start with one person as the passive partner and the other person as the active partner, and then the partners switch roles. The use of active and passive roles helps eliminate performance pressure and minimizes distractions so you can concentrate fully on touching or being touched.

When you are the active partner in a sensate-focus exercise, do the caress as instructed and try to keep your attention on exactly where your fingertips and skin touch your partner's skin. Touch for your own pleasure. Don't worry about what your partner may be thinking or feeling, and don't speak to your partner during the exercise or ask for feedback unless it's part of the exercise. Assume that the caress feels good to your partner. If something bothers your partner, he or she will tell you. Your only task when you are active is to focus on your own sensations. When you are finished doing a caress, tell your partner.

When you are the passive partner, lie in a comfortable position. Relax any of your muscles that feel tense. Focus on the sensations you receive when your partner touches you. Mentally follow his or her hand as it caresses your body. Let your partner know if he or she is doing something that hurts or bothers you. If everything is fine, don't say anything or give any feedback. Just allow yourself to soak up the sensations like a sponge. You don't have any responsibility except to focus on what you are feeling.

You may initially feel some resistance to doing an exercise in which you remain completely passive. I urge you to try. You may find that being in this unfamiliar role and allowing yourself just to receive is quite enjoyable.

Not receiving constant verbal feedback from your partner may seem frustrating or unnatural at first, but it will help you learn which sensations and touches you like. Dividing activities into two specific roles also helps you learn more about your own body—and your partner's—than if you were instructed to touch each other at the same time. By concentrating totally on where your skin touches your partner's skin, you will become fully involved and present in what is happening. Although only one partner is active at a time, both partners have the same point of focus. You will find this more sensually arousing than when you and your partner do different activities at the same time. This passive role/active role approach also fosters a climate of sharing and trust.

When sex therapists first started having their clients do sensate-focus exercises, the instructions were somewhat different than the ones you just read. Sex therapists used to tell their clients, "When you are active, try to please your partner. When you are passive, tell your partner everything you like and don't like." They found soon enough, however, that these instructions could create a lot of performance pressure.

From working with clients, my colleagues and I have found that when people are instructed to touch for their own pleasure, they enjoy more and learn more—and so does their partner. If you start your touching practice with exercises that use the active and passive roles, you will actually become more confident about touching your partner than if you engage in mutual touching.

Take the Pressure Off Yourself

We often put even more pressure on ourselves than we do on our partners. During a sensate-focus exercise, try not to have any expectations about how you will feel or respond. There is no requirement that you respond in any particular way during an exercise. Although some of the sensate-focus exercises teach you how to recognize different levels of arousal or erection, there is never any demand that you have a particular level of arousal or erection during any exercise. It is important to remember this before you do these exercises—knowing and being aware of different levels for yourself does not mean you have to reach particular levels for an exercise to give you pleasure.

Some people become concerned because they don't experience sexual arousal during some of the sensate-focus exercises. Don't be concerned. Many of the exercises are sensual, not sexual—they are about touching and sensation, not arousal. Everybody's experience with an exercise is different. For example, I have had clients who did not experience a genital caress as particularly sexual, and I have had clients who experienced a face caress as sexual.

If you feel arousal during an exercise, don't interfere with it. Just let it happen. Don't try to increase your arousal, don't try to fight it off, and don't try to control it. Just take a deep breath and enjoy it, even if your level of arousal goes all the way to orgasm.

Take the Pressure Off Your Partner

In addition to taking the sexual pressure off yourself, don't worry about how your partner will respond when you are active during a sensate-focus exercise. If he or she becomes aroused during a caress, that's fine, but there should be no expectation that your partner *will* become aroused, stay aroused, have an erection, have an orgasm, lubricate, ejaculate, or hold anything back.

It is normal and loving to want to know that your partner is enjoying himself or herself. However, the problem with expecting your partner to respond in a certain way is that your expectations will be communicated nonverbally, even if you don't say anything. You don't have to ask, "Are you aroused?" or, "Did you come?" for your partner to feel pressure. When you have expectations, your touch changes subtly and your partner can pick up on this. If this happens, you and your partner will both have a difficult time focusing on your feelings.

The Benefits of Touching

I grew up in a touchy-feely family. As an adult I didn't realize how much I missed being touched. Sensate-focus touching made me realize how much I had missed that physical affection. — JOHN

Before I started in on a sensate-focus program, I didn't like to be touched too much. I always felt that being touched meant my partner expected something from me, so I was always on edge. But with sensate focus you get to have some time just to relax and enjoy being touched, without feeling like you owe anybody anything. — JOANNE

Why learn to touch in this sensate-focus way? There are a number of benefits that can ensue. Research has shown that touching and being touched provide a number of benefits beyond the obvious increase in sexual pleasure. The first benefit is relaxation, already discussed in Chapter 1. Certain types of touch help our bodies relax, whether we are active or passive. In fact, touching can actually bring physical healing. The "laying on of hands" has been used in many cultures throughout the world with the intention of curing physical illnesses.

Much of the research on touch and health has been brought together by Ashley Montagu in his classic book, *Touching*. Montagu describes the effect of skin contact on the mental and physical health of people of all ages. His book shows that touch is vitally important for humans, as well as for other animals. For example, infant monkeys deprived of maternal touch have sexual problems later in life. Human infants that are deprived of physical contact have higher death rates than those who are touched.

In human adults, being touched has been shown to lower heart rate and blood pressure, and to reduce the effects of stress. Touching may also have a positive effect on the immune system.

Although touch obviously has benefits for adults, there is no research showing that adults *need* touch. But there is no reason to think that our need to be touched ends with infancy or childhood. The desire to be held or touched is a strong motivation for engaging in sexual activities. For many of us, and especially for men, sexual encounters are the only situations in which we are allowed to touch other human beings or enjoy being touched by them.

Touching also makes it easier to share feelings. Patients who are touched in the genital area by doctors or nurses during a physical examination often spontaneously confide personal sexual information. It seems that being touched in intimate areas brings intimate thoughts and feelings to the surface.

Being touched has been shown to have a positive effect on adults in medical settings as well. For example, in one study, patients who were touched by nurses recovered faster than those who were not touched. It is not known exactly how touching helps people get better. It could be that touching promotes relaxation and indirectly affects the immune system. Or it could be that the act of touching communicates the expectation that the patient will get well.

Much of the more recent research on the benefits of touch has studied the effects of "bodywork." There are many forms of bodywork, which is any type of therapy that tries to free up blocked emotions by using specific body movements or postures. Other recent research on touch has included applied research on the benefits of touch for medical patients, elderly people, and children with autism, as well as the medical benefits of touching pets.

Some of us grew up in families that touched a lot, and others did not. Whether or not you are naturally comfortable with touching and being touched, the exercises in this book—which start out nonsexual and gradually proceed to the more sexual—will help you get the wonderful touching you need for relaxation, comfort, and physical and mental well-being. The exercises will develop your confidence in, desire for, and appreciation of touch.

Some General Directions
for the Exercises

Remember the element of predictability that's so important for relaxation? At the start of every exercise, I will tell you if you need any supplies as well as how long an exercise should take. Be sure to read through the directions for an exercise before you do it, so that you don't get to the middle of an exercise and think of something you forgot—or forget what to do next!

In general, most of the exercises you will do by yourself will take about half an hour, and most of the partner exercises will take about an hour. For most exercises, you will need baby powder, some kind of lubricant, and a large towel to protect your bedsheets. Before you begin the program, it might be a good idea to place a basket or nightstand next to your bed where you can keep these supplies. Beyond that, to do most of the touching exercises in this book, you need only the basics—your skin and your partner's skin.

Now, let's take a few pages to review some of the basics about sexuality. The next chapter offers a refresher course on the anatomy of the sex organs, as well as a discussion of the sexual-pleasure cycle.

chapter 3

The Sexual-Pleasure Cycle

by Paul Dahlquist

*L*et's review some basic sexual anatomy as it relates to the body parts you will caress in later exercises. I'll talk about the sex organs that are most relevant to the theme of pleasure.

Biology 101

In men, the penis is the organ for sexual intercourse as well as for urinating and conveying sperm outside of the body. Physically, the penis has two obvious structural divisions, the *shaft* and the *head* (see Figure 2). Men who have not been circumcised have a sheath of skin called the *foreskin* that covers the head of the penis. The head of the penis is very sensitive in most men, as is the *frenulum,* the area on the underside of the penis where the shaft meets the head.

During sexual stimulation, the penis becomes erect because it contains three cylinders of tissue that fill with blood. Two of these cylinders are called *corpora cavernosa* and the third is called the *corpus spongiosum.*

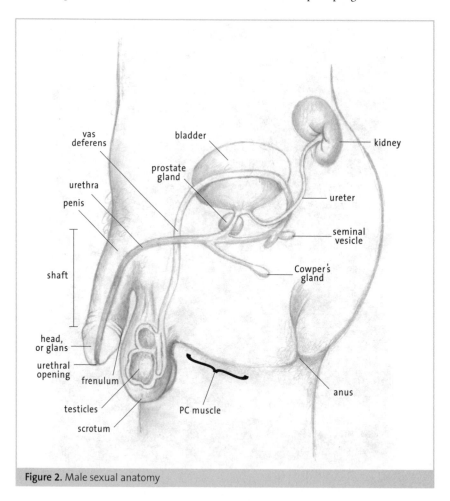

Figure 2. Male sexual anatomy

The *scrotum* is the pouch of skin that hangs between a man's legs and contains the *testes,* the male reproductive organs that produce sperm. The testes also produce *testosterone,* the important hormone that controls a man's sex drive. (Women also have testosterone in their bodies, but in much smaller amounts than men do. It plays an important role in a woman's sex drive, too.)

Men have a muscle group in the genital area that is essential for sexual pleasure. This is the *pubococcygeus* or *PC muscle* that runs behind the scrotum and supports the pelvic floor. In following chapters I'll describe the PC muscle in more detail and explain how to exercise it and use it to create more enjoyment during sex.

The collective name for a woman's external sexual anatomy is *vulva* (see Figure 3a). The vulva includes the *pubic mound,* the outer and inner *vaginal lips,* the *clitoris,* the opening of the *vagina,* and the opening of the *urethra.* The clitoris is very significant because it seems to have no function other than pleasure and is the most common source of stimulation to orgasm for women. Although much smaller than the penis, the clitoris is similar to the penis in structure; the clitoris contains erectile tissue and has a head and a shaft as well as a hood.

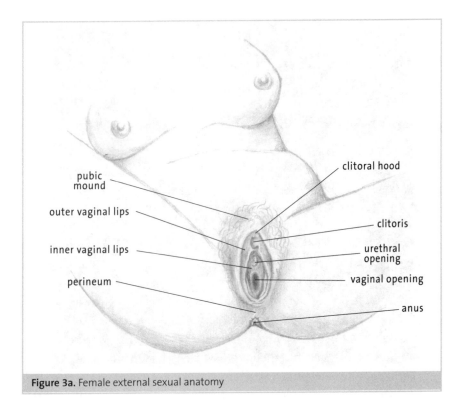

Figure 3a. Female external sexual anatomy

Most women get pleasure from stimulation of all areas of the vulva, including the vaginal lips, the pubic mound, and the vaginal opening.

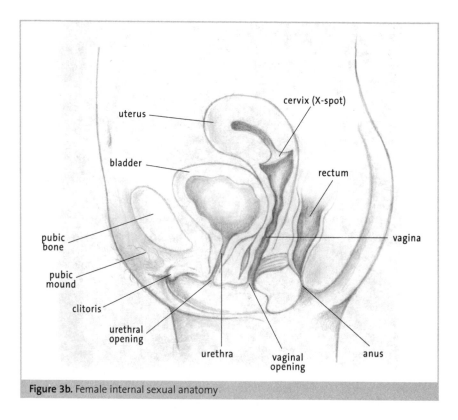

Figure 3b. Female internal sexual anatomy

Women have a *PC muscle* that is located inside the vaginal opening. This muscle is essential for female sexual pleasure because it is the muscle that spasms when a woman has an orgasm. The following chapters will include PC muscle exercises for women.

The vagina is the tubular organ designed for sexual intercourse (see Figure 3b). It also serves as the birth canal. The vagina contains several structures that are significant in terms of sexual pleasure. The *Gräfenberg spot,* or *G-spot,* is located on the upper front wall of the vagina, behind the pubic bone. The G-spot has been the focus of a lot of research in the past twenty years. Many women report that stimulation of the G-spot causes intense orgasm and possibly the release of large amounts of fluid.

The *anterior fornix erogenous zone (AFE or A-spot)* is the area on the front wall of the vagina between the G-spot and the cervix. Manual stimulation of this area has been found to trigger lubrication. Another erogenous zone that can be stimulated in conjunction with the A-spot is the *vaginal sponge,* or *paraurethral sponge*. This is a squishy area that surrounds the whole urethra and clitoris internally. It is on the front wall of the vagina right in front of the G-spot.

The *cervix* is the opening to the uterus. The penis often makes contact with the cervix during deep penetration in certain intercourse positions. Some women find this arousing, and others report that it feels slightly painful, like a cramp. The cervix is sometimes called the *X-spot*, or *ecstasy spot*.

The *cul de sac* is the end of the vagina that extends beyond the cervix. It is normally only available for stimulation when a woman is very aroused and the uterus lifts up a little bit from the vagina. I've also heard the cul de sac called the *fornix*. If the front wall is the anterior fornix, then the cul de sac must be the *posterior fornix*.

There are two sources of vaginal muscle tone. The first is the PC muscle, which a woman experiences as surrounding the opening of the vagina. Prior to orgasm, a woman has voluntary control of this muscle and can use it to tighten the vaginal opening. The other source of vaginal muscle tone is the striated muscles that run around the vaginal walls. If you were to do a pelvic exam and look at the vaginal walls, they would appear to be somewhat striped or corrugated-looking due to these striations, which are called *rugae*. A sensitive male lover can feel the rugae during intercourse. These muscles alternately grip and release the penis, and this action is what causes many of the highly exciting sensations of intercourse. A woman can learn to exercise these muscles with the use of a sex toy called Ben-Wa balls. I'll describe such an exercise in a later chapter.

Both men and women have an area in the genitals called the *perineum*. In women, it is the flat surface between the rear of the vagina and the anus. In men, it is the flat surface between the back of the testicles and the anus. Both men and women report that they experience pleasure when this area is stimulated.

Masters and Johnson's Human Sexual-Response Cycle

The sexual-response cycle is the sequence of the physical changes that take place as men and women receive sexual stimulation. Based on their research, the famous sexologists William Masters and Virginia Johnson advanced the theory that human sexual response proceeds in four stages: excitement, plateau, orgasm, and resolution (see Figure 4). Their findings were based on laboratory studies of male and female volunteers who agreed to be monitored as they engaged in sexual activity. Masters and Johnson recorded heart rate, blood pressure, skin temperature, and respiration rate as well as genital changes to figure out how the body responds as people become sexually excited and approach orgasm.

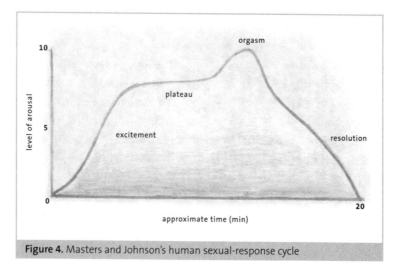

Figure 4. Masters and Johnson's human sexual-response cycle

The first three stages of the sexual-response cycle (excitement, plateau, and orgasm) are accompanied by two processes called vasocongestion and myotonia. In the case of sexual response, *vasocongestion,* or *engorgement,* is an accumulation of blood in the genital region, causing swelling or erection. *Myotonia* means muscle tension. As men and women become more and more aroused on their way to orgasm, many of the muscles in their bodies experience increased tension, especially the muscles in the pelvic area, including the PC muscle.

The Excitement Phase

In the excitement phase of the sexual-response cycle for men, the most dramatic physical change is the appearance of an erection (caused by increasing vasocongestion). The testes and scrotum may also elevate slightly.

In women, the genital response that best corresponds to the male erection is lubrication of the vaginal walls. This occurs when blood flows to the muscular middle layer of the vagina and lubrication is literally pushed through the vaginal walls. This is called "vaginal sweating." Let me make clear what vaginal lubrication means and doesn't mean. A lot of men wait to start sexual intercourse until their partner has lubricated, because they believe vaginal lubrication is a sign of arousal. Vaginal lubrication is a sign of physical readiness for intercourse, but not necessarily of psychological readiness. A woman could lubricate because she has been touched on her A-spot or G-spot, but she may not necessarily feel psychologically turned on, so it's always best to use other signs of arousal as well, such as rapid breathing and increased heart rate.

In addition, during the excitement phase, the clitoris and labia may swell, and the uterus may elevate slightly. Many women experience breast swelling during the excitement phase.

We don't normally think of women as having erections, but of course the clitoris becomes erect because it contains two corpora cavernosa. A woman's erection ability is somewhat more diffuse than that of a man. The clitoris has two long roots and is anchored by ligaments onto the pubic bone. This entire part of the clitoris that you can't see becomes erect. The G-spot is directly behind it. The whole area surrounding the urethra, which is called the vaginal sponge or paraurethral sponge, contains tiny blood vessels that swell when vasocongestion takes place.

The sex flush, in which the face and neck and chest turn red, may occur in both sexes during the excitement phase. Both men and women start to experience increased blood pressure and heart rate as well as rapid breathing.

The Plateau Phase

In the plateau phase, the man gets his full erection. The penis may turn a dark red and the head may turn purple. The testes and scrotum swell and elevate even more. *Cowper's glands,* located at the base of the penis, may produce a couple of drops of clear fluid that appear at the tip of the penis. The function of the Cowper's gland fluid (which is also called *preseminal fluid)* appears to be to neutralize and cleanse the urethra after urination.

The plateau phase can be accompanied by some major physiological changes in women. The inner and outer vaginal lips may turn a very dark red. This is called the *sex skin.* The muscles and ligaments that support the uterus may tighten and cause the uterus to lift up off of the vaginal canal. Masters and Johnson called this response uterine "tenting."

Part of the outer or middle third of the vagina may tighten noticeably. Masters and Johnson called this the formation of the "orgasmic platform." *Bartholin's glands* (located under the skin of the inner lips about halfway between the top and bottom of the vagina) may secrete a couple of drops of clear fluid, although this is often not noticeable due to the presence of other lubrication. The areolas may enlarge and give the nipples a cone-shaped appearance. (I use the word "may" in these descriptions instead of "will" because every woman is different and not all women experience all of these changes.)

During the plateau phase in both sexes, the sex flush continues, and breathing, heart rate, and blood pressure reach high levels and stay there for a while. Men and women may also experience short muscle spasms in the hands, feet, and face.

The Orgasm Phase

Orgasm is the reflex that occurs when vasocongestion and myotonia have reached peaks and can't go any higher. This triggers spasms of the PC muscle, which force the collected blood out of the genital area. According to Masters and Johnson, a man was judged to have had an orgasm if his heart rate reached a certain level and his PC muscle spasmed rhythmically and he ejaculated.

Ejaculation takes place in two phases: emission and expulsion. *Emission* occurs when semen begins to move from the testes, receives more lubrication from the prostate gland, and collects in a swelling of the urethra near the prostate called the *urethral bulb*. Psychologically, men experience this as the point of no return or the point of inevitability (POI). This is the feeling that an ejaculation has reached a stage where it is going to happen no matter what. Physically, the man has a feeling of fullness at the base of the penis.

The second phase of ejaculation is *expulsion*. In this phase, the PC muscle starts to spasm and semen is expelled from the penis. If a man pays close attention to his ejaculation, he will be able to identify these two distinct phases and to feel how intense the pleasure is with each spurt of semen.

Ejaculation results when the PC muscle contracts, causing semen to be expelled from the penis. This does not always occur at the point of orgasm. Some men can experience a sensational full-body orgasm without an ejaculation. (Some Eastern philosophical and religious traditions advocate this practice because they believe that ejaculating too often can deplete a man's vital essence.) There are also men who ejaculate but experience no pleasurable or orgasmic sensations. This is true of some men who have premature ejaculation. Most men, however, do experience orgasm and ejaculation as one combined pleasurable sensation. But it is possible to focus on them separately and appreciate each one more, as you will learn in Chapter 13. Learning to recognize subtle differences during orgasm and ejaculation will make these moments of pleasure seem to last much longer.

Masters and Johnson believed a woman had an orgasm if her heart rate reached a certain level and her PC muscle spasmed rhythmically. They did not at that time have information about female ejaculation, a phenomenon that can occur with stimulation of the G-spot.

In this discussion of anatomy, I have described several orgasmic triggers in women's bodies, and I will teach you exercises to use them in Chapter 12. However, genital changes are not the whole story of orgasm. Orgasm is systemic—it occurs throughout the whole body. In addition to contractions of the PC muscle and other pelvic muscles, most people experience muscle spasms of the anus, buttocks, back, legs, arms, and shoulders. An intense orgasm is sometimes accompanied by facial grimacing. Tingling in the fingers and toes can occur as blood flows back to the extremities.

Some people have unusual or idiosyncratic reactions to orgasm. They may experience uncontrollable sweating, laughing, or crying, because an orgasm can be such a huge emotional release, especially if you haven't had one for a while and you've been under a lot of stress. When you have an orgasm, your brain releases endorphins—natural pain-killing, pleasure-causing chemicals that are released during states of intense physical activity. People who have orgasms experience anything from a mild pleasant feeling of relief or release to an intense, rock-your-world sensation that may include feelings of ecstasy or an altered state of consciousness.

When most people have an orgasm with a partner, they feel increased intimacy and emotional attachment. This is due to the action of a hormone called *oxytocin,* which many men and women release at orgasm. Oxytocin is known as the "bonding hormone," because it is also the hormone that is secreted by pregnant women during breast-feeding.

Other people have unusual emotional reactions after orgasm. Some people feel slightly sad, melancholy, or depressed. A small group of people experience intense migraine headaches after orgasm due to changes in blood flow.

The Resolution Phase

In the resolution phase, the body returns to its unaroused state. Men lose their erection and the testes and scrotum return to their normal position. In women, blood gradually leaves the genitals, and vaginal and clitoral swelling go down. Men experience a refractory period in which they are unresponsive to sexual stimulation for some time after they have an ejaculation and lose their erection. In a young man the refractory period may be negligible, but as a man gets older, he may find that it takes him longer to get another erection after he ejaculates.

Problems with Masters and Johnson's Conclusions

Masters and Johnson's work on sexual response was groundbreaking, but it was not without its flaws. Over the years the human sexual-response cycle, as defined by Masters and Johnson, has been criticized on a number of levels. The most obvious criticism is that the model is 100 percent physiological and doesn't include any psychological concepts. Being human, we give psychological meaning to our sexual activities, and Masters and Johnson ignored that fact.

This point was brought to the fore by Helen Singer Kaplan, another well-known sex therapist and researcher. Her contribution to the sexual-response cycle was the addition of a "desire" phase: a mental stage that occurs before any direct stimulation starts. This is a very important insight—in fact, I consider it so important that I've devoted an entire chapter to it later in this book.

Most sexual encounters begin in the minds of the participants well before any direct physical stimulation starts. The problem with the desire phase is that Kaplan and others who came after her have been unable to really define what sexual desire is. Synonyms that have been suggested for it include sexual interest, desired sexual frequency, attraction, erotic love, lust, sex drive, chemistry, and passion.

It has also been suggested that the sexual-response cycle should include five phases: interest or desire, arousal, physiological readiness (erection or lubrication), orgasm, and psychological satisfaction. An attempt to use these concepts and make the sexual-response cycle more psychological is David Reed's *erotic stimulus pathway* model. In this model, rather than excite-

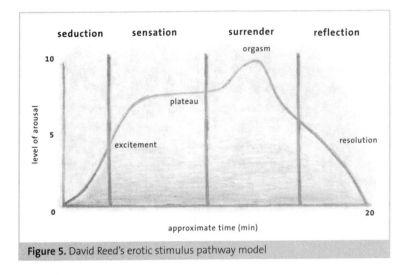

Figure 5. David Reed's erotic stimulus pathway model

ment, plateau, orgasm, and resolution, the stages are seduction, sensation, surrender, and reflection. These four psychological stages can be overlaid on Masters and Johnson's four physiological stages (see Figure 5).

Seduction is twofold. It is a person's understanding of both how to find another person seductive and how to make herself or himself seductive to a desired partner. The roots of our feelings about seduction generally begin in the early adolescent years and have much to do with sexual self-esteem. In the sensation phase, input from all five senses becomes important, not just touch. In the surrender phase, we relinquish control and allow ourselves to become vulnerable enough to have an orgasm. In the reflection phase, we think about the recent sexual encounter and give meaning to it. If we judge the encounter to have been positive, this will fuel our desire for the next encounter.

A significant issue that Reed has noted is that couples who have been together longer (in other words, who are beyond the courtship phase) often lose their skills at seducing their partner or making themselves appealing to their partner. Please keep this idea in mind as you read the rest of this book. Use my exercises as jumping-off points to learn to seduce your partner and make yourself more sexually desirable. The seduction and sensation phases of Reed's cycle can provide an opportunity to get creative and think of new ways to desire and arouse your partner.

Sex by the Numbers:
A Focus on Pleasure

Masters and Johnson have been criticized from a historical point of view, a clinical point of view, a feminist point of view, and a scientific point of view. (If you would like to read more about these various viewpoints, see the book listed in "Suggested Reading" titled *Sex Is Not a Natural Act*, by Lenore Tiefer.) My main problem with Masters and Johnson is an experiential one—in other words, their model includes nothing about how people really experience their sexual acts on a moment-by-moment basis. During sex, many people don't even pay attention to things that Masters and Johnson thought were important. They only know how they feel as the sexual act continues. The Masters and Johnson model is a *response* cycle when it should be a *pleasure* cycle. If we call it a response cycle, we imply that sex is essentially reactive, whereas I believe if we call it a pleasure cycle, we imply that sex is a creative act.

Given that so many sex researchers have criticized the sexual-response cycle, which one do we use? I've come up with a very simple sexual-pleasure cycle that I call "sex by the numbers." This pleasure cycle relies primarily on a concept called *peaking*. When you peak, you allow your arousal to increase in a predictable series of wave-like ups and downs. Because I use this sex-by-the-numbers approach, throughout the book I will refer to an arousal scale of 1 to 10. Please look at Figure 4 on page

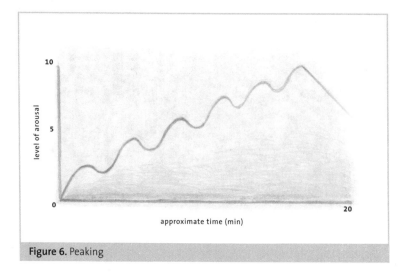

Figure 6. Peaking

30, which depicts the typical Masters and Johnson sexual-response cycle, and Figure 6, which depicts a pleasure cycle that involves peaking.

You can see from Figure 6 that level 1 is no arousal and level 10 is orgasm. Level 8 would roughly correspond to Masters and Johnson's plateau phase.

In the chapters that follow, I'll introduce you and your partner to the peaking process. First, let me explain the theory behind it.

I believe that men and women each have two pleasure scales that they can use to enhance their sex lives. Men have an arousal scale and an erection scale. Women have what I call a physical scale and a psychological or subjective scale. All are simple-to-use, 1-to-10 scales.

The Male Arousal Scale

The man's arousal scale ranges from feeling a slight twinge around the penis up through orgasm. This scale measures perceived closeness to orgasm and ejaculation. Level 1 is no arousal. Levels 2 and 3 are slight twinges in the genital area. (Note that this is not the physical erection we are talking about; it's a psychological or subjective state.) Level 4 is a steady low level of arousal. Levels 5 and 6 are medium levels. Level 7 is the strong feeling that you would seriously like the stimulation to continue. The best indication that you have reached level 8 is awareness of your heart rate and breathing, and a sense of blood rushing in your ears. Level 9 is the level right before the point of no return, and level 10 is orgasm, which usually includes ejaculation.

The Erection Scale

The erection scale is a little more complicated. Erection is the filling of the penis with blood. You can have an erection without feeling aroused, or you can feel very aroused but not have an erection, although the two usually go together.

I usually describe erections as having four phases: initiation, filling, rigidity, and maintenance. *Initiation* is the mental mechanism that has to "let go" and tell you it is okay to have an erection. This is an unconscious process; in most men, erection is not under conscious control, but rather under the control of the autonomic nervous system.

Filling is the stage of erection in which blood begins to flow into the penis and the penis thickens. On the 1-to-10 scale, level 1 would be no erection, and levels 2, 3, and 4 would correspond to increased filling.

Erection is controlled by small valves in the blood circulation system at the base of the penis. *Rigidity* is achieved when enough blood has flowed into the penis so that the valves start to close off, trapping blood in the penis. The penis now has a "spring back" quality to it—if you push it down with your hand, it will resist and become erect again. On the 1-to-10 scale, level 5 is the start of rigidity, and levels 6 through 10 indicate a progressively harder penis. Here's where things start to get a little tricky, because every man's erection ability is a little bit different. There are some men who never get a level-10 erection (which I have described in my classes at various times as "the theoretically hardest erection that could exist," or a "diamond cutter"). On your personal erection scale, level 10 is *your* level 10—the hardest erection that you get. Adjust your scale downward accordingly. Your hardest possible erection is usually the level of erection you wake up with in the morning.

Rigidity can also be described using the angle of the penis. For example, an erection that points straight up toward the navel is usually very hard, whereas an erection that points straight out may not be as hard.

The closing off of the valves at the base of the penis causes an erection to maintain itself, since the blood does not go in or out of the penis. It is normal, however, to have your erection decrease or increase a couple of levels during the course of a sexual encounter. For some men, when direct stimulation of the penis stops, their erection starts to flag a bit. If this is true for you, it does not mean that you have erection problems. It is also normal to feel your erections go up and down within a range from 6 to 10 during intercourse. Again, this does not indicate any erection problems and is no cause for concern.

It is also normal to require direct stimulation, like fondling or kissing of the penis, before you become erect. Many men do not have spontaneous erections. I know that some men believe that if they are nude with a partner they find attractive, they should have an erection quickly, as in: "Two minutes have gone by—why don't I have an erection?"

The truth is that most men do not have an automatic erection just from being nude with a partner. So try to get rid of those internal timetables and experience your partner's touch without worrying about how long it takes you to become aroused or erect.

In general, a nice full erection creates a tight fit in your partner's vagina, and this means more pleasure for both of you. Just be aware that a level-10 erection may not always be the most enjoyable for your partner.

I've found that most women prefer erections that are about a level 8. A full or level-10 erection may be difficult for a woman's vaginal muscles to grip continuously. There are some great exercises in Chapter 10, "Getting Better and Better (Erections) All the Time," for making your erections even stronger than they are now.

The Female Physical-Arousal Scale

Women can also use 1-to-10 scales to describe the degree of their arousal. The physical-arousal scale refers to any changes that happen for women in the genital area. This is similar to the man's erection scale, but it doesn't refer only to erection of the clitoris. It refers also to vaginal lubrication and swelling in the vaginal sponge area, as well as uterine tenting, exposure of the cul de sac, and formation of the orgasmic platform.

As with the male scale, every woman has a different degree of highest physical arousal. Some women would feel they are at level 10 when their clitoris becomes very hard. Other women might experience a 10 as being copious vaginal lubrication due to stimulation of the A-spot or G-spot. Other women might consider it a 10 when they can feel that their G-spot has swollen up, or when they sense that their cul de sac has opened up or that the middle section of their vagina has tightened.

The best I can do here is to give you some very general guidelines based on my own experience. Level 1 would be no arousal. Level 2 or 3 would be slight twinges in the genital area. Level 4 would be the beginning of clitoral erection and lubrication. Levels 5 and 6 would be swelling of the G-spot and vaginal sponge. At levels 7 and 8, the clitoris is at its maximum erection level, and the inner third of the vagina may tighten. At level 8, you will be aware of an increasingly rapid heart and breathing rate and a sense of blood roaring in your ears. I generally consider levels 9 and 10 to be maximum swelling of the G-spot and vaginal sponge and full exposure of the cul de sac.

I've described this physical-arousal scale based on intercourse. Your physical scale will be slightly different, because most women use the clitoris for self-stimulation, so a level 10 for self-touch might be maximum lubrication and erection of the clitoris. Women who stimulate their A-spot or G-spot or cul de sac with a dildo during self-pleasuring would probably use the sensations in one of those areas to describe level 10. So during self-pleasuring, you can be creative. You have many options for different erogenous zones to stimulate.

The Female Subjective, or Psychological, Scale

The use of this scale is very important, because a woman could be very physically aroused but not at all be turned on from a psychological standpoint, or she could be very psychologically aroused, even to the point of orgasm, but not lubricate and need to use some external lubrication. The woman's subjective-arousal scale measures her psychological sense of how close to orgasm she is.

This scale is similar to the man's arousal scale. Level 1 is no subjective arousal. Level 2 or 3 is a twinge feeling in the genitals. Level 4 is a steady low level of arousal. Level 5 or 6 is a medium level of arousal. At level 7 or 8, you really feel strongly that you don't want this stimulation to stop. Level 9 is the level right before the point of no return, and level 10 is orgasm, whether it is triggered by an external trigger, like the clitoris, or an internal trigger, like the G-spot. I'll have a lot more to say about this in the later chapters on female arousal and orgasm.

A Final Word on the Numbers Approach

Please don't be turned off by the idea of using numbers to describe your sexual response. It might make the arousal process sound mechanical, but trust me, once you learn to use the approach, the numbers drop out of your consciousness, and you learn to use particular sensations to gauge your physiological and psychological arousal.

Drugs and Sexual Pleasure

This is probably as good a place as any to comment on the use of recreational substances to artificially alter the sexual-pleasure cycle. Throughout history, people have looked for substances to alter their sexual desire and arousal as well as their general state of consciousness. Aphrodisiacs are foods or drugs that cause an increase in sexual desire or arousal. Unfortunately, no true, tested aphrodisiacs are known to exist. So people have instead turned to many legal and illegal drugs to alter their state of sexual consciousness. Some of the drugs that have been used for this purpose are alcohol, amphetamines, cocaine, Ecstasy, and marijuana.

Alcohol generally does not have a positive effect on a person's sex life, although a couple of drinks may temporarily potentiate testosterone in a woman and make her feel horny. A couple of drinks can relax a man enough to delay his ejaculation reflex, if that is a concern. However, long-term excessive use of alcohol can dampen your sex drive and cause problems with erection, arousal, and orgasm, especially in men. Men who are chronic alcoholics often cannot get erections at all, because alcohol potentiates estrogen in men, which inhibits erections.

Stimulants like amphetamine and cocaine have reputations as erection enhancers because they stimulate blood circulation. Again, this may be true in the short term. Use of cocaine or amphetamines can sometimes cause a man to have a harder erection than normal and for a longer period of time. However, he may have trouble ejaculating. Long-term excessive use of cocaine or amphetamines can degrade the erection response and possibly even damage erectile tissue.

Ecstasy (also known as MDMA, X, or the love drug) is a mild hallucinogen that causes general feelings of well-being and has a reputation for increasing positive emotions. It is sometimes referred to as the "love drug." It increases feelings of love and sensuality rather than sex drive or desire. Its effects have been compared to alcohol without the hangover. However, I believe that using it is dangerous because, as a hallucinogen, its effects can vary widely every time you take it.

Marijuana is also a mild hallucinogen that has a reputation for making people horny and causing distortions of space and time that make sexual encounters unusual, to say the least. Sexually, the main effect of marijuana is that it seems to cause time to speed up and slow down so that you are able to focus intently on your sensations. As you can imagine, this effect could be very good for sex. However, long-term excessive use of marijuana by men can cause breast enlargement, amotivational syndrome, and possible fertility problems. If marijuana is smoked, it can also cause lung problems.

Nicotine and caffeine are two mild stimulants that don't have any positive effects at all on sexual pleasure. In fact, use of either can be seriously damaging to your sex life. Caffeine and nicotine constrict the tiny blood vessels in the skin. Guess where in the body those blood vessels are located? In your genitals, mouth, and fingers—all of which are essential for sexual pleasure. Nicotine is especially harmful to erections. If you smoke and are at all concerned about erections, quit smoking now.

In general, it appears that some drugs may have a short-term positive effect on sexual pleasure. But to my knowledge the long-term effect of all of these drugs is to degrade a person's sexual experience. Plus, intimacy problems can happen in a relationship when one or both partners have sub-stance-abuse problems. If you think you or your partner has a substance-abuse problem, please arrange to see a professional counselor.

Prescription drugs can also interfere with sexual pleasure. The most common offenders here are the SSRIs—the selective serotonin-reuptake inhibitors like Prozac, Paxil, and Zoloft. These commonly prescribed antianxiety/antidepressant drugs can inhibit both sexual desire and orgasm. They should never be prescribed for men or women who have difficulty with desire or orgasm, and yet this happens all the time.

Some medications used to lower blood pressure can interfere with erections, and so can some ulcer drugs. Antiandrogen drugs that are prescribed for men with prostate problems can cause problems with male desire, erection, and orgasm. Even seemingly harmless over-the-counter allergy medications can temporarily interfere with erection and lubrication. If you are having problems with your sexual response and pleasure, it's a good idea to check with your doctor to find out if one of the drugs you are taking might be the culprit.

The next chapter gets into the fun stuff. It describes ways of touching yourself to enhance your sexual pleasure. Learning the pleasures of self-touch lays the foundation for increasing your sexual pleasure with a partner.

chapter 4

Self-Pleasure: Learning the Ways of Your Body

by Paul Dahlquist

*N*ow *that you are familiar with the basic principles of sensate focus and the male and female sexual-pleasure cycles, you are ready for some exercises that will teach you more about your body and its natural sexual response. Practice these sensual and sexual exercises by yourself before you go on to the partner exercises. I would like you to practice the breathing exercises and exercises for control of the pubococcygeus (PC) and pelvic muscles every day from now on, and to practice the self-caressing, "peaking," and "plateauing" exercises* *at least once, but more often if you can. Taking time alone to explore your own response to touch will help you learn to take yourself to higher and higher levels of arousal and will add immeasurably to the excitement you create with your partner.*

This is particularly true for women. In my practice, I have seen many women who have never really touched their genitals or even looked at them. Few women explore their bodies enough to discover what really turns them on. Often this lack of self-knowledge is the only thing stopping them from becoming aroused enough to reach orgasm. Fortunately, this is easy to remedy. For such women, the peaking exercises can radically change their experience of intercourse. These exercises build sexual charge and make orgasm that much more explosive.

I want to stress, however, that each of these self-pleasuring exercises is beneficial for both men and women. The ideas of pleasing yourself, knowing your own body, and learning about your natural sexual responses are so important that I have emphasized them throughout the book. Learn to trust yourself and your own feelings. Even if you're older, it's never to late to learn to pleasure yourself.

In this chapter you will learn the art of self-touch and self-pleasuring, which are not necessarily the same thing as masturbation. Masturbation is self-touch of the genitals for the purpose of pleasure, but for most people the goal of masturbation is orgasm. The self-touch techniques you will learn in this chapter don't have to lead to orgasm. They are done to increase your awareness of all of the different levels of your arousal, and many of them involve body areas other than the genitals.

The Benefits of Self-Touch

Given that self-touch is so much fun and gives us so much pleasure, how in the world did it ever get such a negative reputation? For many centuries, masturbation was seen as a sin. This belief has its roots in the Old Testament of the *Bible*. Masturbation was generally forbidden because it could not lead to procreation. In the 1700s and 1800s, the view shifted to the idea that self-touch of the genitals was physically bad for you. It was believed to cause everything from tuberculosis, nervous diseases, insanity, impotence, and homosexuality to hairy palms, epilepsy, memory loss, and blindness.

We now know that there is no evidence whatsoever that self-touch is bad for you. In fact, self-touch has several benefits. Most people, especially women, report that the orgasms they have with masturbation are the most intense. Women who masturbate as teenagers are more likely to be orgasmic during sex with partners as adults. Self-touch techniques are often prescribed for people who have sexual problems, such as low desire or difficulty with arousal and orgasm. Self-touch is probably the best way to become aware of your personal pleasure cycle. It has also been shown to increase sexual self-esteem.

Too Much of a Good Thing?

There is only one situation I am aware of when masturbation can become a problem, and that is if it becomes compulsive. A behavior is compulsive when you have no control over it. Compulsive masturbators start out masturbating to relieve sexual tension and to feel pleasure, but gradually they feel more and more anxiety if they don't masturbate, so they masturbate more and more often to get the same level of anxiety reduction. This can become a problem because excessive masturbation (twenty or more times a day in some cases) can be maladaptive, meaning that it interferes with your life goals. It can also interfere with your social and occupational functioning.

A person whose only sexual outlet is masturbation when other partners or outlets are available is said to have an autoerotic sexual orientation. Autoeroticism is a sexual orientation in which you are not interested in other partners but instead are only interested in having sex with yourself.

I hope you feel free to touch your own genitals without guilt or shame. These self-awareness exercises will teach you the basic elements of peaking and get you more in tune with your own responses so you can be a better lover for your partner and experience more arousal and pleasure yourself. The first few exercises below condition your body for pleasure, and the exercises presented later in the chapter help you discover your natural arousal patterns. These are the first steps on the path to heightened sexual pleasure.

✑ *Exercise 1.* **BELLY BREATHING**

Here's a simple breathing exercise to do for ten minutes each day. I start with this one because proper breathing is essential for sexual arousal. In fact, it is impossible to become sexually aroused if you are holding your breath. If you do this breathing exercise every day, it will lower your heart rate and blood pressure, and it will allow you to relax so you can do the rest of the exercises that follow.

To start, lie comfortably on your back. Place one hand on your abdomen. Slowly breathe in through your mouth while inflating your belly (not your chest) and then slowly exhale. Your stomach should rise and fall with the breath.

Do two or three belly breaths and then breathe normally for a couple of minutes. Then belly breathe again. While belly breathing, pause for three seconds between breathing out and breathing in. Don't pause between breathing in and breathing out—the inhale and exhale should be one continuous process.

✑ *Exercise 2.* **RELAXATION BREATHING**

If you are especially anxious or have a lot of stress in your life, you should also try the following breathing exercise. Blow all of the air out of your lungs through your nose rather rapidly. Now take all of the air that you can back in through your nose, slowly. Think of it as caressing the inside of your lungs with air. Relax your stomach muscles. As soon as you have as much air as possible in your lungs, start exhaling it slowly. Don't hold your breath at all.

Your breath is now under your conscious control. Do this five or six times. It will slow down your heart rate and lower your blood pressure. This simple breathing exercise can create all of the relaxation you need in order to do any of the exercises in this book.

I don't have space in this book to describe as many breathing exercises as I would like. If you are interested in learning more breathing exercises to both relax and invigorate you, find a book on yoga. It will most likely contain entire chapters on breathing techniques to relax, greet the day, or prepare for sex.

✐ *Exercise 3.* DEEP MUSCLE RELAXATION

In addition to breathing, a second element of relaxation is muscle relaxation. When you were lying on your bed to do belly breathing, your body probably became very relaxed the longer you lay there. What follows is a more advanced muscle-relaxation exercise. Allow about thirty minutes.

Lie on your back in bed. Starting at your toes, systematically tense each muscle group and then relax it. Start with your feet and work your way up through your calves, thighs, buttocks, abdomen, stomach, chest, shoulders, fingers, lower arms, upper arms, neck, and all of the parts of your face. Systematically tensing and relaxing each muscle group will allow you to recognize more clearly the difference between when the muscle group is tense and when it is relaxed. After you have practiced this exercise a few times, try combining groups. For example, to do one leg, tense the toes of your right foot, then the whole foot, then the calf, then the thigh, then the whole leg.

It can sometimes be helpful to listen to relaxing music while you do this exercise. Choose something restful or new age, or a CD of nature sounds. Combine your deep-muscle-relaxation session with breathing exercises. You may also be able to find a CD or tape that guides you in the progressive tensing and relaxing of muscle groups.

✐ *Exercise 4.* THE DAILY PC MUSCLE EXERCISE

The other daily exercise that I would like you to do involves a particular group of muscles in your pelvic area. The full name for it is the *pubococcygeus,* or *pubococcygeal muscle group,* but it is often called the *PC muscle* for short. This muscle group runs from the pubic bone in the front of the body to the coccyx, or tailbone, in the rear, and it supports the pelvic floor.

In men, this is the muscle that spasms when ejaculation occurs. In women, this is the muscle that spasms during orgasm and gives the vagina a feeling of tightness.

A strong PC muscle contributes to your sexual pleasure in several ways. If you exercise it daily, you will build the muscle mass in the pelvic area, which will increase the amount of blood flowing to your genitals and allow for more pleasurable sensations during sex. In addition, a strong PC muscle can tighten the vagina and make orgasm and ejaculation stronger and more enjoyable. An added benefit is that a strong PC muscle often prevents bladder and prostate problems. In fact, correcting bladder problems in pregnant women was how this muscle was first "discovered," and the PC muscle exercises are sometimes called *Kegel exercises* after the obstetrician who first recommended them. In the chapters ahead, I'll give you more specifics on working with the PC muscle to heighten your arousal, but in this chapter I'll show you how to do the basic muscle exercises.

To exercise the PC muscle, you must first learn to identify it. Here's how. Men, to locate your PC muscle, lightly place one or two fingers behind your testicles. Pretend that you are urinating and want to stop the flow by tightening an internal muscle. That is the PC muscle. You may notice that your penis and testicles move up and down a little bit as you tighten the muscle.

Women, to locate your PC muscle, either lightly place one or two fingers on your inner vaginal lips or insert a finger about an inch into your vagina. Now squeeze as if you were urinating and wanted to stop the flow. The muscle that you feel tighten as you do this is the PC muscle. Try to flex only that small muscle and keep your thigh and abdomen muscles relaxed.

Now that you know where the PC muscle is, here is the daily PC muscle exercise I want you to do. Flex the PC muscle and hold it for about two seconds. Then release. Don't hold your breath while you are holding the muscle in. Just breathe normally. Do twenty-five repetitions three times a day. The great thing about this exercise is that you can practice it any time of the day. You can do the exercises during your morning shower, immediately after you use the toilet, while you are driving, while you are brushing your teeth, while you are watching television, or during any activity that you repeat every day. I had you touch the PC muscle to help you locate it, but when you do the exercises you do them internally, so you don't have to touch yourself. If you have trouble isolating the PC muscle from other pelvic muscles, either keep your finger on it the first few times you do the exercises or exercise the muscle while you urinate and see if you can stop the flow.

There are two common mistakes that people make when first trying these exercises. One is to overdo the repetitions by doing too many at one time or doing the exercises too frequently during the day. Like any other muscle, the PC muscle can become sore. The second mistake is to squeeze other muscles instead of the PC. When you do PC muscle exercises, the muscles in your buttocks, thighs, and abdomen should not be tense at all. They probably will be tense the first few times you do the PC muscle exercises, but work on relaxing the other muscles so you can isolate the PC.

It takes about three weeks of daily exercises for your PC muscle to get in shape. Once it is in shape, you should still exercise it every day to keep it strong and enjoy the benefits.

✑ *Exercise 5.* **THE ADVANCED PC MUSCLE EXERCISE**

After you have been doing twenty-five repetitions of the simple PC muscle exercise three times a day for three weeks, try the following, more difficult exercise. Add ten slow repetitions. Try to tense the muscle for a count of five seconds, hold for five seconds, and then release or push out on the muscle for five seconds. It's reasonable to expect to be able to work up to ten repetitions three times a day after one month, even if you're older. Or it may take more time. That's okay. Just do as many as you can.

Because of how much the PC muscle contributes to sexual health and sexual pleasure, I cannot overemphasize the importance of doing these exercises—at the recommended levels. When you begin to experience the results, you will get hooked on them, too.

✑ *Exercise 6.* **PELVIC THRUSTS AND ROLLS**

The next two exercises can help you loosen up the muscles in your pelvic area, especially your hips, thighs, and buttocks. They are also good for your back. A flexible pelvis can help you engage in more sexual positions and allow you to become more sexually aroused. Too much muscle tension in the pelvic area limits your arousal and can interfere with sensations of sexual pleasure.

Pelvic thrusts can be done either standing up or lying down. To do them standing, plant your feet about shoulder width apart and gently but firmly rock or tilt your pelvis from back to front without moving any other parts of your body.

If you are lying down, put your feet flat on the floor with your knees up and rock or tilt your buttocks slowly up and down so they are the only part of you that moves off the floor. Do the thrusts at a comfortable pace and repeat them about twenty times. Keep your other muscles relaxed and breathe evenly. You can also practice pelvic thrusts while walking. Just thrust your pelvis forward with each step.

Pelvic rolls are similar to thrusts. While either lying or standing, move your hips sideways in a continuous, rolling motion. Try to imitate the motion you would use with a hula hoop. Practice rolls at different speeds and practice some as slowly as you can. Combine thrusts and rolls and try to do them for five or ten minutes a day. Do them to music if that feels good. Try closing your eyes so you can really feel your body.

Enhancing Touch with Oils and Lubricants

In the next exercise and in most of the exercises throughout this book, I will suggest you use an oil, lotion, or other lubricant for your caress. Oils and lubricants will increase your pleasure; the sense of touch seems to linger when you use lubrication. Lubricants also enhance the sensations you feel by keeping your skin moist and preventing your touch from grabbing or sticking to the skin. For many of the advanced exercises during which you will give or receive prolonged stroking, lubricants are essential for maintaining the most pleasurable level of touch.

I prefer to use plain mineral oil because it stays warm on the body and tends to last a long time. Water-based lubricants, such as K-Y Jelly, are safe to use with condoms, but they tend to feel cooler and don't last as long on the body, so you have to keep reapplying them. Recently, many lubricants have come on the market that simulate vaginal lubrication. These can be very enjoyable, but they also tend not to last long on the body.

Some couples enjoy using scented or edible oils and lotions because they spark other senses and can be sexy and fun. The practice of aromatherapy is based on the idea that different scents have relaxing or stimulating effects. These types of oils are usually available in adult boutiques or specialty bath shops. Other couples prefer to use an entirely natural lubricant, such as vegetable oil, which has no scent and is very compatible with the body.

There are many good lubricants available to you. The lotions and oils you choose can affect and enhance the pleasurable sensations you and your lover feel, so experiment with them to find the ones you enjoy most and that work best for you. If you do try a new oil or lotion, start out with a small amount, because it may cause irritation. If it does, stop using it and try something else later. You can also try varying your oils and lotions according to the exercises and your mood, to see what sensual pleasures they bring out.

ℭ *Exercise 7.* SIMPLE SELF-CARESS

Now you will learn to practice the basic sensate-focus techniques you read about in Chapter 2. Practice these first on your own body before you do any touching exercises with your partner. This is a very important part of the sensate-focus program. Again, I strongly recommend that you practice self-caress techniques and get to know your own sensual responses before you move on to practicing with a partner.

Before you begin, have some baby oil or lotion handy. Choose a small area of your body, such as your arm, chest, or thigh, for your first caress. Touch yourself slowly and lightly on the skin surface—don't massage the muscles. Focus on the exact point of contact between your hand and your body. If your mind starts to wander off to something else, bring it back to exactly how your skin feels.

Remember to breathe evenly as you do the caress. Pay attention to the temperature and texture of your skin. Is it warm or cold, smooth or rough, firm or soft? If you have trouble focusing, slow down. Spend at least ten to fifteen minutes on this caress.

ℭ *Exercise 8.* GENITAL SELF-CARESS

After you have practiced the simple self-caress a couple of times on a couple of different body parts, you are ready to do a similar caress on your genitals. This is not the same as masturbation—the goal is not to head straight for orgasm. You will caress your genitals slowly so that you can learn about what kind of touch you prefer on your genitals. Allow about fifteen to twenty minutes for this exercise and use some baby oil or other lubricant that can be used on the genitals.

Before you do any exercise in which you touch your genitals or your partner's genitals, and especially when you will be inserting a finger into the vagina, be sure to wash your hands, trim your nails, and make sure the area under your nails is clean. Women, to do this exercise, lie or sit naked in a comfortable position. Put some baby oil on your fingers and slowly begin to touch your inner thighs and your vaginal lips. Remember to breathe and to keep your pelvic muscles, including the PC muscle, very relaxed. Slowly stroke your clitoris and inner lips, and then insert a finger into your vagina.

Focus on the point of contact between your hand and your genitals. If your mind starts to wander off to something else, bring it back to the exact point of contact.

Pay attention to the temperature, texture, and shape of your vaginal lips and clitoris and the area inside the vagina. If you become aroused during this exercise or even have an orgasm, that's fine—but it is not the goal of the exercise. Don't try to make it happen, don't force it, and don't push it away. Just experience it. Whatever happens is all part of getting in touch with your own pleasure—enjoying yourself and learning about your body.

Men, to do this exercise, sit or lie naked in a comfortable position. Use some baby oil or lotion on your fingers. Slowly begin to stroke the skin of your penis and scrotum. Remember to go very slowly; this is not a masturbation stroke. Don't try to get an erection, but if you have one, enjoy it.

Concentrate on the exact point of contact between your hand and your genitals. Pay attention to the temperature, texture, and shape of your penis and scrotum. If your mind wanders off to something else, slow your touch down and bring your mind back to the point of contact. Remember to breathe and to keep your pelvic muscles, including the PC muscle, as relaxed as possible.

After you have spent fifteen or twenty minutes on this caress, if you want to have an orgasm and ejaculation, go ahead. Just don't feel like you have to have one if you're not really in the mood.

Practice this genital self-caress exercise at least once, but preferably a few times. Repeat it as often as you like. Caressing yourself in this way will teach you to focus on touch, to breathe deeply, and to relax your muscles— three of the most important basics for continued sexual pleasure.

♂ *Exercise* 9. **AROUSAL AWARENESS**

The foundation of the sexual pleasure program that I describe in this book is to become aware of your arousal and learn to manipulate it. This is the "sex by the numbers" approach that I discussed in Chapter 3. "Peaking" is a process in which you learn to modulate your arousal, whether you are pleasuring yourself or receiving a caress from your partner. When you peak, your arousal goes up and down a series of levels that are under your control. Doing this increases your staying power and builds up sexual charge.

The first step to peaking is arousal awareness: Before you learn to peak, you have to be able to recognize how sexually aroused you are. The way to do this is to think of your sexual arousal on a scale from 1 to 10, as I described in Chapter 3. Using this number system may sound clinical and may seem to contradict what I said in earlier chapters about getting away from a performance orientation. Please don't get the impression that I am asking you to evaluate yourself in any way. Rather, these numbers are to help you *describe* your sexual responses. The idea is not to see how high you can go in any one exercise, but to help you become aware of the differences in how you feel at each level. In other words, reaching a level 9 in any exercise is not better than reaching a level 5; it's just different. As one of my clients, Paul, said, "At first I thought it was really strange to use this 'numbers' approach to arousal, but it turned out to be user-friendly, since everybody understands the concept 'on a scale from 1 to 10.'"

If the idea of numbers bothers you, you might think instead of a musical scale, in which the notes get higher and higher. We'll be using this arousal scale throughout the book, and I promise you it will get easier to work with. After you get used to it, the numbers will just drop away and you'll be left with the sensations. Men, remember, the scale I'm talking about here describes how close you feel to orgasm, not your erection level. That's a separate scale that we'll be using in a later chapter.

To review, on this 1-to-10 scale, a 1 is no arousal and a 10 is orgasm. Consider a twinge feeling in the genital area a 2 or 3. A 4 is a steady, low level of arousal. A 5 or a 6 is a medium level of arousal. By the time you reach level 7 or 8, you may feel a little short of breath, or you may feel your heart pound or your face flush. A 9 is the point right before orgasm, and a 10 is orgasm.

To do the arousal awareness exercise, begin a slow genital self-caress as you did in the previous exercise. Caress yourself exactly as you did last time, breathing, relaxing, and paying attention to the point of contact between your fingers and your genitals.

During a twenty-minute exercise, every five minutes or so, ask yourself, "What arousal level do I feel I am at now?" Don't try to reach any particular level of arousal. Just notice it and try to estimate your arousal level on the 1-to-10 scale. At this stage, don't try to manipulate or control your arousal level in any way.

Caress your genitals in the way that feels best to you and remember to go slowly to make it easier to stay focused. If you want to have an orgasm at the end of this exercise, go ahead.

ℰ *Exercise 10.* **PEAKING**

In this exercise you will actually peak—that is, you will modulate your arousal so that it goes up and down in a series of hills and valleys. Allow about twenty to twenty-five minutes for this exercise and have lubrication ready. Refer to Figure 6 on page 36 to familiarize yourself with the peaking pattern. To begin, caress your genitals until you think you are just past the "twinge" stage (level 2 or 3). Then stop the stimulation and allow yourself to go back to level 1. Start caressing again and this time go up to level 5. Stop the stimulation again and allow your arousal to go down two levels, to level 3.

Repeat this cycle a few times and try peaking at levels 6, 7, 8, and 9, if you can. Each peak should last about three to five minutes, including both the up and down phases. If you're really aroused at the end of the exercise, go ahead and have an orgasm.

Try not to forget the basics. Pay attention to the exact point where your hand touches your genitals. Be lovingly slow with your touch. Breathe, and keep your muscles, including the PC muscle, very relaxed.

Repeat this exercise as often as you feel like it. To vary it a little, do one whole peaking exercise where you only play with the lower levels (2, 3, 4, and 5) and another exercise where you only play with the higher levels (6, 7, 8, and 9). Or you could do several peaks all at the same high level. You may find that the peaking process makes your orgasm stronger if you do decide to have one. The whole peaking process seems to allow for the optimal release of endorphins that I described in Chapter 1. The gradual buildup of sexual energy that happens during the peaking process will help your body prepare for the exercises you will do with your partner later in the book.

ℰ *Exercise 11.* **PLATEAUING WITH BREATHING**

Plateauing is an advanced form of peaking in which you allow your arousal to go up to a certain level and stay there for a period of time, from a few seconds to as long as a couple of minutes. Plateauing is illustrated in Figure 7. You plateau by using several techniques you have already learned, as well as a couple of new ones. The techniques include

> breathing
> pelvic movements
> using the PC muscle
> switching focus

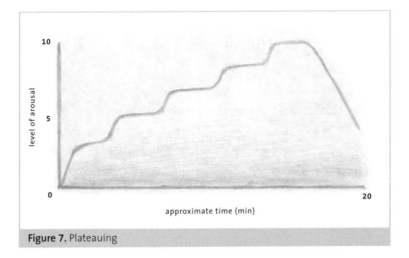

Figure 7. Plateauing

I recommend that you practice using them one at a time, so that you thoroughly learn each technique before you add the next one. While this may seem complicated at first because of all of the numbers involved, remember that you already have experience recognizing your arousal levels from the peaking exercises.

For this first exercise, begin with a genital caress. Remember to caress yourself in the slow sensate-focus style. Breathe and keep your pelvic muscles relaxed.

Comfortably allow your arousal to go up to a level 4. You will try to plateau at level 4 by changing your breathing. As you reach a point slightly higher than level 4, slowly take two deep belly breaths. This will allow your arousal to go down slightly. When your arousal dips a little bit below level 4, speed up your breathing so that you are almost panting. This will cause your arousal level to go back up. See if you can hover around level 4 for thirty seconds or more just by changing your breathing. The technique here is to slow your breathing down to lower your arousal and speed your breathing up to increase your arousal.

The way to plateau is to visualize the in-between levels. In other words, when you sense that you are slightly above level 4, you are actually recognizing level 4½, and when you sense that you are slightly below level 4, you are actually recognizing level 3½. Continue this exercise, plateauing at levels 5, 6, 7, 8, and 9, if you can. Finish the plateauing exercise with a climax if you're in the mood.

✑ *Exercise 12.* **PLATEAUING WITH PELVIC MOVEMENTS**

In this version of the plateauing exercise, you will use changes in your pelvic movements to help you plateau. These are the same pelvic movements you did in the pelvic thrust and roll exercise. To begin, caress your genitals, using some lubrication. Remember to caress yourself slowly and to breathe and relax. When you reach a level 4½, stop stroking. When you dip down below level 4, start touching yourself again and also start some slow pelvic rolls and thrusts. See if you can plateau for about thirty seconds at level 4 by stopping the touch if you go too high and doing pelvic thrusts and rolls if you go too low. The basic technique is to speed up or put more energy into your pelvic movements to become more aroused, and slow down your pelvic movements to become less aroused.

Use these changes in pelvic movement to plateau at levels 5, 6, 7, 8, and 9, if you can. See if you can hold any of these plateaus for longer than thirty seconds. Finish the exercise with an orgasm if you feel like it. Going through all of these different plateaus will make it second nature to you to modulate your arousal by moving your pelvis.

✑ *Exercise 13.* **PLATEAUING WITH THE PC MUSCLE**

Begin with a genital self-caress, using lubrication. Remember to focus on your slow touch and to relax and breathe. When you reach a point just beyond arousal level 4, stop caressing and squeeze your PC muscle a couple of times. This should take your arousal level down. When your arousal level dips below level 4, start caressing yourself again. See if you can plateau for thirty seconds at arousal level 4 just by using this combination of starting and stopping the touch and squeezing your PC muscle.

Men, when you use the PC muscle to plateau, you have to watch out that you squeeze just hard enough so that your arousal level goes down but not so hard that the squeezing makes your erection go down. It may take a little practice to know how many squeezes to do and how hard to squeeze so that you affect your arousal but not your erection. If this PC squeezing does affect your erection, just start the plateauing exercise at a higher arousal level when you have a firmer erection.

Continue the exercise, plateauing at levels 5, 6, 7, 8, and 9, if you can, just by using the combination of stopping and starting your touch and squeezing the PC muscle. Finish the exercise with an orgasm if you are in the mood.

⌇ *Exercise 14.* **PLATEAUING BY SWITCHING FOCUS**

This exercise uses changes in your focus in order to plateau. During any kind of sexual activity, it is possible to focus on a number of different things that are going on. In all of the touching exercises that you have already done, I had you focus on the exact point of contact where you were touching yourself. That's the basis of sensate focus. But it's possible to use sensate-focus techniques to touch one area and focus on another area.

When you do a genital caress on yourself, it's possible to focus on how your hand feels touching your genitals or on how your genitals feel when they are being touched by your hand. You can practice consciously switching your focus back and forth between these two aspects of the touch.

Let me make a couple of analogies—one to a symphony orchestra and one to a finely prepared meal. If you are listening to a symphony orchestra for the first time, you probably experience the music as one combined sound. But with a little more experience, you can pay attention to the different sections—the strings, woodwinds, etc. If you have experience playing a musical instrument yourself, you may even be able to pick out the sounds of the individual instruments.

Or let's say that a famous chef has prepared a special meal for you. You will probably really enjoy the meal whatever your background, but if you have an extensive cooking background, you will probably be able to pick out the tastes of the individual spices, the same way that wine experts can pick up subtle flavors.

By learning the skill of switching focus, you can become a sexual virtuoso or gourmet chef. To begin this version of the plateauing exercise, caress your genitals, using some lubrication. Focus intently on the area you are touching. When you reach a level slightly above level 4, continue touching yourself but focus on the way your genitals feel being touched by your hand. When your arousal level dips down slightly below level 4, just focus normally. Now go up to a level slightly above level 5. Continue touching yourself but now switch your focus to the way your hand feels touching your genitals. See if you can plateau at level 5 for thirty seconds by switching your focus back and forth between what your genitals feel like when they are being touched by your hand and what your hand feels like when it is touching your genitals.

Whew! This one takes a little bit of mental effort, doesn't it? There's yet another way to do this. When you reach a desired level, switch your focus to some part of the genitals you are not currently touching. This will make your arousal dip down slightly. For example, when you reach a level slightly above level 6, if you are stroking the head of your penis, keep stroking the head but shift your focus to what the shaft feels like. When your arousal dips down below level 6, switch your focus back to the area that you are currently touching. Or if you are caressing your clitoris and you reach a desired plateauing level, switch your focus instead to how the opening of your vagina feels.

See if you can plateau through the whole range of levels by either switching your focus from hand to genitals and back, or by switching your focus from the area you are currently touching to another area.

When you have mastered all of the plateauing techniques—breathing, pelvic movements, using the PC muscle, and switching focus—you can practice using them all in the same exercise by using a different plateauing technique for each level. Then, when you get really good at these techniques, try combining them. When you reach a desired plateau level, slow down your breathing, squeeze your PC muscle, and switch your focus. When you want your arousal level to rise, use pelvic thrusts and rolls. Pretty soon these techniques will all become second nature and you will do them automatically whenever you feel your arousal level change. At that point, you won't have to worry about numbers anymore.

The next chapter takes a look at the nature of sexual desire, and then we get into sensate-focus exercises that partners can do together.

chapter 5

Thoughts on the Nature of Sexual Desire

by Morgan Cowin

*W*hen *people ask me my favorite sexual position (and a surprising number of people do ask me that, mostly my students), I always say, "A philosophical one." As part of that approach, what I have done in this chapter is make a series of observations about sexual desire. I figure maybe if I talk around the topic, some of these observations will resonate with you and give you insight that can help increase desire in your life.*

I've placed this chapter between the one on self-pleasuring exercises and the one on introductory partner exercises for a simple reason: If you are going to engage in sensual or sexual activites with another person—such as the sensate-focus exercises that are presented in the next chapter—it helps if you feel at least *some* sexual desire for that person. Yet whether or not you feel desire for your partner doesn't depend purely on your respective moods. Sexual desire between two partners who care for each other can actually be enhanced—and doing sensate-focus exercises with your partner is one way to stimulate desire, as I discuss in more detail in the next chapter. Meanwhile, in this chapter I present some basic information about desire and how it is experienced differently by women and men. I also offer suggestions for increasing your sexual desire.

Sexual Desire, Libido, and the Zest for Life

What is sexual desire? No one has really pinned it down or defined it to my satisfaction, yet a lot of people are convinced that they have problems with it. In fact, reduced or "inhibited" sexual desire is one of the primary sexual complaints of our culture. I'm not so sure everyone who worries that they have a problem with sexual desire actually *does* have a "problem," in the clinical sense of the word. I think desire springs from a fundamental longing for union with another person. It seems to involve a mental state of readiness, a certain enlivening of the body, and a focusing of attention on what can satisfy that hunger. Still, how we feel about ourselves, our partner, and the circumstances of our lives will make an enormous difference in whether we feel desirous—and desirable—or not.

Libido, or sex drive, is an aspect of sexual desire, but it does not account for all of it. Libido is the psychic energy we get from our basic biological urges. It is also a measure of how often the body feels ready to have an orgasm. Libido is at least partially affected by genetics. It can also be influenced by our diet, by depression, and by other chemical and hormonal changes. Like sexual desire, libido fluctuates. Nobody has the same sex drive all the time, nor do we always feel the same level of desire.

We know that sexual desire includes a strong component of testosterone-based sex drive, especially in men. What we lack is a coherent theory about the psychological components of sexual desire. The good news is that there are several factors that are absolutely known to increase sexual desire. The bad news is most relationships are not set up to include these factors. These factors are

- novelty
- risk
- being forced to be apart
- exploration
- leisure time
- the absence of adult responsibilities

Let's talk first about *novelty*. Most people in committed relationships are not willing to go out and have sex with someone else just to boost their general level of sexual desire (although it will work). What you could do instead is boost novelty by using fantasy. Most people find it okay to fantasize about other partners.

That exciting sense of taking a *risk* also contributes to sexual desire. The problem with trying to insert an element of risk into your relationship is that probably the reason you wanted to be in a relationship is so you don't have to go out there and risk rejection. So you can use fantasy to insert this element. Or you and your partner could get out of the same old rut and actually try a few new things sexually.

Couples who are *forced by circumstances to be apart* often experience increases in sexual desire. An example of this is the "Romeo and Juliet" effect. Young couples who are forbidden to see each other by their parents are often much more attracted to each other than they would be if the parents don't interfere. You and your partner probably aren't teenagers, but if one or both of you travel a lot, use that fantasy life of yours again. Pretend that you and your partner can't wait to be together and some evil force is keeping you apart. This actually makes for pretty good fantasy material.

The *exploration* element may also be a little difficult to inject into your relationship if you've been with the same partner for a long time. You probably feel as if you know every inch of his or her body. That's why the sensate-focus program will increase your desire. It will give you a new perspective on your partner's body and create a climate of exploration.

Think back to some of your first relationships when you were a young adult. Remember how horny you were, and how you couldn't wait to be with your partner? Do you wonder why you don't feel that same level of desire for your partner now? Look around you. The context of your relationship is completely different. Back then, you may not even have known how you were going to pay the rent next month, but that thought definitely didn't keep you from wanting to have sex. Now you probably work a lot and worry about money. You may even have kids to support. All of these things can be real sexual-desire killers.

I don't think you should abandon your family and move to a commune just to get your libido back. But try to recognize the considerable impact your *adult responsibilities* have on your level of sexual desire. You may be unable to avoid these responsibilities, but you can temporarily put them on the back burner by arranging for a few days away by yourselves and agreeing not to worry about being responsible for that time. Budget the money for the time off, and pay for as much of it ahead of time as you can so you don't have to make any financial decisions or worry about money.

Another word for desire is enthusiasm. You can go to bed with your partner and have sex and experience a lot of pleasure, or you can leap into bed because you can't wait to jump your partner's bones. To me, the biggest problem with Masters and Johnson's work is not just that they failed to include a desire phase of the sexual-response cycle. They also failed to note that how people respond in a planned sexual encounter in a laboratory is probably profoundly different from the way they would respond in a sexual encounter with someone they were madly in love with and couldn't wait to have sex with. I mean, ask yourself, "What if I were in one of Masters and Johnson's studies? My partner and I would go into the lab and get all wired up, and then Masters and Johnson would tell us to have sex the way we usually do. How would it feel?" You would probably go through with it, but it might be a little intimidating or even kind of boring.

Now, picture yourself in a different scenario. You've been madly in love with someone for years, and circumstances have prevented you from having sex with this person. You have literally been lusting after this person for years. You think about this person the first thing every morning when you wake up, and you think about this person the last thing every night before you go to sleep. How do you think you'd respond if you finally had the chance to have sex with this person? If you were in Masters and Johnson's laboratory, you'd probably blow up all of their equipment!

My point here is that sexual desire has an object, whereas sex drive does not. You could be horny due to the action of testosterone, and in most cases having sex with just about anyone would probably satisfy your sex drive. But when you sexually desire someone, all of your psychic energy, lust, enthusiasm, and love are directed toward that person and no one else.

Sexual desire is like *élan vital*—a fancy French phrase that means life force or joy in living. Sigmund Freud believed that the libido was so powerful that it was the driving force in the development of the personality. (He also said that love was exaggerating the difference between two women, or something like that, but never mind. He had his own problems.) I talk to people all the time who say they have low sexual desire or they wonder how to get their desire back. For the most part, these people lead boring or even depressing lives. If you are a boring person in all of the other areas of your life, why in the world would you expect to be a dynamo in bed? Your level of sexual desire is reflective of your connection or involvement with other important areas of your life. Sexual desire is what integrates your sex life with the rest of your life.

This view implies that if you want to increase your level of sexual desire, you need to develop an enthusiasm for other areas of your life. What is it that floats your boat? I'm not talking about taking up a new hobby or developing an obsessive interest in something. People often become obsessed with exercise or other hobbies as a way of avoiding sex or as a substitute for sex.

What I'm talking about is something I've noticed for a long time about sexual desire. The people I've observed who seem to enjoy the highest levels of sexual desire are those who have a curiosity and enthusiasm about life in general. These are the people who are fully present in everything they do, whether it's interacting with their family, working at their job, or pursuing a goal like community activism. They aren't trying to do twenty-seven things at once. Multitasking is an enemy of sexual desire. As an antidote, try to deepen your level of involvement and connection with things that are important to you. You'll see the benefits reflected in your sex life.

Male-Female Differences in Sexual Desire

This section is primarily directed toward women, but some men will find it applicable too. There are several major differences in the way that the average man and the average woman experience sexual desire—though there are always exceptions. A woman's psychological sense of her sexual desire also tends to be much more influenced by sociocultural factors, such as her perception of her role as a woman or her permission to be sexual.

One of the biggest differences is that for most men, sexual desire and sex drive are pretty much synonymous. In other words, most of a man's sexual desire is testosterone-based sex drive. While women need a certain level of testosterone to feel horny, for a lot of women testosterone is not enough. For many women, sexual desire is inextricably connected to moods, relationship issues, physical appearance, and any number of other contextual issues.

Social scientists put it this way: A man's sexual desire is primarily governed by nature, but a woman's sexual desire is primarily governed by culture. Or to say it in a very simplified way, men tend to look inward to determine what their level of sexual desire is, and women tend to look outward. Here's an example. A man has a sensation in his groin. He looks down at his penis and sees that he has an erection. He thinks, "I'm aroused." He doesn't think, "I wonder if I'm aroused."

On the other hand, a woman could notice that she's lubricating, and we have no way of predicting her thoughts. She could have any number of reactions. Sure, she could be thinking "I'm aroused." But she could also be thinking, "I wonder why I'm aroused," or, "Look at this clown I'm with— I couldn't possibly be aroused," or, "Do I look fat?" or even, "I'm wet— that's disgusting."

Women who react this way aren't in denial. It's literally possible for a woman to lubricate but not feel a psychological sense of sexual desire or arousal.

An example of how women may be influenced by social stereotypes has to do with the notion of the sexual peak. Have you ever heard the stereotype that men reach their sexual peak at age eighteen and women reach their peak at thirty-five? Like most stereotypes, this one has a grain of truth. Research has shown that when we talk about a man's sexual peak, we are talking about the time of his life when he is able to get an erection most quickly, whereas when we talk about a woman's sexual peak, most people understand that to mean the years when a woman has the highest level of desire and is able to have an orgasm most easily.

A woman's sex drive is most likely to be at its peak between the ages of about seventeen and twenty-five, because that's when a woman's body produces its highest testosterone levels. Those levels start to decline as early as the late twenties. However, a woman could feel her highest levels of sexual desire at any time in her life. It's probably true that by the mid-thirties most women are fairly confident in their ability to have orgasms.

Another area where societal expectations can short-circuit a woman's sex drive has to do with our stereotype about the typical woman with low sexual desire. Our stereotype of the woman with low desire is usually a woman who has been married for a number of years and has kids and no longer wants sex with her husband.

But what about single women? They could have desire issues too. I know of no research comparing sexual desire issues in monogamous women versus women with several partners. If I had to guess, I would say that non-monogamous women probably have higher levels of sexual desire, because there may be some question about where or when they are going to be able to have sex next (or with whom). That uncertainty creates the exact kind of circumstance that makes for higher levels of desire.

Here's a value judgment. I believe that the best of all possible worlds for most people would be to have one partner but have huge amounts of desire for that partner. For most of us, that's probably not possible. What if you had to choose between the following:

1. You could have a monogamous relationship with a partner whom you loved and who loved you. You would enjoy sex but not really feel sexual desire or testosterone-based lust for your partner.

    OR

2. You could be the horniest woman on the planet, but no one would love you enough to have sex with you.

When you look at it that way, you see that your problems are important to you, but everybody's dealing with her or his own problems. (In a way, the example is kind of off the wall, because I think if you were the horniest woman on the planet, somebody would be interested, no matter how unlovable you were.)

Besides social beliefs that have an impact on our expectations about male and female sexual desire, another reason that women's desire issues are more complicated has to do with hormones. Both men and women have testosterone. Men have more, which is why a man's sex drive tends to be stronger on average than a woman's. In addition to testosterone, both men and women have a brain chemical called *dopamine* that appears to influence both sexual desire and sexual pleasure. Dopamine is not a hormone, it's a neurotransmitter, which is a brain chemical that allows brain cells to communicate with each other. Dopamine has many functions in the brain, one of which appears to be inspiring and motivating the pursuit of pleasure. People who are depressed and don't show their usual level of interest in sex and other pleasurable pursuits often have low levels of dopamine activity.

The late Theresa Crenshaw, M.D., was a sex therapist and researcher and the author of *The Alchemy of Love and Lust,* among other books. She believed that women have several different types of sex drive or sexual desire based on different hormones. She believed that testosterone was responsible for a woman's "aggressive" sex drive—the type of lusty sex drive that a woman would have in common with a man. She also believed that high levels of dopamine, estrogen, and oxytocin (the bonding hormone) influence what she called a woman's "seductive" sex drive—the urge to attract a man. Dr. Crenshaw believed that high levels of estrogen and serotonin (another neurotransmitter, also implicated in depression) influence what she called the "receptive" sex drive—the urge to be penetrated or be the recipient of sexual intercourse. For many women, receptive desire is a reaction to a stimulus rather than a spontaneous impulse.

So you can see that female sexual desire is more complicated than most of us think. If you are a woman and you believe that you have low sexual desire, please take the information in this section to heart. The nature of your sexual desire may change daily, weekly, monthly, or yearly. Testosterone-based lust is not the only form of sexual desire for you as a woman. Through the use of the exercises in this book, try to recognize when your desire takes the form of your wanting to be the receptive partner in intercourse, wanting to seduce your partner, wanting to sexually dominate your partner, or wanting to be intimate with your partner. These are all forms of sexual desire. Don't limit yourself to a male-based view of sexual desire.

Another area where men and women differ has to do with Masters and Johnson's sexual-response cycle (see Figure 4 on page 30). One of the major criticisms of the sexual-response cycle over the years has been that on average the cycle is more reflective of a male pattern of response than a female pattern, which is true. When Helen Singer Kaplan added the desire phase, this issue became even more complicated. Men are more likely than women to have the stages go in order: desire, excitement, plateau, orgasm. However, for women, sexual desire and sexual excitement (or arousal) often occur at the same time. For example, once a woman starts to lubricate, she may also feel a surge of desire. Or a woman might not really desire sex until she is very aroused or even close to orgasm.

Desire Killers

This section is also primarily intended for women. As my colleagues and I have noticed over the years, psychological issues that can intrude on sensational sexuality seem to run along gender lines. For men, the big issues are penis size and performance fears. Women, on the other hand, have several issues that can dampen desire. Actually, these issues can affect all phases of the sexual-response cycle, not just desire, but I decided to include them in this chapter because desire is where it all really starts. These issues include the permission factor, poor body image, lack of masturbation experience, performance pressure, lack of assertiveness, a history of sexual abuse, and intrusive thoughts.

Many women seem to have difficulty giving themselves permission to enjoy their sensuality and their sexuality. One reason for this is that unenlightened attitudes and double standards persist, even today. I still hear comments like the following from clients and students who are in their twenties: "I was told that only 'bad girls' enjoy sex," or, "I was taught that you have sex because it's your duty; I didn't know it was possible to enjoy it."

This attitude is unfortunate and unfortunately common. Many women who have problems with sexual desire say they wish they could have sex for their husband's sake because they feel sorry for their husbands. If that is your attitude, you really owe it to yourself to do the sensate-focus exercises in the next chapter and in the chapters on arousal and orgasm. Unless you give yourself permission to enjoy sex and want to have sex for yourself, it's going to be really difficult for you to experience the ultimate in sexual pleasure.

Another reason women sometimes hold back or lose their desire for sex is poor body image. I know too many women who would rather skip sex because they feel fat and unattractive. As one client told me, "I don't feel okay about having sex because I don't feel comfortable having my partner look at my body."

Most women I talk to have a problem with their body image. Even the most beautiful women in the world find something to dislike about their own bodies. This is because we have become captive to a media-generated ideal that has little to do with reality. When you look at yourself in the mirror every day, you probably compare yourself consciously or unconsciously with models, actresses, socialites, and other celebrities—all inhabitants of a fantasyland. Try to remember that the reflection that stares back at you from the mirror lacks the benefit of an image stylist, a professional makeup artist, perfect lighting, and the right camera angles, not to mention the best plastic surgery and personal fitness trainers money can buy.

Don't allow a negative body image to stand in the way of your sexual enjoyment. Your partner probably appreciates your body the way it is and finds you very desirable. Women are much harder on themselves than their partners are. In surveys, men indicate that their standards of attractiveness are much more relaxed than women's. Have you ever heard the old joke "What does a woman have to do for a man to find her desirable?" Answer: "Show up." Again, like most stereotypes, this one contains a grain of truth.

You may find your breasts or thighs unattractive, for instance, but chances are that your partner likes the way they look and feel. In fact, studies have shown that many men prefer their partners slightly heavier and softer than the women would ideally like to be. To deny yourself sexual enjoyment because you think you don't meet certain standards of attractiveness is a huge waste. You can enjoy your sensuality and sexuality no matter what you think your body looks like—and your body will look better for it!

Of course, changes that make you feel better about yourself will help your sex life. Sex feels better when you are in good health. So try to exercise moderately, quit smoking, and eat healthy foods. Doing so will improve your skin tone and muscle tone—your overall fitness—which do have a bearing on how much you enjoy sex. (The same goes for men, too!) Remember that a woman's sexual desire needs more maintenance than a man's, and one of the best ways to help maintain it is with physical exercise, because exercise boosts dopamine. Moderate weight loss has also been shown to boost sexual desire.

Another very common reason that women have problems with low sexual desire is because they often have sex with a partner before they have explored their own bodies. Most men have masturbated for years before they ever have sex with a woman. But for many women, touching their own genitals has been taboo, and this lack of masturbation experience means that they have learned nothing about what stimulates them and pleases them during lovemaking.

Women are often shy about communicating their sexual desires and needs to their partner. Part of this is rooted in the old "nice girls don't do it, and they certainly don't enjoy it" myth. This is an attitude destined for the dustheap. It is up to you to take full responsibility for your own sexual enjoyment and make sure that your desires are fulfilled. If communicating about your sexual desires is difficult for you, you will find exercises in Chapter 14 that can make doing so easier. They show you how to give your partner instructions and feedback about your desires in a very structured way, in order to minimize any discomfort you might feel.

Being unassertive is one thing, but some women actually sabotage their sexual desire. They do this by making sure that they don't have time for sex, or that the only time they have available is very late at night when they know their partner will be too tired for sex. Are you scheduling every hour of the day because you have very little desire for sex? If so, it's time to change that now. Ask yourself whether you are subverting possible sexual situations rather than creating them.

Sexual abuse as a child or adolescent, or a sexual trauma as an adult, can have serious consequences for your sexual desire. It is common for those who have been sexually abused as children to become afraid of sex. These women shut down their feelings so that they won't be hurt again. They feel betrayed, powerless, mistrustful, and out of control regarding sexuality.

If you have been sexually abused, you may need to see a counselor to help you recover from the experience and move beyond it to enjoy a full sexual life. You may find that the exercises in this book, especially those in Chapters 4, 6, and 14, can help you rebuild your sexuality from the ground up—particularly if you have a loving partner you can share them with. Keep in mind that you will probably have to take it slowly to learn about sex in a nontraumatic way and to regain your sexual desire.

Men and women think differently. This comes as no surprise to anyone. There are a number of research findings regarding the different ways that men and women process information. Men seem to have an easier time compartmentalizing—that is, they seem to be more able to experience one thing at a time (like sex) and tune out everything else—whereas women tend to have more intrusive thoughts. This becomes very apparent in our sexuality. Women have a much more difficult time than men clearing the details of the day from their heads to free themselves for sex. Then when they have sex, thoughts or worries about the day still intrude. Women tend to be more other-focused than men. This means that it's important for women to make some kind of transition between whatever they were doing before they had sex, and sex. Good transitions include meditation, listening to music, physical exercise, relaxation exercises, or massage.

Men seem to have the opposite problem. They deny that anything else could be on their minds, and they go ahead and try to have sex if it's offered to them. But sometimes they're really not ready. This is one reason why men experience the performance problems they do.

Neither way of thinking is good. There must be a happy medium, in which you can clear your mind to allow yourself to focus on sex but can accept your feelings enough to know that something is bothering you that you need to deal with before you try to have sex.

Sensate-focus exercises are very helpful for the problem of intrusive thoughts, because they give you a mental device, something to focus on so your thoughts don't intrude. The better your sensate-focus abilities become, the better you will be able to deal with those intrusive thoughts when they hit.

Drugs to Enhance Sexual Desire

As mentioned earlier, sex drive in both men and women is primarily a function of the hormone testosterone. For women, this is the aggressive or assertive component of sexual desire. Whether you are a man or a woman, if you experience a precipitous decline or shutdown of your sex drive after a period of having a normal sex drive, you probably should have your testosterone levels checked.

There are testosterone skin patches and injections available for men, but they only work if a man has abnormally low levels of testosterone. There are also testosterone-based creams for women that are designed to be rubbed onto the thighs on a daily basis. The FDA has approved only one testosterone-based oral medication for women. It's a combination of estrogen and testosterone called Estratest. It's usually given to women after menopause. It's not specifically prescribed to improve sex drive, but anecdotal evidence indicates that it can. If you believe that a decrease in your sex drive has been caused by hormonal problems, you may need to consult with an endocrinologist and have him or her recommend a special compounding pharmacy that can make a custom blend of hormones for you.

Some women have found that taking DHEA (dihydroepiandrosterone, a steroidal hormone used by the body to create testosterone) can lead to an improvement in their sex drive. DHEA supplements are sold in health-food stores.

There is also a new supplement on the market called Avlimil. Again, it is primarily recommended for women who have experienced a lowered sex drive after menopause. Avlimil is a nonprescription daily supplement that contains herbs and roots like black cohosh, sage leaf, capsicum pepper, damiana, and ginger root. The website for Avlimil claims that it promotes blood flow, increases both relaxation and libido, results in large improvements in desire, arousal, and orgasm, and generally enhances sex and improves satisfaction.

Recall that the neurotransmitter dopamine is responsible for the seductive component of female sexual desire. Dopamine motivates people to pursue pleasure. There is a drug called *apomorphine* that supposedly works on dopamine in the brain. It is still in the testing stages, and it will be interesting to see whether it works. (It is in testing to see if it improves men's erections by helping to start the initiation phase of erection, which is mostly mental.)

If you are having problems with low desire, it is hard to tell if it could be due to low dopamine activity, because it's difficult to measure dopamine in the brain. A brain scan is required to measure dopamine activity. However, an antidepressant called Wellbutrin is known to boost dopamine activity in the areas of the brain that have to do with pleasure. And don't forget that any kind of physical movement—for example, exercise or bodywork—will boost dopamine.

As I've mentioned several times, one of the best ways to enhance sexual desire is to participate with your partner in some basic sensate-focus exercises. So let's do it!

chapter 6

Partner Caresses That Kindle Desire

by Paul Dahlquist

I*n Chapter 4 you took the time to explore your sexuality with simple self-caresses. Now it's time to experience your partner's body in a whole new way. The basic sensate-focus caresses presented in this chapter are delightfully relaxing and will get you in just the right mood to explore your sensuality and set the stage for pleasure. That's why I'll have you do one or more of these caresses as a prelude to most of the advanced exercises ahead. You will find that they really do ignite your desire, even if you don't exactly feel de-*

72

72

sirous when you begin the exercises. Am I suggesting that you shouldn't wait until "the moment is right" to do sensate-focus exercises? Yes, and here's why.

Most people operate under the myth that spontaneous sex is the best kind—the more surprise, the sweeter the interlude. Somehow the idea of penciling a lovemaking session into your datebook the way you would a business luncheon or a dentist appointment seems rather, well, crass.

If you feel this way, you probably assume that you have to wait until you feel mutual desire to try one of these exercises with your partner. I would counsel you not to wait. Instead, make a date to do them when you both have time. My experience with clients has shown that if you schedule time for these exercises, over time your desire will actually increase, whereas if you wait for the "right" time, it could be a very long wait! I don't mean to discount spontaneous sexual desire; spontaneous sex is great. But the truth is that sexual desire will happen more frequently only if you make the time for it.

The series of caresses I introduce below can help. They stimulate desire, and that is a boon in this modern age, when the hectic pace of life can cause a temporary loss of interest in sex. (Here I use the term *interest* synonymously with *desire.*) Believe it or not, poor time management is one of the most common causes for the loss of sexual desire. Fatigue, stress, and boredom also take their toll. Fortunately, there are solutions. I am assuming that your healthy sexual desire is what led you to buy this book. But if fatigue, stress, and plain boredom are issues for you, the exercises in this chapter can help bring your desire back.

How Sensate-Focus Exercises Stir Up Desire

Remember what I said about the importance of relaxation for sexual desire and arousal? The basic sensate-focus exercises you are about to learn activate the relaxation response. Try them, and you'll see how the slow, pleasurable touch can restore a deep sense of calm. But the benefits don't stop there. Since the exercises are new to you, they will alleviate sexual boredom (in the last chapter I mentioned the importance of novelty and exploration for enhancing sexual desire). Because you have to plan and schedule time to do the exercises, you will get accustomed to making sexual activity a higher priority in your life. The exercises will also gradually increase your sexual arousal. Sexual desire and sexual arousal are not the same thing. The relationship between the two of them is complex. In the discussion in Chapter 3 about Masters and Johnson's human sexual-response cycle, I mentioned that another well-known sex therapist and researcher named Helen Singer Kaplan had added a desire phase to the response cycle. This desire phase supposedly precedes the excitement phase, the idea being that you have to have some base level of desire to motivate you to begin sexual activity.

But this isn't necessarily true. Many people begin sexual activity when they don't really feel desire. Most of us believe that the relationship between attitudes and behaviors is that attitudes cause behaviors; in other words, you want to do something and that causes you to do it. But this relationship can be reversed. Many times doing a behavior causes us to have a better attitude toward it.

To think about this in terms of sex, compare sex to an exercise program. A lot of people would like to exercise, but they just can't seem to get started. They really don't have the desire to exercise, and they make all kinds of excuses for why they can't do it. But if you force yourself to get out a couple of times and start walking, a funny thing happens. Physically you feel better, so you want to walk more. Plus, you look back at your behavior and say to yourself, "I must like walking more than I thought."

The same thing will happen with sex. Once you start doing these basic sensate-focus exercises, they'll energize you and cause endorphins to be released, and that will motivate you to want sex more often, and that's the definition of desire. Plus, you'll look back on how much you enjoyed an exercise and you'll say to yourself, "I must really want sex more than I thought."

To do these next few partner exercises correctly, remember the sensate-focus principles I discussed in Chapter 2. First, remember to focus on the sensations you feel at the exact place where your skin meets your partner's skin. Second, try to keep your awareness in the here and now. If you let your mind drift off to the chores you have planned for later in the day or the project due at work, your sexual desire won't even have a chance. But if you allow yourself to focus, appreciation builds. When you can appreciate your sensual experience with a partner, your desire for that contact increases, and your pleasure in it grows.

Finally, focus on nondemand interaction, a basic concept I explained in the second chapter. When you are the active partner, caress for your own pleasure. Don't aim for—or expect—any particular response from your partner. When you are the passive partner, allow yourself to follow the sensations and enjoy them, without feeling that you have to respond.

Now let's try the first of the sensate-focus exercises for partners.

✑ *Exercise 15.* **THE FACE CARESS**

This exercise will really relax you. Like the back caress that follows, it is a short, nongenital caress that can be used to make the transition to other, more sexual exercises. Just because it is not a genital exercise does not mean it isn't sexual or sensual. For the reasons discussed in the previous section, these nongenital exercises can increase desire.

To do the face caress, you will need some type of lotion that both you and your partner like. Make sure that you both find the scent and texture appealing. You will also need a quiet room where you won't be disturbed for one hour and a clock or watch to time the exercise.

The partner who will be active first sits up with his or her back against a headboard or wall with a pillow on his or her lap. The passive partner lies between the active partner's legs, head on the pillow, face up. You can do this caress with clothes on, nude, or partially nude, whichever is most comfortable. I would suggest you wear something really comfortable like a sweat suit or a robe, or you could even wrap yourself in a blanket.

Here are the instructions for the active partner. Slowly caress your partner's face and neck. Cover the area from the top of the head to the collarbone. Caress for your own pleasure, using the sensate-focus techniques you read about in Chapter 2. Caress as slowly as you can. Pay attention to the temperature, texture, and shape of your partner's face. Experiment with using all of your fingers, the knuckle of just one finger, or circling leisurely with the back of your hand. Just remember that this is not a massage. If you were doing a massage, you would try to feel and manipulate the muscles under the skin. In a caress, you are trying to increase skin sensations.

Focus on the exact point of contact. If your mind drifts off to something else, bring it back to the sensations in your hand.

Caress for fifteen to twenty minutes, covering your lover's forehead, cheeks, bridge of the nose, chin, neck, and ears. If you start to get bored or lose focus, slow your touch down to about half the speed it was before. Pay attention to the various contours of the face and the places where skin texture changes. How do the eyebrows feel beneath your fingertips, or the lips?

If you think your partner is starting to fall asleep, give him or her a light tap on the shoulder. If you feel any sexual arousal during this caress, even if it's only minor, take a deep breath and allow the arousal to spread throughout your body. Don't fight off any arousal, and don't expect yourself to feel more than you are feeling.

Here are the instructions for the passive partner. As your partner caresses you, pay attention to the exact point of contact where the fingertips are touching your skin. Does it bring a sense of warmth or cause the muscles to relax? Is it a little ticklish or deeply comforting? If your mind drifts off to something else, consciously bring it back to the sensations you are feeling at the place where you are being touched. As long as the sensations of the caress are pleasurable, don't say anything to your partner. Give your partner feedback only if he or she does something that bothers you.

Remember that this is a nondemand exercise. This means there is no pressure on either partner to perform in a particular way. I hope you feel completely free to lie back and enjoy the caress without feeling pressured to give feedback. Just enjoy the sensations that come from having your face lovingly stroked. And remember to relax all of your muscles. Stay passive; don't move around, sigh, groan, or do anything because you want your partner to feel he or she is doing a "good job."

Keep your PC muscle relaxed, too. If you feel any of your muscles tensing up, consciously try to relax them. If you feel any sexual arousal during the face caress, take a deep breath and allow the arousal to radiate throughout your body.

After one person has been active for fifteen to twenty minutes, switch roles for another fifteen to twenty minutes. After the caress is over, lie down and belly breathe together for another couple of minutes.

Having your face stroked is very comforting, isn't it? For some people, it provides a physical experience of nurturing they have not felt since childhood. Doing the face caress brings you back into touch with sensuality at its most basic level, which is pure body gratification. Here's what my client

Connie said about this exercise: "I was skeptical that having my partner touch my face would increase my sexual desire. At first during the face caress I thought I would fall asleep. But then as my partner caressed my ears and neck I started to feel warm all over, and I realized I was actually thinking about having sex with him."

If you can return to this state of basic enjoyment of your body, I believe your ability to feel strong sexual desire will increase.

⟋ *Exercise 16.* THE BACK CARESS

The back caress introduces some new elements. Since you do it in the nude, it may stir arousal. This caress includes the whole back of the body, from the shoulders to the feet. You will touch the buttocks but not the genitals. You can do it in bed or on some other roomy surface. Use a large towel to protect your bedsheets.

Before you begin, have some baby powder ready. Set aside about an hour for this exercise. Each of you will take a twenty- to thirty-minute turn as the active partner.

Here are the instructions for the active partner. Sprinkle some baby powder on your partner's back, from the shoulders to the feet. Put yourself in close body contact with your partner, lying or sitting right next to him or her. Now, slowly caress the skin on each part of your partner's back, including the shoulders, arms, mid-back, buttocks, thighs, and calves. Again, this is not a massage of the back muscles. Your touch should be light.

Use one hand to caress the upper body. Then move to a new position when you are ready to caress the lower body. You can also sit comfortably and do the caress with both hands if you prefer. Don't try to do the caress in a massage position by leaning over your partner's body. You need to stay comfortable.

As you are touching, pay attention to what you feel at the end of your fingertips or on the back of your hand or your palm. Notice how different parts of the back feel when you stroke them with your palm rather than your fingertips. Take plenty of time to appreciate the slopes and valleys of your partner's body, as the lower back becomes the buttocks, and the buttocks give way to the legs. Notice the direction the hair grows down the legs and arms. You may find it especially enjoyable to touch the back of the neck, the spine, and the thighs right beneath the buttocks.

If your mind wanders off while you are doing this, bring it back to where you are touching. If you get bored, close your eyes and slow your touch to half the speed it was before. Remember to caress for your own pleasure, and don't worry about what your partner is thinking or feeling. If you feel any sexual arousal during this exercise, take a deep breath. This will allow the arousal to spread throughout your whole body.

If your partner falls asleep, give him or her a light tap on the shoulder. Don't let your partner miss out on the sensations. If you feel your partner tensing up, give a light tap on the area that is tense.

At the end of the exercise, use your hair, breasts, or whole body to caress your partner for a couple of minutes. Then lie on top of your partner or right next to him or her and hold yourself close for a minute to finish up. This will help you continue to feel connected.

Here are the instructions for the passive partner. Lie comfortably on your stomach with your arms and legs slightly spread. Relax and enjoy the caress. Focus on the exact point of contact. If your mind wanders off to something other than the caress, practice bringing it back. Keep your mind in the here and now. Let your partner know if he or she is doing anything that bothers you. Don't say anything to your partner unless something hurts or bothers you. If you feel sexual arousal during the caress, take a deep breath so that the arousal will spread. Don't try to fight off the arousal, and don't try to force yourself to become aroused.

Relax all of your muscles. If a particular muscle tenses up, your partner will tap it. This will remind you to relax it. Keep your PC muscle relaxed.

After you've gone through the exercise once, switch roles. Then lie together and breathe normally for a few minutes.

The way I usually do the back caress is to snuggle up against my partner and use one hand to reach as many parts of his back as I can. Then I change positions so I can reach his legs and feet. I usually use some type of body powder to do this caress. Powder can increase the sensual arousal of this caress, especially if your hands tend to perspire.

⚘ Exercise 17. THE FRONT CARESS

Set aside about an hour for this session. If you have been looking forward to touching your partner's genitals, you'll get your turn in this exercise. In this caress, you will explore the front of your lover's body, from the shoulders to the feet. Do this exercise in the nude.

For this caress, as well as all of the others that follow, first spend five to ten minutes doing the back caress. This will focus you, help you make a transition from whatever you were doing before, and help both of you relax before the main exercise. It will also help you review and reinforce the basics of sensate focus before you try something new. In the book's later exercises, when I ask you to do a "focusing caress" before an exercise, a good choice is usually the back caress or face caress—anything that will relax you and allow you to make a transition between whatever you were doing before and the main exercise.

Before you begin, have baby powder, mineral oil, and a large towel on hand.

As the active partner, sprinkle some baby powder on the front of your partner's body from the shoulders to the feet. Choose a comfortable position in which you can maintain as much body contact as possible with your partner. Keep at least one hand on your partner at all times so you don't startle him or her with a sudden touch. Caress for your own pleasure. Don't worry about what your partner might be thinking or feeling. Slowly caress each area, including the shoulders, chest, arms, stomach, abdomen, genitals, thighs, and calves. Focus on the exact point of contact. If your mind drifts off, bring it back to what you are feeling right here, right now. Experiment with different patterns of touching and see how sensual you can make your touch. If you start to get bored, close your eyes and slow down your caress to half the speed it was before.

As you reach your partner's feet, start moving your caress back up toward the genitals. When you reach the genitals, pour a little mineral oil on your hand and caress the genitals for a few minutes. Then wipe the mineral oil off on the towel and continue the caress (with powder) back up to the shoulders.

In this exercise, as in any sensate-focus exercise, there is no right or wrong way to caress. If you are caressing the skin lightly, doing it for your own pleasure, and doing it in a slow, sensuous way, you are doing it right. If your partner starts to tense up, lightly tap the tense muscle as a reminder to relax. If you get aroused during this caress, take a deep breath to allow your arousal to spread.

Caress for about twenty minutes. At the end of the caress, use your hair, chest, or the whole front of your body to caress your partner. Then lie on top of or right beside your partner to end the exercise. After holding each other for a minute or so, switch roles.

Here are the instructions for the passive partner. Lie comfortably on your back with your arms and legs slightly spread. As your partner caresses you, focus on the exact point of contact. If your mind drifts off to something else, bring it back to the exact point of contact. Keep all of your muscles completely relaxed, including your PC muscle.

Tell your partner if he or she does anything that bothers you; otherwise, don't say anything. If you feel any sexual arousal during the caress, just enjoy it. Take a deep breath to help the arousal spread throughout your whole body. After you have switched roles and completed the exercise a second time, lie together for a few minutes and belly breathe or hug.

ℰ Exercise 18. THE GENITAL CARESS

For this exercise you will need baby powder and lubrication. Finding the type of lubrication that is right for you can make the exercise even more sensuous, so you might want to experiment. I suggest using either an oil-based lubricant, like baby oil or mineral oil, or a water-based lubricant, such as Astroglide or K-Y Jelly. You may want to test the lubricant on your skin before you use it on the genitals, because some people are allergic to different lubricants.

Set aside an hour for this exercise. Before you start, you should become familiar with several important areas of the male and female genitals. For the female genitals, you will need to be able to locate the pubic mound, the clitoris, the clitoral hood, the outer vaginal lips, the inner vaginal lips, the perineum, and the vaginal opening. All of these structures are visible. Below, I tell you how to locate the G-spot, the anterior fornix, and the cervix, which are internal and not visible.

For male anatomy, you need to be able to locate the following areas: the shaft of the penis, the head of the penis, the frenulum, and the scrotum. If you have trouble locating any of these male or female organs, please refer to the discussion and illustrations in Chapter 3.

Once you know how to find these areas on yourself, take your partner on a tour of your genitals. If you are a woman, sit, spread your legs, and put some lubrication on your genital area. Show your partner your pubic mound, clitoris, clitoral hood, outer lips, inner lips, and perineum. You can do this either by touch or using a mirror.

Then have your partner put some lubrication on one of his fingers and insert it about an inch into your vagina. Squeeze your PC muscle to show your partner its location. Have your partner insert his finger all the way into your vagina so he can feel the texture of the vaginal walls.

To show your partner where your G-spot is, lie on your back with your knees bent. Have him hold his hand palm up and insert his middle finger straight into your vagina. When his finger is inserted as far as it will go, have him hook it back toward himself, as if he wanted to point to the pubic mound from inside. The spot he is touching that provides an intense pleasurable sensation for you is the G-spot. To your partner, this area will feel a little rougher or more textured than the rest of the vagina. Have your partner slowly move his finger around on the G-spot. He will feel it swell and start to pulse.

Show your partner your anterior fornix area (A-spot). To do this, sit leaning against a headboard and spread your legs. Have your partner hold his hand palm up and insert his middle finger straight into your vagina as if he were going to touch your G-spot. But instead of curving his finger, he should keep it straight and run it up and down along the front wall of your vagina right above the G-spot. That's the A-spot.

To show your partner your cervix, lie down on your back. Have him slowly and gently insert his longest finger and reach as far as he can into your vagina along the upper wall. The cervix will feel like a knobby area about the size of a half dollar. He will probably find it on the upper wall on either the right or left side. You will know when he touches it because you know the feeling of something touching your cervix from having a pelvic exam with a Pap smear. Be sure to tell your partner if he is stroking the cervix with too much force, because it can be very sensitive.

If you are a man, sit with your legs spread and put some lubricant on your hand. Show your partner the head and shaft of your penis. If you are uncircumcised, show her how to pull back your foreskin. Show her your scrotum and have her feel your testicles inside it. Show her the perineum, between the testicles and the anus, and show her the frenulum, the highly sensitive area on the underside of the penis at the base of the head.

Now that you are both familiar with each other's anatomy, you are ready to start the genital caress. Before you begin, do short back caresses of five to ten minutes for each partner. Set aside another forty minutes so you can take a twenty-minute turn in each role.

Here are the instructions for the active partner. Spend some time on a front caress. Remember to caress as slowly as you can. Caress for your own pleasure rather than to turn your partner on. Let your focus follow your fingers or hand as it moves along your partner's skin. If you get distracted, bring your mind back to the area you are touching. If you feel yourself becoming mechanical or staying in one spot too long, slow down and pay attention to the temperature of the skin and the various textures in the genital area. If you feel your partner tense up, lightly tap the tense muscle as a sign to relax.

If your partner is a woman, use lots of lubrication and slowly move your fingers over her vaginal lips, perineum, and clitoris. Then slowly and gently insert a finger into her vagina. Stroke the PC muscle and the vaginal walls. Insert your finger a little deeper and gently stroke the G-spot until it starts to swell and pulse. Notice how this pulsing feels against your finger. Gently stroke the anterior fornix area and the cervix.

Do the first part of this caress sitting next to your partner and stroking her from the side. Then move around and lie down between your partner's legs so that you can see the areas as you caress them.

If your partner is a man, put some lubricant on your hand and slowly caress his penis and scrotum. Avoid using a masturbatory stroke; just caress the skin's surface lightly. It doesn't matter if your partner has an erection or not. If he gets so aroused he ejaculates, apply a warm towel to the area where you and he are sticky, and continue the caress.

Here are the instructions for the passive partner. Lie on your back with your legs slightly spread and close your eyes. Stay passive even if you become aroused. You may find that it is even possible to go all the way to orgasm without moving.

Try to keep all of your muscles, including your PC muscle, as relaxed as possible. Focus on exactly what you are feeling. If your mind drifts off, bring it back to the point of contact. Give your lover feedback only if he or she does something that bothers you.

If you feel yourself getting aroused, take a deep breath. If you feel like you might have an orgasm, go ahead. Don't fight it off, but don't try to force one either. If you don't feel aroused, don't worry about it. Many people actually experience this caress as sensual rather than sexual.

Each partner should spend twenty minutes caressing the other. Then lie together and breathe for a couple of minutes when you are done.

If you want, before you switch roles, you can set aside some time to talk about what each of you liked. Each partner can describe one or two things that felt especially good. The passive partner can ask for a new kind of touch and can guide the active partner's hand if that helps to show exactly what kind of touch is desired.

A Few More Suggestions for Cultivating Sexual Desire

(In the Introduction I suggested that you might want to read all the way through the book before you attempt any exercises. Here's an exception. Don't read this section until you've had a chance to do the partner exercises described in the chapter. Just skip this section and go on to Chapter 7.)

Did you enjoy the exercises in this chapter? During any of the exercises, did you look ahead and wish your partner would move on to a more sexual caress? When your partner was doing the genital caress, did you wish he or she wouldn't stop until you had an orgasm, or did you wish you could continue the exercise so that you could have intercourse?

I'm betting that at some point you had one of the above thoughts. And guess what? That's one definition of sexual desire: wanting to move on to the next step.

Remember from Chapter 2 how one of the sensate-focus principles is to stay in the here and now? That means you concentrate on what is happening right now rather than thinking ahead about what's going to happen next. I gave you those instructions on purpose. Being able to stay in the here and now is a really good skill that helps you focus on touch. It's also really good reverse psychology. Don't beat yourself up if you had trouble staying in the here and now because you kept looking ahead to more overtly sexual activities. That "looking ahead" means you have sexual desire!

The difference between sexual desire and sexual arousal is that arousal means deriving pleasure or sexual satisfaction from what's happening right now. Desire is wanting the next thing or wanting something you don't have right now. By definition, desire includes an element of unfulfilled anticipation. If you are always sexually satisfied, you will not feel desire.

This implies that maybe sometimes you should back off from sex a little and allow a sense of desire to build up. Doing so is especially important for women. To experience horniness, sometimes you must temporarily go without satisfaction.

In general, a woman's sexual desire requires more maintenance than a man's. What happens to many women is that at the beginning of a relationship, both the woman and her partner desire sex a lot. Then a woman's sex drive starts to go south, maybe for hormonal or other reasons, but her partner still wants a lot of sex and she doesn't want to turn him down, so she has sex when she doesn't really feel like it. Doing this is good for maintaining your level of intimacy with your partner, but it's not very good for maintaining your level of sexual desire. As a woman, you need to find the optimal frequency of sexual arousal for you that will keep your sexual desire and your love for your partner in balance. Sometimes that's difficult. Two ways to do it are to use sexual fantasy and to substitute other activities for sexual intercourse once in a while.

The Uses of Fantasy

A wise person once said, "As long as you're making plans, you're in good shape," implying that as long as you have something to look forward to, you're living. This philosophy has huge implications for sexual desire. Are you the type of person who looks forward to things? Do you read books because you can't wait to find out what happens? Do you watch movies because you want to find out how it all comes out in the end? When you are hiking or cycling, do you follow an unknown path just to see where it leads? If so, you have cultivated the ability to know the difference between desire and pleasure. You enjoy a sense of unfulfilled anticipation.

If you are not this type of person, how could you become this type of person, especially sexually? I have four suggestions. Three of them involve fantasy. Fantasy is a private mental experience that contains thoughts or images that are sexually arousing to a particular person.

The first suggestion is to use "fantasy interruptus." This is a technique in which you relax and allow yourself to have a fairly detailed sexual fantasy. You can touch yourself while you are fantasizing if you want to. The point is to have a fantasy with a narrative structure and follow it along in chronological order. Right before you get to the payoff (the part in the fantasy when you have an orgasm), stop fantasizing. Just leave it right there and get up and do something else. I guarantee you will walk around horny all day, thinking about how you can't wait to finish that fantasy.

The second technique is to cultivate that unattainable object of desire. Think of the one person on this planet whom you would absolutely kill to have sex with. It could be a celebrity, someone you know, or someone who's forbidden to you. For now, put aside the thought that this person doesn't know you, doesn't want you, or doesn't love you. Make up a narrative sexual fantasy involving how you would meet this person and exactly what the two of you would do together. Repeat this fantasy as often as you want, changing details or embellishing it.

Some people worry that if they fantasize about a forbidden person, sooner or later they'll lose control and try to act out their fantasy. Research shows that this really doesn't happen. The majority of people seem to have a grip on the difference between fantasy and reality. (In fact, research shows that some people actually have a chance to act out their unattainable-object fantasy because the person suddenly becomes available. Most people who have this experience report that they wish they hadn't acted on the fantasy because acting on it ruined the fantasy for them! Most people who have had this experience report that the fantasy was better than the reality.)

A third fantasy technique involves reliving past experiences. These could be experiences with your current partner or with a past partner. An experience with a past partner works best, if you have one. A lot of people feel that they are somehow being unfaithful to their current partner if they fantasize about a past partner. I say, "No way! You are free to fantasize about anything you like. It's not *1984*—we don't have the thought police." If you try to shut down sexual feelings about a past partner because you feel guilty about them, you risk shutting down your sexual desire for your current partner. Your libido doesn't discriminate.

Research shows that in general, people don't have very good memories for past sexual experiences or milestones. However, many of us have had a few sexual encounters that are etched into our brains. I have a few of these that I've used so many times that if they were videotapes, they would have worn out a long time ago. I still run through my first experience of sexual intercourse once in a while.

If you don't have any past sexual experiences that were good enough to use as fantasy material, what are you waiting for? Get busy generating some!

Which brings me to the final technique for enhancing sexual desire. Sex is a creative act. As a sexual being, you are the writer and director of your sex life. Instead of passively responding and experiencing your sex life, start to embrace the perspective that you need to *create* a sexual experience for yourself and your partner that's so wonderful that your partner can't wait to see what happens at the end. That's where the enthusiasm factor that I discussed in the last chapter comes in.

Now that we've laid a foundation with some basic exercises for partners, the next two chapters present more ways to create sexual pleasure with your partner, through oral sex and intercourse.

chapter 7

Oral Pleasures

by Paul Dahlquist

*O*ral *sex is any contact between the mouth and the genitals. Oral sex done on a woman's genitals is called* cunnilingus. *Oral sex done on a man's genitals is called* fellatio. *(Contact between the mouth and the anus of anyone of either sex is called* anilingus.*)*

Why Is Oral Sex So Popular?

There's a short answer to that question and a long answer. The short answer is that oral sex is one of the most pleasurable sexual caresses you can receive. Many people find oral sex more pleasurable than intercourse. For men, receiving oral sex is an activity that is fantasized about second only to intercourse. Women on average tend to be more orgasmic during oral sex than they are during intercourse. Given that oral sex is so popular and pleasurable, I feel that it deserves a whole chapter to itself.

The long answer to the question has to do with changes in sexual practices over the past sixty years or so. The question here is really, "Why is oral sex so much more popular than it used to be?" Oral-genital sex has been practiced throughout recorded history, but it's only in about the last sixty years that it has become increasingly common in the United States. There are several reasons for this.

First, fifty or sixty years ago, people were less affluent than they are today, and therefore they had less privacy in which to engage in sex. When couples wanted to be alone together, they often had to do so in a car. This is not a conducive situation for oral sex, especially cunnilingus. Also, couples were often in a hurry, so they generally went right for the "main event."

Second, prior to the sexual revolution, there were many states in which any sexual activities other than penile-vaginal intercourse were against the law! Even male/female consensual oral sex fell under sodomy laws that were meant to forbid male/male anal intercourse and sex with animals.

Third, fifty to sixty years ago, there were still many areas of the United States in which standards of personal hygiene were poor. People who do not wash their genitals on a regular basis are rarely objects of desire for oral sex.

Finally, the biggest factor in the growing popularity of oral sex has been the increase in educational level among many sectors of the U.S. population. Many more people attend college and graduate than they did years ago. It's not that people are being taught how to have oral sex in college; it's that higher education is a liberalizing influence. When you go to college, you are exposed to people from all backgrounds and therefore become more open to sexual experiences other than intercourse. So we could say that oral sex is really the educated person's sexual choice.

Positions for Oral Sex

Although fellatio is commonly referred to as a "blow job," it does not involve any blowing. It involves licking or sucking the penis. There are a number of positions you can use for fellatio. The most common is the man lying flat on his back and the woman kneeling or bending over him, either between his legs or to one side. Or the man can sit on the edge of the bed and the woman can kneel in front of him, or he can stand up and lean against a wall and she can kneel in front of him.

Cunnilingus involves licking or sucking the vulval area, including the clitoris, outer lips, inner lips, and vaginal opening. The most common position is for the woman to lie on her back and spread her legs. The man lies on his stomach between her legs. She can put a pillow underneath herself and bend her knees. In this position, the man is looking at the vagina in such a way that the clitoris is at the top. Cunnilingus can also be done the opposite way—he can lean over her so that he is approaching the vagina so that the clitoris, from his perspective, is at the bottom. This is the same position that is used for mutual oral sex, the "69" position, in this case with the man leaning over the woman.

Another commonly used position is for the woman to sit on the man's face. He lies on his back and she straddles his face. She can also stand up and he can kneel in front of her, or she can sit in a chair and he can kneel in front of her.

Which of these positions is the most pleasurable? Everybody has his or her favorite. It depends not only on the level of physical stimulation but also on the visual stimulation. I know a lot of men who get intense pleasure from watching a woman kneeling over them and giving them oral sex. From the woman's standpoint when she is the receiver, I think it's easier to have an orgasm when you are on your back and your knees are raised and your feet are planted flat on the bed to give you more leverage. From a psychological standpoint, some women enjoy the idea that they are straddling their partner's face, but I think it's harder to have an orgasm in that position, because for the vaginal muscles to spasm you are fighting gravity.

Before I discuss the sensate-focus approach to oral sex, here are a few basic tips to make oral sex more pleasurable in general.

Make Oral Sex
More Fun

Be sure to wash your genitals thoroughly before oral sex. Women, don't just wash the outside. Insert a finger as far as it will go into your vagina and kind of run it around the inside to clean off any of the normal daily discharge that your vagina produces.

Shaving the genital area can make oral sex a lot more pleasurable for a number of reasons, especially for women. The reason that women's genitals often have an odor is that vaginal lubrication and sweat get trapped in the pubic hair. A lot of men like a very musky vaginal odor, but some don't, especially close up, and if you shave the outer lips and just leave a small "landing strip" up the pubic mound, you will have less vaginal odor.

Another reason pubic shaving is good for a woman is that it makes it much easier for her partner to find her clitoris, and therefore she will receive more stimulation. I haven't read any studies on this, but I'd be willing to bet that women who shave are consistently more orgasmic during oral sex than women who don't shave. Don't take my word for it—find out for yourself! (Of course, there are some men who prefer a woman with a lot of pubic hair.)

Pubic shaving is equally important for men. First of all, it makes your penis look larger when it's flaccid. Shave all the hair off your shaft and your scrotum. Also shave a patch about an inch square right above your penis, and the area in the crease between your thighs and your scrotum. The same thing applies to a man that applies to a woman: If you shave, you will increase your sensitivity.

When I began to suggest to clients that they shave or trim their pubic hair, initially some of them were against it. So I offered to shave it for them. After they saw the difference it made in how they felt, they were all for it.

If you feel that daily shaving is too much of a chore, you could opt for laser hair removal. This can be done for either men or women and may take two or three sessions.

Another factor that enhances oral pleasure is the use of lubricants. Most lubricants that are safe for the genitals are safe for oral contact. However, not all lubricants provide the same degree of pleasure. For example, I find that water-based lubricants, like K-Y Jelly, generally do not feel good for oral sex. I prefer baby oil, which feels really good on the lips, but some people might find it too greasy. If you don't like the taste of genitals, adult stores sell all kinds of flavored lubricants that somewhat mask the taste. These lubricants come in different flavors, including chocolate. I prefer genital lubricants that contain glycerine. When you apply these to the genitals and blow on them, they warm up on the skin.

Some people use food on the genitals to make them taste better. For the most part, it's safe to put foods on the penis, but I wouldn't insert any kind of food into the vagina, as it could upset the normal pH balance. And, romantic as it might sound to drink a sip of champagne and go down on your partner, don't do it. Alcohol burns!

Women, it's a good idea, before you begin doing fellatio on your partner, to let him know whether you are comfortable with his ejaculating while his penis is in or near your mouth. A sensate-focus oral caress may or may not bring him to the point of ejaculation, but you should still discuss this. As an option, you can stop the caress before it gets to that point and switch to intercourse. Some women are comfortable with their partner's ejaculating during oral sex, and some are not. Don't do anything that makes you uncomfortable.

✐ *Exercise 19.* THE SENSATE-FOCUS APPROACH TO ORAL SEX

There are few things as pleasurable as giving or receiving a sensual, nondemand oral caress. The tongue has a lot of nerve endings, and you may find it fun to discover which parts of your tongue are most sensitive and receptive to certain tastes and textures.

In the sensate-focus approach to oral sex, the genital caress includes your lips and tongue as well as your hands. Remember to explore freely and do only what feels good. Think of sensate-focus oral sex with your partner as simply using your tongue instead of your hand. The same instructions apply. In other words, do it slowly, focus on the touch, and do not pressure your partner to respond.

One problem that people sometimes have with sensate-focus oral sex is that they revert to their old way of having oral sex rather than trying it the sensate-focus way. Many people keep their tongue and neck stiff when they do oral sex. For an oral sensate-focus caress, you should completely relax your lips, tongue, and neck. One of my clients, Natalie, put it this way: "When I used to give oral sex, I always felt like I was working at it. The best thing about the sensate-focus approach to oral sex is that you remember to relax all of your face muscles so you don't get tired or sore. Now I can go down on my partner for long periods of time."

Set aside about an hour for your first sensate-focus oral caress. Give each other relaxing back caresses first.

Here is the active partner's role. Start with a manual caress on the front of your partner's body for a few minutes. Then focus on the genital area and caress the genitals with your hand for a few minutes. Then, if you feel like it, lean over your partner and try to caress in the same way with your lips and tongue as you did with your hand.

Men, when you are active, lick your partner's clitoris, her inner and outer lips, and the opening of her vagina. Slowly insert a well-lubricated finger into her vagina and stroke it at the same time. Women, rub your lips over the shaft and head of your partner's penis, and lick his penis and scrotum. Fondle his penis and scrotum with your hand at the same time or keep one hand on the base of his penis so that you control the depth of penetration and you are comfortable with it.

Do the oral caress for your own pleasure. Focus on exactly what you are feeling. Notice how concentrating on your own sensations makes you much more attentive to the little things: the warm spots, the places where the skin is most delicate, the areas of extreme sensitivity. How does it all feel against your tongue?

If your mind drifts off to something else, either bring your focus back to what you are doing or change to doing something that will keep your attention. Don't pressure your partner to become aroused or wonder what he or she is thinking or feeling. If you feel any performance pressure, stop the oral part of the caress and back up to a stage in which you felt more comfortable. If you feel your partner tensing up, lightly tap the tense muscle as a signal to relax. Continue for fifteen or twenty minutes before you switch roles.

If you are the woman and are active, don't worry about whether or not your partner has an erection. In fact, it's often good to start the oral sex before he has an erection. From a personal standpoint, I find it a huge turn-on to feel my partner get an erection as I am doing oral sex.

Here's a special hint for women when they are active during oral sex. Position yourself so that you are rubbing your clitoris on your partner's shinbone. Or kneel back on your heels so that you can rub your clitoris against one of your own heels to stimulate yourself.

If you are the passive partner, lie on your back with your legs slightly spread and close your eyes. Keep all of your muscles, including the PC muscle, as relaxed as possible.

Pay attention to the sensations you experience. If your mind drifts off, return the focus to your sensations as soon as you catch yourself. Let your partner know if he or she does anything that bothers you.

Each time you feel your arousal increase, take a deep breath. If you become very aroused or even have an orgasm or an ejaculation, that's fine. Don't try to hold back your arousal or force it to happen.

Women, if your partner does ejaculate, you can either take it into your mouth or remove your mouth from the penis and catch the ejaculate in your hand or remove your mouth from the penis and allow the man to ejaculate on his stomach. If you choose to let your partner ejaculate in your mouth, when you feel his PC muscle start to throb, tighten your lips around the penis and suck. If you are comfortable swallowing the ejaculate, do so; otherwise, spit it into your hand or a towel.

I'm not going to try to talk you into allowing your partner to ejaculate in your mouth if you are just not comfortable with it. However, from a personal standpoint again, I have to tell you that whether this feels good depends 100 percent on your feelings about the partner you are with. I have been with some men and felt that I really didn't want them to ejaculate in my mouth, whereas with certain others, it was a huge turn-on to feel their PC muscle throb and feel them start to ejaculate. This can be a very special pleasure with someone you really care for.

Once you are able to enjoy this basic sensate-focus approach to oral sex, increase your pleasure by moving your hips and doing pelvic thrusts and rolls as your partner is going down on you. As long as you do the thrusts and rolls in a relaxed way, you won't put any pressure on your partner to perform in a certain way.

Safer Sex

Since this is the first chapter in which I've discussed activities that might involve the exchange of body fluids, I need to talk about safer sex. Oral sex is a behavior that could put you at risk for HIV and other sexually transmitted diseases (STDs). So is unprotected intercourse. Before you do any exercises that might involve the exchange of body fluids, I urge you and your partner to take the precaution of being tested for HIV and other sexually transmitted diseases. If your tests are negative but you have any cause for doubt, use condoms for three months and then get tested again. Be aware that the HIV virus can remain undetected for long periods of time.

I have not incorporated safer-sex techniques into the sensate-focus exercises that involve oral sex and intercourse. One reason for that is because I wrote this book for couples who know each other well enough that this should not be an issue. If you do not know your partner well enough to be sure about his or her sexual practices, you probably don't know him or her well enough to be having sex. Another reason is because sensate focus emphasizes feeling as much as possible, and condoms tend to desensitize the penis.

Please don't put yourself at risk. If there is any chance of infection, use a condom to practice the sensate-focus partner exercises or wait until you and your partner have received a clean bill of health.

chapter 8

The Many Pleasures of Intercourse

by Brie Childers

*B*efore *I get to the chapters on lasting longer, erections, and female arousal, I need to talk about the specific pleasures of sexual intercourse. Many of the exercises for arousal, erection, and lasting longer include intercourse.*

Motivations for Intercourse

Couples are motivated to have sexual intercourse for a number of reasons. The most common reasons are to relieve sexual tension and to reproduce. But since we now have such a wide range of semireliable forms of contraception available to us, sexual intercourse does not necessarily have to result in pregnancy. The most important implication of the availability of birth control is that couples are now likely to have intercourse for other reasons besides reproduction. Relieving sexual tension is still an important motive, but the major motive for sexual intercourse for most couples is to share pleasure: to receive pleasure for oneself and to give pleasure to the other person.

Intercourse Positions

Sexual intercourse is any activity in which the penis is inserted into the vagina. This can be accomplished in any number of physical positions. There are no intercourse positions that are bad or wrong, and none that are inherently good or the best for everybody. Which intercourse positions you and your partner like is strictly a matter of personal taste and mutual agreement.

Although there are probably hundreds of possible intercourse positions (check the *Kama Sutra!*), we generally classify positions into four basic types: male superior, female superior, side-to-side, and rear entry. Each of these positions has its own physical and psychological benefits that contribute to a pleasurable experience for a couple.

Male Superior, or Man on Top

A male-superior position is any position in which the man is physically on top of the woman. The most commonly used version of the male-superior position is the *missionary* position, in which the woman lies flat on her back and the man lies on top of her. In other variations, the man can support himself on his elbows or on his elbows and knees or even on the palms of his hands and his knees.

From a physical standpoint, the male-superior positions are generally very arousing to men. Therefore most men tend to have the least amount of ejaculation control in these positions. This is because in a male-superior position, the man's center of gravity is in his chest and he is supporting himself with his arms, a position that can often lead to fatigue. Plus, when you have to expend a lot of energy concentrating on supporting your weight, it's difficult to focus on the pleasurable sensations in your genitals.

From the physical standpoint for a woman, the male-superior positions, especially the missionary position, tend to be the least physically arousing. This is because these positions do not allow for much depth of penetration (the angle is wrong), and it's difficult to receive much clitoral stimulation in these positions.

Given that there are physical problems that can decrease pleasure for both partners in these positions, why are they still so popular? From a psychological standpoint, the male-superior positions have a lot going for them.

First of all, the male-superior positions are very intimate. In the missionary position the partners have full body contact. In all of the male-superior positions the partners are face-to-face and can gaze into each other's eyes and kiss.

Second, these are the positions that seem to have been programmed into us by our culture. When we see mainstream movies or read stories about couples who are in love, generally they have intercourse in one of the male-superior positions. Many couples also like these positions because they reflect traditional conceptions about the male and female roles in sexual intercourse: that the man is the aggressor or initiator and the woman is receptive.

There are a couple of variations on the traditional missionary position that can provide more physical stimulation for the woman and more staying power for the man. The first is the *coital alignment technique (CAT)*. This position was described by Edward Eichel in his book *The Perfect Fit*. It is a version of the missionary position in which the man moves his whole body up toward the woman's shoulders so that when they have intercourse, his penis moves up and down into her vagina rather than in and out horizontally. The position is recommended in order to provide more stimulation of the woman's clitoris, because the pubic bones of the two partners grind together with every thrust.

An even better male-superior alternative to the missionary position is a position that has not yet been given a name in the "official" sex-therapy literature. *(Cosmopolitan* magazine calls it the "Cosmo Butterfly," and throughout this book I'll refer to it as the *butterfly* position.) In this position, the woman lies on her back but tilts her pelvis so that her legs are up in the air. She can either spread her legs, rest them back on her body, or even rest her knees on her shoulders if doing so is comfortable. (A pillow placed under her hips will help.) The man then kneels between her legs and inserts his penis. It's important that he kneel straight up so that his center of gravity is in his legs and hips rather than in his arms and chest.

From the standpoint of the woman, this position allows stimulation of the clitoris, because in addition to the stimulation she gets from intercourse itself, because her legs are spread, the man can withdraw his penis and use it to caress her clitoris, or he can caress her clitoris with his fingers. When a woman is in this position, her vagina is somewhat curved and shortened. Thus it's more likely that her partner will be able to stimulate her G-spot during intercourse. The position allows the man to penetrate deeper, meaning that his partner will receive more stimulation of the A-spot, the cervix, and the cul de sac. This is the position in which a woman is most likely to have a vaginal or uterine orgasm.

To me, the best part of this position is that it allows stimulation of the woman's PC muscle. In this position the man's center of gravity is in his legs, giving him total control of the depth of penetration and allowing him to use his penis to tease the woman's PC muscle. This is really important because the PC muscle is the muscle that spasms when a woman has an orgasm. Sometimes just teasing it by using a little shallow penetration can trigger an orgasm if the woman is already highly aroused.

From a psychological standpoint, the butterfly has all of the benefits of the standard male-superior positions and more. It enhances intimacy because the partners are face-to-face. They can easily gaze into each other's eyes, and the man can lean down so they can kiss. In this position, both partners have a better view of each other's bodies, which can be a turn-on. Both partners can watch the penis go in and out of the vagina, which is also very arousing.

Also, since in this position a man is not supporting the weight of his chest, he will have more stamina and will last longer. I have also found that this position seems to be the best for a man to practice multiple-orgasm techniques.

There are other variations of the butterfly position that can be extremely pleasurable. In one of them, the woman grabs the arches of her feet with her hands. This creates leverage that allows her partner to stroke faster. In another version, the woman tilts her pelvis back so far that her vaginal opening is pointing straight up. This variation allows for the deepest penetration into the cul de sac. In other variations, the woman can put her legs around her partner's waist, put her legs on either side of his head, or do sort of a half twist and put both her legs on one side of him.

Female-Superior Positions

A female-superior position is any position in which the woman is physically on top. In the most common version of the female-superior position, the man lies on his back and the woman kneels straight up on top of him so that her center of gravity is in her hips and thighs. In other variations the woman can lie flat on top of her partner and move back and forth rather than up and down, or she can squat on top of him, balancing herself with her feet and the palms of her hands.

From a physical standpoint, this position is generally good for male arousal. For most men it is not as physically arousing as the missionary position. Some men find it difficult to become aroused in this position because they physically need to move more to become aroused enough to ejaculate.

For women, this position is acknowledged by most sex experts to be the best from a physical standpoint. It allows the woman to have complete control of the depth, angle, and speed of penetration. By lowering her upper body onto her partner, a woman can change the angle so she can receive stimulation of the G-spot. When she is moving straight up and down, her G-spot and cul de sac are stimulated. If she wants more clitoral stimulation than she gets just from the penetration itself, she can climb off the penis and rub it against her clitoris. Also, in female-superior positions, either the man or the woman can reach down and stimulate the clitoris.

From a psychological standpoint, the female-superior positions have the same benefits as the male-superior positions: There is a great degree of intimacy since the partners are face-to-face. Some men have psychological discomfort with this position because they prefer to be the aggressor or initiator during sex. Some women have psychological discomfort with this position because they feel that their partner thinks they are being too aggressive. Also, this position is associated in popular culture with the "bad girl" stereotype (think Sharon Stone in *Basic Instinct)*. Of course, many men enjoy feeling that they are being dominated, and many women enjoy the empowering feeling of being on top.

A hint for men in the female-superior position: As you thrust into your partner, grab the bottom of her buttocks with both hands and gently spread her cheeks so you get deeper penetration.

Another aspect of the psychology of a particular position, believe it or not, is aesthetics. Women especially care about how they look while they are having sexual intercourse. Some women are uncomfortable with certain positions that they believe present their bodies in an unflattering light. These concerns can interfere with a woman's pleasure.

For example, women generally feel they look their best when they are lying on their back, which suggests that they would look their best in the male-superior position. When you lie on your back your face relaxes and you look younger. The man's body covers up most of your body. On the other hand, in the female-superior position a woman's face is likely to look older, especially if she is leaning over. Gravity takes over, and many women feel that their breasts and stomachs look too flabby or saggy when they're on top.

These concerns might sound pretty shallow, but I assure you that many women have them. Some women even stop having sex entirely because of these concerns. If such concerns interfere with your pleasure enough to cause you personal distress, it's a problem. Solutions include using positions in which you are most comfortable or making love in dimmer light.

Side-to-Side Positions

This group includes any positions in which both partners lie on their sides. In one of these positions, the partners lie on their sides facing each other, and the woman wraps her top leg over her partner's hip. In another version, called the *scissors* position, the man lies on his right side. His partner lies on her back perpendicular to him, and they insert his penis and interweave their legs.

From a physical standpoint, the side-to-side positions provide a lot of pleasure because neither partner has to support his or her body weight. These positions are physically relaxing and are often recommended for people with physical limitations such as knee problems or arthritis. However, these positions tend to be less sexually stimulating than the male-superior and female-superior positions. In the face-to-face version I described above, really deep penetration is generally not possible. In the scissors version, deep penetration is possible, which is sometimes enough to stimulate the G-spot, the cul de sac, and the X-spot (cervix). The side-to-side positions are often recommended for men who would like to last longer.

Couples can be very intimate in the side-to-side positions, especially the face-to-face version. This position allows for mutual eye gazing, kissing, and the stroking of each other's bodies. Since this position is so relaxing, many couples prefer to just insert the penis and not thrust. Rather, they lie next to each other and talk and kiss just to feel connected.

From a psychological standpoint, the side-to-side positions tend to convey more equality between the partners. I generally think of a side-to-side position as kind of an "I'm not sure I really want to make the effort to have an acrobatic session of lovemaking first thing in the morning, so let's put it in and see if anything happens if we move around a little bit" position.

Rear Entry

This includes any position in which the man enters the woman from behind. In the most common version of the position, the woman is on her hands and knees and her partner kneels straight up behind her. The rear-entry position can also be done with the woman lying flat on her front and her partner lying flat on top of her. Also, she could kneel at the edge of the bed, and he could stand up behind her, or they could lie on their sides like spoons, with her back against his front.

From a physical standpoint, the rear-entry position can be extremely stimulating to a man, because a lot of men get pleasure from the feeling of a woman's buttocks against their penis. This position allows for deep penetration, and I believe it is the best position for stimulating the cervix and the G-spot if the penis is curved. It's difficult to get clitoral stimulation from intercourse alone in this position, but either partner can reach down and stimulate the woman's clitoris with their fingers.

The rear-entry positions have the potential to provide the most speed and the best friction, especially if the man grabs the woman's hips. So if you like really vigorous pounding on your cervix, this is the position for you. In my opinion, there's one other version of this position that's especially good. If you are a woman, instead of kneeling on all fours, bend over and rest your elbows on the bed and your head on your upper arms. In this position your butt is straight up in the air. This will allow your partner to thrust into you with more force, because you have changed the angle of your body and much of the energy of your partner's thrusting is absorbed by the mattress. The bed does all the work and you get all the pleasure!

From a psychological standpoint, some people object to the rear-entry position because they find it primitive, impersonal, and animalistic. On the other hand, a lot of people like the rear-entry position because they find it primitive, impersonal, and animalistic. (There's no accounting for taste, is there?) The position also has a bad reputation because the physical position itself is associated with anal sex, and it also suffers from the unfortunate nickname "doggy style." (Maybe if we could think up a new, more flattering name for it, more people would use this highly satisfying sexual alternative.) True, it's more difficult to feel intimate in this position, but all it takes is for the woman to turn her head and gaze into her partner's eyes.

Women sometimes object to this position not only because of the lack of intimacy, but also because the position highlights an area of the body (the buttocks) that many women consider to be their least attractive body feature. The good news (whether you believe it or not) is that your butt looks a lot better pointed straight up in the air than it does when you're on top. Trust me!

Your Attitude

In my mind, one of the main goals of sexual intercourse is to feel and be aware of every pleasurable thrust. The secret to being able to do this is to use minute position changes that keep you interested from moment to moment. For example, I had a lover who preferred to use the male-superior position most of the time. This was fine with me, as I usually put my legs up and did a version of the butterfly position. I could always tell when he got really aroused, because he would lie down flat on top of me and put an arm around my neck. Because I knew that this movement meant that he was about to ejaculate, every time he did it, I would get more and more turned on to the point that I would have an orgasm from the stimulation of feeling his arm around my neck.

I think everybody has a subtle change in position or movement that signals that his or her arousal is increasing. Now that you have an understanding of sensate focus, it should be easy to pay enough attention to your partner's response so that you will be able to figure out what that subtle change is. Here are a couple of examples:

Men, when you're using the butterfly position, every once in a while stop your thrusting, lean over, and give your partner a deep kiss. If you stop your thrusting and focus on your penis inside her vagina, you'll probably feel your partner's PC muscle tighten involuntarily around your penis. You may even feel her have a surge of lubrication. Or every once in a while, stop thrusting and lean over and gently suck on one of your partner's nipples. She'll probably have that involuntary PC squeeze again. Or you may actually feel her clitoris harden up a little.

Another secret to enjoying intercourse as much as you can is to recognize the fine line between boredom and burnout. Boredom occurs when you always use the same position all the time or always do the same exact type of foreplay in the same order. On the other hand, burnout can occur if you are so concerned about becoming bored that you become a fanatic about using every position in every sexual encounter. The secret is to use the same positions often enough to get an excellent sense of your own and your partner's responses, but also to vary things enough to keep your sex life interesting.

There are many other variations of the four basic positions. For example, I haven't mentioned anything about having intercourse while sitting in a chair or while standing in the shower, both of which are possible and both of which are enjoyed by many couples. If you are going to use a wild or exotic position, make sure you're both physically up to it. You don't want to use a position that's so complicated or physically uncomfortable that it becomes difficult to pay attention to all of the pleasurable sensations in your genitals. (You also don't want to use a position that's so physically dangerous that you end up the victim of some MTV *Jackass* stunt! Practice safe sex—and I don't just mean by wearing a condom!)

Besides positions, there are other interpersonal issues that couples have to decide upon regarding intercourse. Two of these issues are frequency and the amount of time spent on intercourse versus foreplay. The stereotype is that men typically want to have all kinds of sexual contact more frequently than women do. (Like most stereotypes, there's a grain of truth here.) So you have to talk about these issues before they become huge areas of disagreement.

Contraception

If you are having sexual intercourse and you don't want to become pregnant, you need to use some form of contraception. Using contraception is not fun. There are no contraceptive methods that contribute to our sexual pleasure. The best you can do is find a method that doesn't interfere with your pleasure too much.

Furthermore, there is no perfect contraceptive method. (Even male and female sterilization have failure rates, although they are negligible.) For a method of contraception to be perfect, it would have to work 100 percent of the time. It would have to be completely reversible, and it would have to have no disadvantages or side effects. In addition, for it to be perfect, it would have to be free.

Having said this, let's review the main currently available contraceptive methods to see how much they interfere with sexual pleasure. I've never seen them analyzed this way; in fact, I tried to find a study that compared contraceptives in terms of whether users were satisfied with them and, surprisingly, no such study has ever been done.

Spermicides

Spermicides are chemicals that kill sperm. They are available in the forms of foams, gels, creams, or suppositories that are inserted into the vagina. The time frame required for spermicidal use limits sexual pleasure. They must be placed in the vagina no more than an hour before intercourse. If you are using a spermicide, you need to check the directions on the packaging, because some spermicides also need to be inserted again after ejaculation. Spermicides are not a good choice for the woman who becomes energized after sex and feels like getting up and getting active. This is because in order for spermicides to be effective, they need to remain in the vagina for a certain amount of time after ejaculation. If you get out of bed and start walking around, the spermicide will leak out.

In addition, spermicidal chemicals feel unpleasant during intercourse because using them precludes the use of other lubricants. For me, the biggest problem with spermicides from a pleasure standpoint is that they are not good for a couple whose sexual repertoire includes a lot of cunnilingus. They taste horrible and should never be put into the mouth. Some people are allergic to the chemicals in spermicides, and these chemicals can cause itching or stinging. In addition, they are messy.

Diaphragm, Cervical Cap, and Contraceptive Sponge

Using the diaphragm or cervical cap involves inserting a plastic or rubber barrier into the vagina and placing it over the cervix. Once either of these is correctly inserted, it cannot be felt and so does not interfere with the sensations of intercourse. However, to work correctly they must be used in combination with a spermicide, so all the problems related to spermicides apply here as well. The biggest problem with the diaphragm and the cervical cap is that their failure rate is unacceptably high; also, inserting them breaks the mood of a sexual encounter if it has already started.

The contraceptive sponge is kind of a combination of a barrier method and spermicide. The sponge was taken off the market for a while, but I believe it is being sold again. To use the sponge, you moisten it and gently tap on it to release the spermicide. Then you insert it and place it near the cervix similar to the way a diaphragm would be placed. Because the sponge contains spermicides, all of the problems with spermicides also apply here.

Condoms

Condoms are latex sheaths that fit over the penis and catch the ejaculate so that it doesn't get into the vagina. A lot of men don't like to use condoms because they decrease penile sensitivity during intercourse. In addition, certain lubricants cannot be used with condoms; so if your enjoyment of intercourse is increased by the use of oil-based lubricants, you do not get that extra source of pleasure if you use condoms. Using condoms sometimes requires a couple to adjust their position or slow down their thrusting if they feel the condom is creeping down the shaft of the penis or falling off. Condoms are difficult to use if a man's erection is typically less than hard.

Female condoms are also available. They are made of polyurethane and have two flexible rings. One ring is inserted into the vagina and placed around the cervix like a diaphragm. Because they are made of polyurethane, female condoms provide more sensitivity for the man than regular condoms. However, they are somewhat difficult to use, because the outer ring that fits around the penis tends to slip.

Hormonal Methods

These methods include birth control pills, Depo-Provera, and the Norplant implant. Birth control pills are hormones that are taken every day and prevent pregnancy by fooling a woman's body into thinking it's already pregnant. Depo-Provera is administered in injection form every three months. Norplant is inserted under the skin of the upper arm and lasts five years; although some people are still using it, the product has been taken off the market.

Hormonal methods of contraception don't interfere at all with sexual pleasure during intercourse. One reason they are so popular (besides their high effectiveness at preventing pregnancy) is that you don't have to interrupt your sexual encounter to use them.

But hormonal contraceptives (especially the pill) can possibly interfere with your sexual pleasure in long-term and insidious ways. There is some evidence that long-term use of birth control pills can depress a woman's sex drive. This happens because the pill either depresses a woman's testosterone production or changes the way her body uses testosterone. If you have been on the pill for several years and are experiencing a loss of sexual desire, you should have your testosterone levels checked. It may be time to switch to another contraception method.

This effect is especially pronounced if, in addition to taking birth control pills, a woman also takes Prozac, Paxil, or Zoloft (the selective serotonin-reuptake inhibiting antidepressant/antianxiety drugs). These SSRIs have long been known to inhibit both sexual desire and the ability to have an orgasm.

There is an irony at work here in the sense that if you are on the pill, you are using the most effective contraceptive available, and therefore this should increase your sex drive and sexual pleasure because you should feel free to have intercourse at any time without fear of pregnancy. However, if the pill has decreased your libido, you may not feel like having sex at all!

The effect can be especially insidious because often when women start taking the pill, they report that they feel unusual surges of sexual desire. These are testosterone-rebound effects caused by the fact that the pill is really inhibiting your testosterone. Pretty soon those rebound surges of testosterone go away, and you may find that you have a decreased sex drive.

Birth control pills, especially those that are estrogen-based, can cause pleasure-destroying side effects such as weight gain, bloating, and nausea. Depo-Provera can cause side effects as well, with the downside being that once the shot is in your body, it takes three months for it to wear off. Some women report that after they have been on Depo-Provera shots for a few months, they often stop having menstrual periods. This could be a huge plus because the woman no longer has to deal with the mess and inconvenience involved in menstruation.

Intrauterine Devices

Intrauterine devices (IUDs) are small plastic and wire devices that are inserted through the cervix and remain in the uterus. Some of them also secrete hormones. They are effective for about two years.

IUDs work because they create a hostile environment in the uterus so that a fertilized egg cannot implant itself in the endometrium (inner lining of the uterus). The IUD can interfere with sexual pleasure because it can cause cramping, pain, and excessive or prolonged menstrual bleeding.

IUDs are used by only 1 percent of women of reproductive age in the United States, but by about 100 million women worldwide. There are currently three types of IUDs available in the United States:

- Copper T380A, marketed as ParaGard IUD

- Levonorgestrel-releasing intrauterine system, marketed as Mirena

- ProgesteroneT, marketed as Progestasert

Sterilization

In the male sterilization operation, the *vasectomy,* the doctor makes incisions in the scrotum and cuts and ties off the two vas deferens, the tubes that carry sperm from the testicles to the abdominal cavity. The operation is done under local anesthesia. In the female sterilization operation, the *tubal ligation,* the doctor severs the fallopian tubes, the tubes running from the ovaries to the uterus, where fertilization usually takes place. Because this is abdominal surgery, it's done under general anesthetic.

Once the sterilization surgery has been completed and the patient has healed, these methods do not interfere with sexual pleasure at all. The downside is that you will experience discomfort (in the case of tubal ligation) or pain (in the case of vasectomy), and you will be unable to have intercourse for a few days (in the case of tubal ligation) or a couple of weeks (in the case of vasectomy).

Newer Methods

A few new contraceptive methods have been approved recently, and for detailed, up-to-date information, I recommend looking at a copy of *The Hot Guide to Safer Sex* by Yvonne Fulbright. One of these new methods is the NuvaRing, a hollow plastic ring that is inserted into the vagina and fits around the cervix like a diaphragm. It dispenses hormones and lasts a month. It cannot be felt during sexual intercourse. The hormones may cause side effects similar to those of the pill.

There is also a skin patch that dispenses hormones for a week. It is placed on the lower body, usually on the buttocks. It can interfere with sexual pleasure in that it looks ugly and the adhesive is so strong that it can pull and irritate the skin when you have intercourse.

There is also a nonsurgical, permanent sterilization option called Essure. In this method, plastic implants are inserted through the cervix and uterus into the fallopian tubes. They block the tubes, and over a few months scar tissue forms over them and prevents pregnancy.

Given that so many of the current contraceptive methods interfere with sexual pleasure, what's a person to do? Most people make their decision about contraception based on factors other than the aspect of pleasure (cost and effectiveness rate, for example). If you are positive that you never want children, I would recommend sterilization. For everyone else, the pill seems to be the best method of choice. If you choose the pill, do be aware of the potential consequences for your libido and health. Some women can get into a vicious cycle: They take the pill and become depressed because they have no sex drive, so they take antidepressants, which lower their libido even further. Don't let yourself get caught in this spiral. If you take the pill, use some of the techniques described in Chapters 5 and 6 to be proactive and maintain your sex drive.

From here, we'll move on to the five chapters addressed specifically to men or women.

chapter 9

Making the Pleasure Last and Last

A Chapter for Men

by Michele Serchuk

A*s I pointed out in the Introduction, I have a reason for arrang-*
ing the next several chapters as I've done. I believe that the better
a man functions sexually—in terms of his ability to control his
ejaculation or to maintain an erection—the more likely his female
partner is to be orgasmic. For this reason, when sex therapists treat
couples, they typically deal first with the man's issues, whether they
involve premature ejaculation or erectile dysfunction. Treating the

man's issues first usually helps the woman reach orgasm more easily and consistently.

The order of the next five chapters reflects this reality. In this chapter we address men's ejaculatory control. In the next we deal with improving men's erections. Both of these are skills a man can improve with great success, especially if he has a loving partner who will join him in the endeavor by participating in the exercises presented in these chapters. Once a couple has enjoyed some success with these issues, a woman's arousal levels and her ability to reach orgasm—the two topics covered in Chapters 11 and 12, respectively—will probably be enhanced. Then we turn again to men in Chapter 13, which deals with ways to enhance men's experience of ejaculation and orgasm.

Although each of these chapters is addressed primarily to men or to women, readers of both sexes will benefit from reading all five of them.

Why Last Longer?

I think lasting longer is always a concern for men. I know it has been for me. I tried using a condom to last longer and even thought about taking Prozac, but the peaking process worked for me. Plus, it feels great! — GEORGE

As a man, one of the best things you can do to increase your pleasure is to learn to last longer before you have an ejaculation and orgasm. This is true whether you are receiving manual or oral stimulation or having sexual intercourse.

Lasting longer, especially during intercourse, has a number of benefits. If you can last as long as you want to while you are having intercourse, this means that you can stay intimately connected with your partner for a longer time. Lasting longer allows you to experience those unique delicious sensations inside your partner's mouth or vagina for as long as you want.

Another reason to last longer is to please your partner. Look at Figure 4 on page 30. When you are ready to begin intercourse, you may already be at an arousal level of 7 or 8, whereas your female partner may be starting intercourse at a lower level, maybe at a 3 or 4. If you can last longer during intercourse before you ejaculate, you will allow your partner to catch up to your arousal level.

Many ancient cultures believed that a man derived his strength and his ability to grow spiritually from extended time spent inside the vagina during intercourse. Taoism and other Eastern religions and philosophical systems also emphasize prolonging intercourse as a way to achieve spiritual growth by becoming exposed to as much of the female essence as possible.

Why Do Some Men Last Longer than Others?

Some men have difficulty lasting as long as they would like to. There are many possible reasons for this.

One reason is that evolutionary pressures influence human males to ejaculate quickly. Like other mammals, humans have in a sense been genetically programmed to ejaculate quickly, as men who ejaculated quickly and impregnated their partners quickly tended to be more successful at getting their genes into the gene pool. It should also be noted that males were literally vulnerable and defenseless when making love, making efficiency a priority.

A second reason why men ejaculate quickly is that there seem to be biological differences in men's responses to pleasurable stimuli like oral sex and intercourse. Some men just naturally seem to have a higher sex drive than others, and that's okay. To co-opt a phrase from the literature on stress reduction, there are turtles and there are racehorses, and while we're probably not going to turn a racehorse into a turtle, there are still many techniques you can use to last longer and increase your pleasure. If you are one of those natural "racehorses," be grateful that you have a high sex drive, because the exercises in this chapter will help you channel that strong drive and realize its full potential.

A third reason why some men ejaculate quickly has to do with their masturbation habits. Most men develop extensive histories of masturbation habits before they ever have sexual intercourse with a partner. Men often feel that when they are pleasuring themselves, there's no benefit to lasting longer, and so they tend to go for the gusto right away.

Cultural Beliefs about Lasting Longer

Fortunately, we've seen a movement in this culture toward lasting longer during all sexual practices, especially intercourse. In the era of famous sex researcher Alfred Kinsey (the 1940s), the average time that men reported they spent in sexual intercourse was about two to three minutes. In more recent surveys (for example, the National Health and Social Life Survey conducted in the 1990s), the reported average was about six to seven minutes. So self-reported time spent in intercourse before ejaculation has doubled since Kinsey's day.

Sometimes it's difficult to answer the question "How long does the average man last in sexual intercourse before he ejaculates?" because many of the surveys on this topic have asked how long a particular session of lovemaking lasts from start to finish rather than focusing on penetration only. But one thing is clear, and that is that men today are interested in lasting longer during intercourse to obtain maximum pleasure.

What Doesn't Work, or How Not to Last Longer

Before I describe exercises men can use to last longer, let me tell you some techniques that don't work, although many men may have heard them from their friends. Creams and lotions that claim to numb the penis aren't a good idea, because, first of all, who wants to have sex with a numb penis? My goal in this book is to teach you how to feel more pleasure. Numbing your penis works against that goal. Besides, those creams can spread to the vagina and numb it also.

The same goes for condoms. Most men experience decreased sensitivity when they use a condom for intercourse. Some men even use two condoms at a time to help themselves last longer. Again, they are feeling less, not more. If you have to use a condom either for contraception or to protect yourself from contracting a sexually transmitted disease, do so, but recognize that there are many ways to increase your sensitivity while using a condom. (For some suggestions, see *The Hot Guide to Safer Sex,* by Yvonne K. Fulbright, listed in the "Suggested Reading" section.)

Some men have been advised to "think about something else" in order to last longer during intercourse. I have heard suggestions of things to think about that include doing math problems in your head, thinking about mowing the lawn, thinking about baseball statistics, thinking about having sex with a really ugly woman, and thinking about having sex with your grandmother. Really! Don't some of those sound absurd? Again, ignoring or blocking your sexual sensations will give you less pleasure, not more.

Some men use drugs (especially alcohol) to last longer. This will work in the short term, because a couple of drinks will slow down your ejaculatory reflex as well as all of your other reflexes. But if you continually use alcohol to try to last longer, you may develop a tolerance effect, meaning that you will need to use more and more alcohol to achieve the same effect. This can be a problem, because if you suddenly stop using alcohol, you may develop rebound premature ejaculation, which can be a scary and frustrating experience. In addition, excessive alcohol use can inhibit erections over time.

Several sex-therapy techniques were developed in the 1950s to help men last longer. You may have heard of some of them. They're called the "squeeze technique," "the stop-start method," and "testicle tugging." These techniques may have worked well in the past for men with severe premature ejaculation, but I do not recommend them. They not only fail to contribute to a pleasurable sexual environment, they actually cause an aversion to sex in most cases. On the other hand, all of the exercises I describe in this chapter are fun to do and increase your sexual pleasure.

Three Basics

There are three things a man needs to do to learn to last longer during any sexual activity. First, he must learn full-body relaxation. Second, he must get control of his PC muscle. Third, he must become aware of his sensations of arousal at all phases of the sexual encounter, especially the sensations that occur in the earliest phases of the pleasure cycle.

To accomplish the first goal, total body relaxation, use the breathing and muscle relaxation exercises described in Chapter 4. Do these for ten or fifteen minutes every day. Deep breathing and muscle relaxation are highly related to the ability to last longer during sexual encounters.

To accomplish the second goal, getting control of your PC muscle, make sure you do the PC muscle exercises described in Chapter 4 on a daily basis. Do both the beginning and the advanced exercises. The PC muscle exercises help you last longer because the PC muscle is the muscle in the pelvic area that spasms when you have an ejaculation and orgasm. Getting control of the PC muscle and relaxing it as you reach high levels of pleasure will help you last longer.

Most of the exercises in this chapter help you accomplish the third goal, which is to pay attention to your sensations instead of ignoring them. Read through all of the exercises so you can get a sense of what they entail. You can work through all of them in order or pick any one that sounds like fun.

Fortunately, the caveman days are behind us, and we have exercises and techniques for prolonging male arousal and pleasure. My goal is not to teach you to last a particular amount of time during your next session of sexual intercourse. My goal is to teach you enough ejaculatory control (for life!) that you will have options. You will be able to have a quickie if you want to. The ability to become aroused quickly and ejaculate quickly is actually an awesome ability. You will be able to be a marathon man if you want to on those occasions when it's all right with your partner. Mostly, I am trying to teach you to stay in the sexual "zone"—that plateau phase during which you are aroused enough to experience maximum pleasure but comfortable enough to be able to last as long as you want to.

⊘ *Exercise 20.* **AROUSAL AWARENESS TO LAST LONGER**

In Chapter 4 you learned to become aware of your arousal level when you were caressing yourself. It was easy to pay attention to your arousal level when you had no distractions. Now you will learn to do the same exercise while your lover fondles your penis and sensually explores you with her tongue and lips.

In this exercise, I want you to focus on your arousal and how close you are to orgasm or ejaculation. You will use the same 1-to-10 psychological arousal scale you learned in Chapter 4 to help you gauge your arousal.

As a quick review, a 1 is no arousal and a 10 is orgasm and ejaculation. A 2 or 3 is that slight twinge feeling at the base of your penis. A 4 is a steady, low level of arousal. A 5 or 6 is a medium level, and by the time you reach a 7 or 8 (corresponding to Masters and Johnson's plateau phase), you may feel your heart pounding, blood roaring in your ears, a flush on your face or chest, or some slight shortness of breath. A 9 is the point right before the point of inevitability.

As you and your partner do this exercise, notice what happens to your arousal if you remain passive and allow yourself to experience pure pleasure with no pressure to perform. Remember to follow the basic sensate-focus principles as you do this exercise and the other ones that follow in all of the chapters. Let's review them:

> When you are active, touch for your own pleasure

> Focus on your sensations

> If your mind drifts, bring it back to the exact point of contact between your skin and your partner's skin

> Stay in the here and now

> If your partner does anything that bothers you, let her know
> Keep all of your muscles relaxed
> Remember to breathe
> Don't pressure yourself or expect yourself to respond in a particular way
> Don't pressure your partner or expect her to respond in a particular way

For this exercise, as usual, you will need baby powder, lubricant, and a towel. Before you begin the arousal awareness exercise, exchange back caresses of about five to ten minutes each with your partner. Stimulate her with a front caress or genital caress before you begin the arousal awareness process.

Lie on your back and take the passive role. Your partner will begin a front caress and then a genital caress, during which she will fondle your penis and scrotum. She can slowly move her fingers around the shaft and head of your penis and gently trace her fingers around each testicle. If she would like, she can then move into an oral caress and use her tongue and lips to lick all over your penis, scrotum, and thighs. She should remember to explore for her own pleasure as she did in the early sensate-focus exercises.

After a couple of minutes, your partner will ask you, "What is your arousal level now?" Tell her your level. If it is higher than a 5, she will back off and allow your arousal to go down. If it is below a 5, she will continue the caress. She should vary her touch so that sometimes your arousal level goes up and sometimes it goes down.

Since you are doing this exercise to begin to learn to last longer, continue the exercise for twenty to twenty-five minutes. During this time, your partner can ask you your arousal level five or six times. Each time you tell your partner a level, take a deep breath and relax your pelvic muscles. Keep your PC muscle relaxed too.

It doesn't matter how high you go or how quickly or how long it takes to get there. If you are really aroused at the end of the exercise, tell your partner and ask her to help you reach an orgasm and ejaculation or to have intercourse.

✑ *Exercise 21.* PEAKING TO LAST LONGER

Remember that a peak is a wave-like increase in arousal. The peaking process allows your arousal to proceed in a wave-like pattern that will help your brain secrete endorphins, those pleasure-giving chemicals. The next several exercises allow you to practice peaking, first as the passive partner and then as the active partner.

Before you begin, you and your partner should do focusing caresses with each other. Pleasure your partner with a front caress or genital caress or some oral sex.

To start the peaking exercise, lie on your back and take the passive role. Your partner will begin a slow front caress and gradually move to your genitals.

When you reach level 3, let her know by saying either "three" or "stop." Your partner will then move her hand to your belly, thighs, or some other part of your body until your arousal has dropped one or two levels. Then she will caress your genitals again until you report a level 4. She will stop and let your arousal go down again.

As you reach each peak, say the number level and then take a deep breath and relax your PC muscle and other pelvic muscles. Do the exercise for about twenty-five minutes. Continue peaking up through levels 5, 6, 7, 8, and 9, and all the way to ejaculation and orgasm at the final peak if you want to. Try to do about six peaks during the exercise.

✒ Exercise 22. PEAKING AT LOWER LEVELS TO LAST LONGER

In order to learn to last longer, it's important to get a sense of all of the different levels on the arousal scale—the low levels as well as the high levels. One way to do this is to devote a whole exercise to peaking at the levels between 2 and 6.

To begin this exercise, you and your partner should do relaxing, focusing caresses. You should then give her a genital caress or oral sex. Then lie on your back and have her caress you with her hands. She should start on an area that's not the genitals, because you want to learn to become exquisitely sensitive to even the slightest rise in arousal. See if you can peak to levels 2, 3, 4, 5, and 6 in a twenty-five-minute session. Then relax and ask your partner to do oral sex or go ahead and have intercourse. You don't want to do too many peaks in any one session, especially at the lower levels. You could experience "peaking burnout," in which you get bored and don't feel turned on anymore. If you want to have an orgasm and ejaculation at the end of the session, go ahead, but if you really don't feel like it, don't force yourself.

ℰ *Exercise 23.* **PEAKING AT HIGHER LEVELS TO LAST LONGER**

It's even more of a challenge to learn the higher levels. You have to pay more attention, because at levels 8 and 9, it could only take a couple more strokes or a simple thrust or other movement to cause you to ejaculate before you're ready. And our goal here is for you to learn your individual time frame so that you ejaculate when you feel you're ready.

Prepare for the session as usual, with focusing caresses and an exercise your partner enjoys. When you move to the main part of the exercise and your partner begins to stimulate you with her hand, have her move to genital stimulation right away. Allow yourself to go up to level 5 or 6 as your first peak. Then peak up to levels, 7, 8, and 9. Stop between peaks just long enough for your arousal to go down about two levels. It is just as important for you to get a sense that your arousal is going down as it is for you to get a sense of your arousal going up.

I have a lot of experience with this exercise, and I can tell you that it is probably the best one in this chapter for enhancing orgasm. There's something about starting at a higher peak and then backing off and moving a little slower that can really make your orgasm explosive.

ℰ *Exercise 24.* **PEAKING AT THE SAME LEVEL**

If you want to, you could design a peaking exercise for yourself in which you overpractice one particular level with manual stimulation from your partner. All you need to do to design your own exercise is to decide on a level and make a plan with your partner about how she should caress you. A good level for this exercise is 7 or 8. What you accomplish if you do five or six peaks at the same level in a twenty-minute exercise is that you learn every sensation that goes along with that level. With practice you will be able to stay at that level for longer and longer amounts of time.

ℰ *Exercise 25.* **PEAKING AS THE ACTIVE PARTNER**

You take the active role in this exercise. Begin it as you would any other, by exchanging back caresses with your partner. Then explore her body with a front caress, a genital caress, or oral sex. When you are done, lie on your back and do any kind of slow pelvic thrust or roll that you wish, as your partner strokes your genitals. Be sure to avoid tightening your stomach, thigh, or hip muscles.

Slowly thrust your penis against your partner's hand. Peak up to level 4. When you reach a 4, tell your partner, stop moving, breathe, and relax your PC muscle. Resume the exercise and continue for about twenty minutes, peaking up to levels 5, 6, 7, 8, and 9 by doing pelvic rolls and thrusts. If you feel like ejaculating or having intercourse at the end of the exercise, go ahead.

✐ Exercise 26. PEAKING WITH ORAL SEX

Remember all those great oral-sex techniques you both learned in Chapter 7? Now is the time for your partner to try them out in the context of peaking.

Begin with focusing caresses. Then lie on your back. Your partner will begin a front and genital caress with her hand. Then she'll start to caress your penis and scrotum with her lips and tongue. In keeping with sensate-focus principles, she should caress you slowly and do whatever feels good to her. Take about twenty-five minutes and peak up to levels 5, 6, 7, 8, and 9. At the end of the exercise, ejaculate if you want to or have intercourse.

When peaking with oral sex, you can use any of the other peaking variations you have learned in this chapter. You can peak using only the low levels (2 through 5). Or you could peak using only the high levels (6 through 10), or you could do several peaks at the same level.

Another oral-sex peaking variation is to become active and thrust into your partner's mouth. When you do this, keep your muscles as relaxed as possible and caress the inside of your partner's mouth with your penis.

✐ Exercise 27. USING YOUR PC MUSCLE TO PUT ON THE BRAKES

Exercising your PC muscle every day, as I recommended in Chapter 4, will give you a good foundation for this next practice. Now you will use your PC muscle to help you last longer.

Learning to use your PC muscle to "put the brakes on" your arousal is a little tricky. Normally, if you reach a certain level of arousal and then quickly squeeze the PC muscle once or twice, your arousal will go down a level. The reason that this takes a little time to learn is that there are many different ways to squeeze. You may have to experiment a bit to see what works for you. It is best to first work with this on your own, before you try it with your partner.

Here are the basic types of PC muscle squeezes:

> One long, hard squeeze
> Two medium squeezes
> Several quick squeezes in a row, similar to the way the PC muscle spasms during ejaculation

As you experiment, try to find the smallest amount of PC squeezing that you can do to take your arousal down a level without affecting your erection. If you squeeze your PC muscle too much before you have a full erection, you may temporarily lose your erection.

To find the best way to squeeze your PC muscle, do a peaking exercise by yourself. During a twenty-minute exercise, slowly caress your penis and peak up through levels 3, 4, 5, 6, 7, 8, and 9, if you can. At each peak, as you recognize the level, squeeze your PC muscle. Experiment with the different ways of squeezing to see which takes your arousal down a level but does not affect your erection.

After you have figured out which pattern of PC muscle squeezes works for you, you are ready to try using the PC squeeze in an exercise with your partner. Begin with focusing caresses. Then have your partner do a front and genital caress with you to start peaking. Peak through levels 4, 5, 6, 7, 8, and 9 during a twenty-five-minute exercise. As you reach each peak, squeeze your PC muscle in your preferred way. Then tell your partner your level, breathe, and relax your muscles. Continue peaking and see if you can use your PC muscle to lower your arousal even at level 9. Make sure you keep all of your muscles other than the PC relaxed. At the end of the exercise, allow yourself to have an orgasm and ejaculation if you wish.

Once you have learned to add the PC muscle into your arousal pattern, try using it during peaking with oral sex. Be careful, though, not to overuse the PC; do a peaking exercise without it once in a while. You don't want to become dependent on the PC squeeze as the only way to last longer, because overuse of the PC muscle can cause delayed ejaculation and can also cause minor, temporary erection loss.

✍ *Exercise 28.* **PEAKING WITH INTERCOURSE**

At last we've reached one of the big payoffs: using your ability to last longer to stay intimately connected with your partner during intercourse. Peaking can be done in any intercourse position. The first time you try peaking with intercourse, you should use the side-to-side scissors position, as it is the easiest.

Before you begin, start your session as usual, with focusing caresses to relax yourselves and promote sensual arousal. Pleasure your partner with a front or genital caress or some oral sex. Then have her give you a genital caress and do a couple of low-level peaks to get started. It doesn't matter if you have an erection initially because you can do this exercise without one, but you should probably have your partner give you a genital caress until you have an erection. Then make sure that your partner is lubricated enough and ready to take you inside herself.

Get into the scissors position. Lie on your right side facing your partner and have her lie on her back perpendicular to you. Scoot up next to each other, interleave your legs with hers, and insert your penis. Thrust until you are at level 4, then back off and allow your arousal to go down a couple of levels. Continue the exercise for about twenty minutes, peaking to levels 5, 6, 7, 8, and 9. Ejaculate if you feel like it at the end of the exercise.

The next time you try this exercise, try the female-superior position. Lie on your back and take the passive role. Have your partner do a front caress, a genital caress, and oral sex if she likes.

Peak up to a 3, and then to a 4 or 5. Be sure to allow enough time between peaks for your arousal to go down one or two levels. Notice how it feels when the blood recedes and then reenters your penis.

Your partner will then climb on top of you and put your penis into her vagina. Remember to keep breathing as you feel yourself enter her. She should start to move very slowly. Notice how wet she is and how it feels to have her moving against you. Let her movements peak you up to progressively higher levels of arousal, even to orgasm and ejaculation if you like. Be sure to allow about five minutes per peak so you are not rushing things.

For the next peaking session, try one of the male-superior positions. You will take the active role in this exercise. Before you begin, make sure you have your preferred lubrication handy. Then begin your session with relaxation and focusing caresses.

Peak up to a 4, 5, and 6 with your partner doing manual and oral stimulation. Then do one or two comfortable peaks with your partner on top.

Next, have your partner lie on her back with a pillow under her buttocks. She should bend her knees, lift her legs up in the air, and spread them (this is the butterfly position described in Chapter 8). If she would like, she can rest her calves against her thighs. This is a good time to apply lubrication to her vagina and your penis.

Kneel, sitting back on your heels, with your penis as close to your partner's vagina as possible. Support your body weight with your legs, not your arms.

Insert your penis and slowly begin to thrust. Move your penis in and out of the vagina by rolling and rocking your pelvis instead of tensing your thighs. Do this as slowly as you can.

Peak up to levels 6, 7, 8, and 9. Take five minutes per peak. At each peak, breathe deeply and relax your PC muscle and other pelvic muscles. Remember to breathe evenly, focus on what it feels like to be inside her, and move in ways that make you feel sensual. At the end of the exercise, have an orgasm and ejaculation if you wish. Notice how strong your orgasm is as a result of practicing this series of peaking exercises.

Once you are able to peak in any intercourse position, add in some of the other techniques I've already talked about. Do one peaking session practicing only the low levels, do one practicing only the high levels, or do one with all of the peaks at the same level. Then add in PC muscle squeezes at some of the peaks to last even longer.

✐ Exercise 29. PLATEAUING TO LAST LONGER

Once you have learned to use the PC muscle to peak, you can learn to plateau. Plateauing can be done with manual or oral stimulation or intercourse. Remember that plateauing is similar to peaking, except when you reach a desired level of arousal, you hold yourself at that level by fine-tuning your focusing, breathing, pelvic movements, and PC squeeze.

The next series of exercises allows you to experience plateauing with your partner. These exercises really increase your staying power at very pleasurable levels of arousal. Practice a separate technique in each session. Always remember to start with focusing caresses and to do a front caress or genital caress for your partner's pleasure so she doesn't feel left out.

For the first exercise, plateau at several different levels by using just the changes in your breathing. Plateau at each level for one to two minutes if you can.

To begin, lie on your back. Your partner will do a front caress and genital caress, lovingly and slowly. Remember to relax, breathe, and focus on the areas where she is touching or licking.

As you reach level 4 on the arousal scale, try to stay there by changing your breathing. The secret to being able to do this is to learn to recognize in-between levels like $3\frac{1}{2}$ and $4\frac{1}{2}$. If you go beyond a 4, slow your breathing down until you are back at a 4. If you go below a 4, speed up your breathing until you are slightly past a 4.

Continue plateauing for about twenty to twenty-five minutes, going through levels 5, 6, 7, 8, and 9 if you can. If you feel like ejaculating at the end of the exercise, do so.

The next time you do a plateauing exercise, try to plateau by doing pelvic rolls and thrusts instead of concentrating on your breathing. If you decide to plateau at level 4, for example, start some pelvic movements at level 4. Roll your pelvis sensually at varying speeds. If you reach a $4\frac{1}{2}$, stop the movements. If your arousal then backs off to a $3\frac{1}{2}$, start the movements again until you are at level $4\frac{1}{2}$. Use your pelvic motions to help you maintain your level. Again, do this for twenty or twenty-five minutes, passing through all of the levels on the way to orgasm and ejaculation.

Next, try to plateau by using your PC muscle to take your arousal down and pelvic movements to bring it back up. Soon you will be able to maintain your arousal level within a narrow range that you will control. Do a whole plateauing sequence using the combination of PC muscle squeezes and pelvic thrusts.

The final plateauing technique involves switching your focus from one part of your body to another, or to a part of your partner's body. For example, peak at level 5 with some hand or oral stimulation from your partner. When you go beyond level 5 to $5\frac{1}{2}$, switch your focus from the part of your penis that is being caressed to some other part of your penis or body. This will lower your arousal level. When your arousal level dips down to $4\frac{1}{2}$, switch your focus back to the area being touched in order to move to the next level. Using this switch-focus technique, do a whole plateauing exercise up through ejaculation.

Plateauing can be done with any kind of stimulation, including all of the intercourse positions. Once you have mastered all four of the plateauing techniques with manual and oral stimulation, do plateauing sequences with the intercourse positions, starting with the scissors position and moving to the female-superior and male-superior positions. Try to do one whole exercise where you plateau in the "zone," which is what I call level 8.

Soon you will find that you can hold yourself at any level of arousal you choose by making subtle shifts in your breathing, your focus, your pelvic muscles, and your PC muscle. You will be able to plateau at level 9 or remain on the brink of orgasm for several seconds or even minutes.

✐ *Exercise 30.* CARESS THE INSIDE OF THE MOUTH AND THE VAGINA

This exercise and the next one are kind of different. They both involve visualizations that help you last longer. In the first one, when you are receiving oral sex from your partner, do a peaking exercise in which you peak by gently moving your penis in and out of your partner's mouth. Actually caress the inside of your partner's mouth with your penis.

Then try the same thing during intercourse. Use the butterfly position, with your partner on her back and you kneeling between her legs. When you are erect, insert your penis and, using the motion of your hips and pelvis, caress the inside of her vagina with your penis, the same way you did with your hand. Feel the vaginal walls, the rugae, the cervix, the PC muscle, the A-spot, and the G-spot with your penis if you can.

✐ *Exercise 31.* "PAINT" THE INSIDE OF THE VAGINA

This exercise is similar to the previous one. The difference is that you visualize your penis in a different way. Think of your penis as a paintbrush, with the penis being the bristles. Think of the handle of the brush as extending in a straight line through your rectum and out your anus. Now, using the butterfly position, caress your partner's vagina as in the above exercise, but move in such a way that you are using all of your hypothetical brush. Use the motion of your hips and pelvis to propel the "brush." I know this exercise sounds kind of wacky, but someone taught it to me, and there's something about visualizing the penis in this continuous way that changes the way you move your pelvis and that really works.

✑ *Exercise 32.* **REPETITIVE PENETRATION**

Many men can last as long as they want to with hand or oral stimulation but ejaculate sooner than they would like to with intercourse. Sex therapists call this "point of penetration" anxiety. It's fairly normal; after all, isn't being inside your partner's vagina the best sexual sensation there is? It's most people's number-one fantasy—no wonder men get so excited thinking about it. Whether or not this is a problem for you, this exercise will help you last longer with intercourse.

Before you begin, exchange back caresses of about ten minutes each and then do a front caress or genital caress with your partner. Make sure you have lubrication handy.

Lie on your back and take the passive role. Do a couple of comfortable lower-level peaks as your partner sensually caresses you with her hands or lips.

Then change positions and have your partner lie on her back. Have her tilt her pelvis back and put her legs up in the air (the butterfly position). Apply lubrication to both your hands. Kneel between your partner's legs and slowly begin to caress your penis with one hand, using a lot of lubrication.

With your other hand, caress your partner's genitals, also with a lot of lubrication. Then start to caress her genitals with your lubricated penis. Caress her outer genitals first (the vulva) and then insert just the head of your penis slowly into her vagina.

Remove your penis from her vagina and caress your partner's genitals with it again. Then insert your penis again, and this time put most of it inside her vagina.

Practice several insertions within a twenty-minute time frame, using peaking to allow yourself to go a little higher on the arousal scale each time. Try to stay within the 4-to-8 range for most of the exercise.

This can be a very erotic and satisfying exercise, and one you and your partner may wish to return to. You can relish each point of contact, and as you move deeper with each instance of penetration, your sexual pleasure will build exponentially.

Your Attitude

Now that you know quite a few exercises to help you last longer, I have some suggestions for your attitude. I've shown you how to last longer through increased awareness of the pleasurable stimuli of oral sex and intercourse, and through the use of the PC muscle, breathing, and pelvic movements to maintain your arousal levels. Try not to get too obsessed with the actual number of minutes that you last during intercourse. Remember, the important thing is that you have more opportunity to be intimate with your partner. It's possible to focus too much on the time frame and lose sight of the pleasure. Keep in mind that when you're doing anything that's highly pleasurable, time seems to fly. You lose your normal sense of time passing, and you may actually underestimate how long you spend having intercourse.

Here's an example of a man who obsessed too much about lasting longer. He was one of my clients. We'll call him Lester. Lester wanted to learn to last longer, so I taught him most of the exercises in this chapter. During every session he would set a stopwatch when we began to have intercourse! I think that's taking the concept a little too far. Take the pressure off yourself and enjoy.

Another piece of advice I would like to offer is don't hold back an ejaculation. The exercises in this chapter are designed to give you enjoyment and control without a sense that you are holding back. Ejaculation is a reflex; if you miss the window of opportunity where you have a chance to maintain yourself in the plateau zone (level 8), well then, so be it. Just let the ejaculation happen and don't try to control it. When you consistently have the feeling that you are holding back your ejaculation, you are actually building some bad habits that can result in less control, not more.

Once you and your partner have practiced these techniques, trust yourself that you will settle into your optimal time frame. Some men have even noticed that when they used these techniques, they spontaneously developed the ability to have male multiple orgasms (MMOs). If you are interested in learning more about this multiple-orgasm process, see my book *How to Make Love All Night* or see *The Multi-Orgasmic Man,* by Mantak Chia and Douglas Abrams Arava (both listed in the "Suggested Reading" section).

Remember, you're lucky to have a high sex drive. It's a lot easier to teach a man with a high sex drive to last longer than it is to try to increase someone's sex drive or teach him how to ejaculate more easily. But doing so is possible, so read on.

chapter 10

Getting Better and Better (Erections) All the Time

A Chapter for Men

by Morgan Cowin

*I*n *Chapter 3, which discussed the sexual-pleasure cycle, I described the processes involved in erection (initiation, filling, rigidity, and maintenance) and the 1-to-10 erection scale. This chapter contains exercises to help you get harder erections. Some of the* *exercises work on initiation, some on filling, some on rigidity, some on maintenance, and some on dispelling a few of the erection myths that can shut you down psychologically. The first three exercises work on initiation and filling.*

✐ Exercise 33. PRIMING THE PENIS FOR QUICKER ERECTIONS

Here is a very effective exercise you can do by yourself to gradually increase your body's ability to generate an erection faster, with or without stimulation. The purpose of this exercise is to "prime" the system of blood vessels that helps you become erect by increasing your blood flow.

If you do this exercise for just five minutes every day, it will work—whether you think it is working or not. Within two to three weeks, you will notice greater hardness in your morning erections and a general feeling of fullness in your penis during the day. You will also notice that it takes you less time to get an erection in sexually arousing situations with your partner. I have found this exercise especially successful with men over fifty and with those who have not been sexually active for some time and have concerns about how long it takes for them to get an erection.

To do the exercise, first complete your daily PC muscle exercises. Then, make sure you are relaxed. You could even do this exercise in the shower if you'd like. Make sure you have a lubricant handy.

Apply the lubricant to your hand and slowly caress the base of your penis, squeezing the shaft and massaging the base. Do this slowly. Do not use a hard or fast masturbation stroke. You might try doing this with the hand other than the one you usually use during masturbation. If you are right-handed, for example, use your left hand for this caress. It doesn't matter if you're aroused or not. Nor does it matter if you have an erection while you are doing this exercise. Continue caressing the base of your penis for five minutes.

Even though the goal is not to get an erection during the exercise, this technique will help your erections in two ways. First, massaging the base of the penis helps you relax the PC muscle; second, a relaxed PC muscle allows the base of the penis to fill with blood more easily. If you're still concerned that not enough blood is flowing in, do this exercise in conjunction with the following one.

⟨𝒢⟩ Exercise 34. RELAXING THE PC MUSCLE FOR STRONGER ERECTIONS

Many men unconsciously tighten the PC muscle when they feel themselves starting to become erect. Men develop this habit because, at first, squeezing the PC seems to pump up their erection. If a man makes a habit of doing this, however, he may start to notice after a while that it takes longer and longer to get an erection, or that he gets an erection and then has trouble maintaining it. If he reacts to this by squeezing harder, he will actually make matters worse. Here's why:

If you squeeze the PC muscle when you start to get an erection, your penis will momentarily fill a little bit, because the blood that was already past the PC muscle flows into the penis. After that, however, the temporary squeezing of the PC muscle prevents more blood from flowing into the penis, and the end result is a net loss. You're actually taking one step forward and two steps back. If, on the other hand, you squeeze your PC muscle when your erection has already reached the state of rigidity, your erection will not be affected, because no more blood could get in anyway.

Squeezing the PC muscle as you are getting an erection also works against your erection in two other ways. First, the sensation of tension actually travels along a feedback loop between your genitals and your brain. When your brain registers this "tension" message, it reacts in ways that interfere with your ability to feel the sensations of the first stages of erection. Your body reacts to the tension by beginning the stress response, including the release of adrenalin, which can inhibit erection.

Second, the fact that you are "doing something" to get an erection shifts you into a performance mode. Psychologically, this decreases your ability to relax and just allow your erection to happen.

Are you squeezing your PC muscle at an inopportune time? Try this exercise to see. Often, one session is all you need to break any bad habits. That may sound too good to be true, but I've seen it work with clients.

This is an exercise that you do with your partner. Start the session with relaxation and focusing caresses. Then pleasure your partner with a nondemand genital caress.

Lie comfortably on your side or back in the passive role. Have your partner spend fifteen to twenty minutes slowly caressing your genitals with her hand and mouth. As you become aroused, if she feels you tighten your PC muscle, she will tell you and then wait for it to relax before she begins the caress again. After your partner has pointed out your unconscious tensing three or four times, you will begin to recognize it yourself, and then you'll be able to keep your PC muscle relaxed without feedback or prompting from your partner. After this caress is done, you and your partner could have intercourse. You can allow yourself to go all the way to ejaculation during this caress if you want to.

⟡ Exercise 35. CARESSING YOUR MORNING ERECTION

For many men, the hardest erections they have are the ones they have during their sleep cycles at night or the ones they wake up with in the morning. Here is an exercise you can do to use this to your advantage.

Figure out about how much sleep you need to get in order to have your best chance of waking up with a morning erection. Allow a little extra time in the morning, and when you wake up, do a peaking exercise (as described in Chapter 4). Do the peaking exercise while paying attention to your arousal levels, not your erection levels (see page 37 if you need to remind yourself about the difference). Peak for about fifteen minutes, going up to levels 5, 6, 7, 8, and 9, and then ejaculating if you want to. This exercise is good for erections because your arousal level will go up and down, but your penis will probably stay relatively hard during the entire exercise.

⟡ Exercise 36. ERECTION AWARENESS

There are some men whose erections are not as hard as they would like because these men have lost their sense of what it feels like to have an erection. They are so used to thinking of erections as an "all-or-none" phenomenon—that is, either a level 1 or a level 10—that they don't recognize the in-between levels that are hard enough for intercourse. The following is an exercise to help you recognize those levels. It is an exercise you do with a partner.

Before you begin the exercise, both you and your partner should familiarize yourselves with the erection levels described in Chapter 3, including the levels that represent initiation, filling, rigidity, and maintenance. (Recall that erection levels are different from arousal levels, which measure how close you feel you are to ejaculating.) Lie on your back and have your partner give you a front caress and genital caress and oral sex. Keep your eyes closed and just soak up the sensations. Every five minutes or so, your partner will ask you how hard you think your penis is. Without looking, give her an estimate. It doesn't matter what erection levels you have during this exercise, and it doesn't matter whether your erection is harder every time she asks you. What matters is that you are aware of your levels and are not underestimating them. Your partner can help you by giving you feedback about whether she thinks you are accurate. Repeat this exercise several times when you are in different types of moods, and see how your erection levels differ according to your mood and whether or not you feel a lot of sexual desire. Finish the exercise by ejaculating or having intercourse.

✐ *Exercise 37.* REGAINING YOUR ERECTION

These next two exercises work primarily on filling and rigidity. There are certain myths that get in the way of getting and keeping strong erections and having fabulous intercourse. One of these myths is the idea that once you have an erection, it should stay at the same level of hardness during the course of an entire sexual encounter until you have an ejaculation and orgasm.

Actually, it is perfectly normal for erections to get harder or softer several times during the course of a sexual exchange. When some men feel their erections start to get softer, whether during intercourse or before, they often tense up—which of course guarantees that the erection will go down even more.

If you begin to feel your erection flagging, "working" to keep it up is the worst thing you can do. The best thing to do is to just let go and enjoy the pleasurable sensations in your penis. Take a deep breath, focus on your lover's touch, and relax your muscles.

Start with focusing caresses. Then, pleasure your partner with a front caress and genital caress. Allow at least twenty minutes for the following exercise.

Lie on your back and take the passive role. Your partner will start a non-demand front caress, genital caress, and oral sex. As always, she should do the caress for her own pleasure. Ask her to notice whether you are staying relaxed and remembering to take deep breaths.

Whenever you have a noticeable filling-level erection response, have your partner stop the caress and allow your erection to go back to erection level 1. Then she can start over and allow your erection to go up to a higher level.

Have her repeat this several times during a twenty-minute exercise, allowing you to go up to several different levels of filling and rigidity. After getting an erection and purposely allowing it to go down and regaining it a few times, you will find that your erection will maintain itself even when your partner stops stimulating you. You will find yourself actually unable to lose the erection because you have done this exercise so well.

If you subscribe to the myth that an erection should stay at the same level of hardness all the way through a sexual encounter, you may feel frustrated the first time you try this exercise. When you feel your partner stop the stimulation, you will probably find that your first impulse is to tense up and squeeze your PC muscle to try to cause an erection. Your partner can point this out to you and remind you to focus, breathe, and relax.

Each time during this exercise when your partner stops the stimulation, try to become more comfortable with the sensation that your erection is going down. You'll get better at breathing and relaxing, and your erection will naturally come back up, allowing you to continue sensation-filled lovemaking.

ℰ Exercise 38. THINK YOURSELF UP

This is a version of the previous exercise that takes place during intercourse rather than during manual or oral stimulation. There are a couple of different ways to do this exercise. Set aside about an hour, and you'll need the usual supplies: baby powder, lubricant, and a large towel.

Begin with short focusing caresses on each other's face, back, or front. In the first version of the exercise, you and your partner should get into the side-to-side scissors position. Put plenty of lubrication on your penis and your partner's vagina, and insert your flaccid penis (for more about flaccid insertion, see Exercise 40, below). Note what level of filling you have. You and your partner should lie as quietly as possible and breathe together. Focus all of your attention on how your penis feels inside your partner's vagina. Without moving, see if you can focus so intently on your penis and the warmth and wetness of the vagina that you can feel your penis start to get harder. Keep your PC muscle relaxed.

This is really a challenge, because the exercise requires you to mentally initiate an erection without pressuring yourself. As you feel yourself start to get hard, thrust a little and then stop. Let your erection go back down a little. Repeat the exercise several times. At the end of the exercise, switch positions and have intercourse until you ejaculate if you feel like it.

In a second version of this exercise, use the butterfly position. Start intercourse when your erection is at about level 5 (the beginning of rigidity). Put plenty of lubrication on your penis and your partner's vagina. Insert your semihard penis and just hold it there without thrusting. Focus intently on the tightness and warmth and wetness of your partner's vagina. See if you can feel your penis harden and expand. Slowly begin to thrust. Feel your penis harden even more. When you reach what you feel is your maximum hardness, go ahead and have intercourse up through ejaculation and orgasm if you wish.

⚭ *Exercise 39.* ORAL SEX WITH THE MAN ON TOP

This exercise works really well for filling and rigidity. Oral sex with the man on top is very stimulating, not only physically, but also psychologically. It's also good if you tend to get up to about a level-6 erection and then have trouble going up further.

Before you begin, lie on your back and have your partner do a front and genital caress with you. When you get to an erection level that is the beginning of rigidity (about a level 5), switch positions and have your partner lie on her back. Get into a comfortable position either kneeling beside her or straddling her chest, provided she is comfortable with that. Don't forget to focus and breathe, despite the excitement of this position.

Your partner can put a pillow underneath her head to raise it up, or she can support her head with one hand. She should give you an oral genital caress in this position by licking the underside of your penis and putting the whole thing in her mouth and sucking on it. She should remember to caress for her own pleasure. The slower she goes with this exercise, the better. You can also hold your penis in your hand and "feed" it to her. Slowly caress your lover's lips with your penis. Thrust into her mouth as slowly as you can.

The toughest thing about this exercise is getting comfortable in a kneeling position, because you will be like that for several minutes. Practice keeping your hips, thighs, and PC muscle as relaxed as possible. The more relaxed you are, the more receptive you'll be to the pleasurable sensations streaming through your penis as it is licked and sucked. The reason this exercise works so well is that when you are in an upright position, you have gravity working for you, causing blood to flow into your penis more easily. Finish the exercise with oral sex or move on to intercourse.

✐ Exercise 40. FLACCID INSERTION

Another myth about erections is that you have to have a level-10 erection to have enjoyable intercourse. This is probably the best exercise I know of to convince you that you don't have to be rock hard to enjoy the intimate pleasures of intercourse. Now that you know the difference between filling and rigidity, you can use the following exercise to show yourself how to enjoy the sweet pleasures of intercourse without an erection. This exercise is usually called "flaccid insertion," but other names for it include "quiet vagina" and "stuffing." It may sound strange, but it actually feels quite wonderful.

Before you begin, make sure you have lubrication on hand. Start with focusing caresses, then pleasure your partner with a front or genital caress.

Get into a side-to-side intercourse position, preferably the scissors position. Lie on your right side facing your partner, as she lies on her back with one leg on top of yours and the other leg between your legs.

Put a lot of lubrication on your penis. Gently spread your partner's vaginal lips with your fingers and apply some lubrication. Take plenty of time with this and enjoy it. You will get the best results from this exercise if your penis is either flaccid or at some stage of filling (level 2, 3, or 4).

Have your partner gently fold your penis into her vagina by pushing the base of your penis inside her. The head will naturally follow. Once you are inside her vagina, breathe and relax your legs and your PC muscle. Notice how warm your partner's vagina is and how wet it feels. See if you are aware of your erection level. Notice whether it changes. You can keep your penis in her vagina without moving, and the two of you can hug, cuddle, talk, or do whatever you want that helps you stay intimately connected. Just close your eyes and focus all of your attention on how your penis feels inside her vagina.

After you have done the quiet-vagina exercise for a while, you may want to start moving around so you get a stronger erection, or you may want to finish the exercise by changing positions and having intercourse.

✐ *Exercise 41.* REPETITIVE PENETRATION FOR ERECTIONS

This exercise helps you dispel the myth that your erection has to stay at the same level of hardness during an entire sexual encounter. Before you begin, exchange focusing caresses and do a nondemand front or genital caress with your partner.

Lie on your back. Have your partner take the active role and do a front and genital caress with you and some oral sex if she wishes. When you have an erection of level 5 or 6, switch positions and have your partner lie on her back with her knees bent and her legs in the air. Kneel between her legs and put a lot of lubrication on your penis and on your partner's vagina. Slowly caress the outside of your partner's vagina with your penis. (You may have heard this practice referred to as "outercourse.")

When your erection is at a level 7 or so, slowly slide your penis into your partner's vagina. Do a few strokes inside and then pull out and again caress her lips and clitoris with your penis. Allow your erection level to decrease one or two levels by stopping the stimulation to your penis. Then stroke your penis again and allow your erection to go up to level 8. Slowly penetrate again and do several long strokes, remembering to breathe, relax, and focus on the pleasurable sensations you are feeling in your partner's vagina.

Repeat several of these erection peaks followed by withdrawal until you are confident you can penetrate with any level of erection. Notice how your penis doesn't have to be supererect to penetrate her vagina as long as you use plenty of lubrication. You are capable of doing this exercise no matter what your level of erection is.

✐ *Exercise 42.* NONVAGINAL REPETITIVE PENETRATION

In this exercise, you will "penetrate" various parts of your partner's body so that you start to think of every part of her body as sexual. Begin with a front caress with your lover. Then caress her genitals with your fingers, lips, and tongue. Put lubrication on your penis (whether it is erect or not) and caress her body with it.

"Insert" your penis into your partner's armpit, elbow, the back of her knee, the space between her thighs, or any other opening you can create. Alternate these insertions with insertions into the vagina. Have fun with each other as you play around with the exercise.

✒ Exercise 43. NONDEMAND PENETRATION

This exercise is good for dispelling the myth that every session of intercourse needs to lead to orgasm and ejaculation. Start with focusing caresses and then do a nondemand front caress or genital caress with your partner.

Lie on your back and have your partner caress you with her hands, lips, and tongue. When you reach erection level 5 or 6, she can climb on top of your penis and have intercourse for a few strokes. You should remain totally passive. There is no demand on you to maintain your erection for any length of time or to have an ejaculation. Your partner will do a few strokes and then return to caressing you with her hands and mouth.

Have her repeat the nondemand intercourse with more and more strokes each time until you are comfortable and relaxed enough to move without putting pressure on yourself to maintain an erection.

✒ Exercise 44. PEAKING FOR ERECTIONS

In Chapter 4 you learned the process of peaking by yourself. In Chapter 9, the chapter on lasting longer, I described the process of peaking with a partner using manual and oral stimulation and intercourse. The peaking process can also be used to help you have firmer erections.

In the chapter on lasting longer, I described the peaking process using the subjective/psychological 1-to-10 arousal scale. If you use the peaking process to help your erections, you can use either the subjective/psychological arousal scale or the erection scale. Using the subjective/psychological arousal scale will help your erections, because focusing on arousal instead of erection takes performance pressure off you. If you would like to peak using the subjective/psychological arousal scale, just do the peaking exercises as described in Chapter 9.

If you would like to peak using the 1-to-10 erection scale, do the following. First, do focusing caresses with your partner. Then have her give you a manual and oral genital caress. Instead of you giving her arousal feedback, she will give you feedback about the hardness of your erection (see Chapter

3, page 37, to review the 1-to-10 erection scale). She'll stop at each peak and allow your erection to go down a couple of levels. After you have peaked at levels 4, 5, 6, 7, 8, and 9, continue the exercise with intercourse or end it however you wish.

You could also do an erection-peaking exercise with intercourse. Start with focusing caresses and have your partner stimulate you manually and orally until you are about a level-5 erection. Then get into the butterfly position and insert your penis. Thrust and peak up to erection levels 6, 7, 8, and 9, and end the exercise however you wish.

You can do this exercise using all of the same variations described in the Chapter 9 exercises for lasting longer. You can do several peaks with low-level erections or several peaks with high-level erections. You could do several peaks at the same erection level. You can be passive or active. You could do erection peaks using any of the intercourse positions. Allowing your erections to go up and down will make them not only harder but also more reliable.

✐ *Exercise 45.* PLATEAUING FOR ERECTIONS

Plateauing using the subjective/psychological arousal scale as described on page 37 will help your erections, as keeping your focus on arousal takes the performance pressure off you. You can also plateau using the erection scale with manual or oral stimulation or intercourse.

Remember that there are four techniques you can use to plateau using the subjective/psychological arousal scale. They are changing your breathing, squeezing your PC muscle, adjusting your thrusting, and switching your focus. To plateau using the erection scale, you'll use an additional technique: changes in the way your partner touches you. The first version of the exercise relies on your partner to gauge your erection level and adjust her touch accordingly.

Start with focusing caresses and then give your partner a front caress and a manual or oral genital caress. Then you should lie on your back, and your partner will start to caress your penis manually and orally. When she sees that you have reached a level-5 erection, she will tell you that you are at level 5. She will take turns slowing down and speeding up her touch to see if you can stay at erection level 5 for a few seconds to a minute.

She should do the same for levels 6, 7, 8, and 9. You should start out the exercise being passive, but as you reach the higher levels, you can start moving and adjusting your thrusting to help you plateau. Finish the exercise any way you both agree on.

Here's an active version of this exercise that takes place during intercourse. Do focusing caresses and then have your partner stimulate you orally up to erection level 5. Then get into the butterfly position and insert your penis. Thrust until you are at erection level 6. Use whatever combination of techniques (changing your breathing, squeezing your PC muscle, changing your thrusting, or switching your focus) helps you plateau at erection levels 6, 7, 8, and 9. With intercourse, I believe the best plateauing technique for maintaining an erection at any given level is alternating the speed of your thrusting between slowing down and speeding up.

✌ *Exercise 46.* SYNCHRONIZING YOUR AROUSAL AND ERECTION

This is a very advanced exercise that combines elements of the arousal-peaking process from Chapter 9 and the erection-peaking process described in this chapter. This exercise requires a high degree of concentration and awareness of your body.

For most men, erections increase as their arousal builds. Although erection and arousal are separate processes, they generally appear to happen simultaneously. Men often have their hardest erections a few seconds before ejaculation. Sometimes, however, you may notice that your erection lags a couple of levels behind your arousal. This usually isn't a problem, but sex feels more pleasurable when the two are in sync.

This partner exercise can help your erection level rise along with your arousal level. It allows you to practice alternating an erection peak with an arousal peak.

While you can't will your erection to become harder so that it matches your arousal level, you can manipulate your arousal level to sink until it matches your erection level. Arousal (which is psychological) decreases faster than erection does. As you do the exercise, you will find that each time your arousal level goes down to come into line with your erection level, the erection level—and your overall pleasure—will increase with your next peak.

Before you begin, refamiliarize yourself with the 1-to-10 arousal scale you used in the self-exercises in Chapter 4 and the erection scale, both described on pages 37 and 38. In this exercise, you will switch back and forth between the two scales.

To begin, exchange focusing caresses with your partner so that you are both relaxed. Then pleasure her with a sensual caress of her choosing.

Lie on your back and shift into the mindset of the passive role. Have your partner caress your genitals with her hands, lips, or tongue. If you approach arousal level 3 and you don't feel any erection filling, have your partner slow down her caressing so that your arousal backs down to where your erection is. Then your partner can start to caress you again.

When you reach a filling-stage erection (level 3 or 4), check your arousal level. If it is higher than your erection level, have your partner stop again so that you can back down. Keep going to higher and higher levels, having your partner back off every time you feel your arousal level outdistancing your erection level.

If you repeat this exercise a couple of times, you will notice that your erection and arousal levels tend to stay together, especially at the lower levels. You may want to repeat the exercise another couple of times to practice this technique at higher levels of arousal and erection. Finish the exercise with orgasm and ejaculation if you wish to.

Erection-Enhancing Drugs

Some men don't get erections that are as hard as they would like, and this can interfere with their sexual pleasure. There are a number of products that can enhance erections. Before I discuss them and how they can contribute to your sexual pleasure, I'll describe how to tell if you are getting the strongest erections your body is capable of. This is a continuation of the discussion about morning erections that began in Chapter 3.

Normal, healthy men who have no medical problems have several erections during the course of a night's sleep. Nobody really knows why men have erections during their rapid-eye-movement or dream sleep phases. It just seems to be the body's way of checking out its circulation system.

If you wake up in the morning with an erection, it is generally the hardest erection your body is capable of. This is the strength of erection you should experience when sharing sexual pleasure with your partner. If you never have nighttime or morning erections, this could be a sign that you have a physical problem (such as circulation difficulties) or psychological issues (such as ongoing anxiety or depression).

The most common situation is a man who has strong nighttime and morning erections but whose erections when he is with a partner are not as hard as his morning ones. If this is the case, you might want to try one of the following erection enhancers. I list them in order from the cheapest and least invasive to the most expensive and most invasive. In general, the first six I've listed here will probably contribute to your sexual pleasure by enhancing your erections. The last two solutions include some serious downsides and should only be used when no other options are available.

Herbal Supplements/Yohimbine

Go to any health-food store and you'll see a whole wall of products that are recommended for male potency. Most of them have not been tested or proven to work. The exception is yohimbine, which is made from a kind of African tree bark. Yohimbine has been shown to improve erections in some men. It is a stimulant. It stimulates the heart and circulation and should therefore not be used by anyone who has heart problems or tendencies toward anxiety.

Viagra

Viagra is currently by far the most popular erection enhancer. It is available by prescription. It works by relaxing the smooth muscle (the PC muscle) at the base of the penis. When this muscle group is relaxed, blood flows into the penis more easily when the penis is stimulated.

I'm a big fan of Viagra. I've seen it work well for a lot of people. In my experience, Viagra is likely to work for men in their forties, fifties, and sixties who are in reasonably good shape and whose erections with a partner are not as strong as their morning erections. In my experience it does not work well for men in their seventies and eighties, perhaps because the smooth muscle at the base of the penis is in bad shape.

Viagra has few side effects, the most common being slight nausea and indigestion. This is most likely to happen if you take Viagra without food. Viagra should never be taken by anyone who is taking nitroglycerin for heart problems.

Viagra does not interfere at all with sexual pleasure. It is taken about an hour before desired sexual activity. It does not produce a spontaneous erection. You and your partner should do the foreplay that you would normally do. In fact, you could make the case that Viagra contributes to sexual pleasure because it helps you take the pressure off yourself and avoid spectatoring.

Levitra

Levitra, an alternative to Viagra, just became available as of this writing. I read through the information sent to me by the drug company that manufactures it. It works in a similar way to Viagra but is less likely to cause indigestion if you don't take it with food. Also, it is purported to work more quickly than Viagra and to have fewer side effects, although it was not directly compared with Viagra in clinical trials. Supposedly, it improves erections for up to twenty-four hours after taking it.

Cialis

Cialis is currently available in Europe. It works within about thirty minutes, and the effects may last for several days. It has some of the same side effects as Viagra: headache, facial flushing, indigestion, and nasal congestion.

MUSE

MUSE (alprostadil) is a small suppository pellet that is inserted into the urethra. After you insert it, you walk around for ten minutes stroking your penis to circulate the medication throughout the erectile tissue. (Viagra works from the base of the penis up; MUSE works from the tip down.)

MUSE is not harmful. I would not use it if fellatio is a big part of your sexual repertoire, as your partner could suck it out of the penis and it tastes terrible. It's probably not a great idea to ingest it.

To me, there is no comparison between Viagra and MUSE. Viagra is the hands-down winner, as long as you can use it with no side effects. I say this because the combination of Viagra and oral sex is fantastic, whereas you can't receive oral sex if you've just inserted MUSE. In addition, Viagra works much more consistently than MUSE, as it does not rely so much on the vagaries of individual metabolism.

Vacuum Erection Device

This is a clear, plastic cylinder that fits over the penis. It's connected to a small battery-powered pump or hand pump. You place the cylinder over the penis and pump air out of it, creating a vacuum that sucks blood into the penis. Then you pull a surgical rubber band off the cylinder and put it around the base of the penis. It acts like a cock ring, keeping blood in the penis.

This device is used for men who have difficulty maintaining their erection due to leaky valves at the base of the penis, but it's also sold as a sex toy or novelty through many adult catalogs. Some men believe it increases the size of the penis if it's used for a few minutes on a daily basis. If used to improve erections, it can break the mood of a sexual encounter that has already started. Also, the rubber band should not be left on for more than twenty minutes, and if it's too tight, it may interfere with ejaculation. This device works well for couples who've been together a long time and have a sense of humor about its use.

Injections

There are several substances that can be injected directly into the penis to produce an erection. Some of these substances are papaverine (a localized vasodilator), phentolamine, and prostaglandin (a hormone). A man can inject these directly into the corpora cavernosa with a fine-gauge needle.

It seems to me that giving yourself a shot in the penis to have an erection would be a last resort, but I've seen people use this method, and it doesn't seem to bother them. It just goes to show you how motivated some men are to continue to receive pleasure from sex. If you use shots, you have to be careful not to overuse them, because if you inject at the same site all the time, you can build up scar tissue. Also, excessive use of these products can cause numbing of the penis or priapism (an erection that won't go down).

Penile Implants

There are some men who can't have erections because they have major medical problems—either diabetes or removal of the prostate gland due to cancer. In these cases, the only solution is really a penile implant: a device that is inserted surgically into the penis.

There are two types of penile implant. The older type is the semirigid rod. This is a bendable device inserted into the penis alongside the urethra. When the man wants to have an erection, he just bends the penis upward, and it stays there until he is through using it, at which point he bends it back down. This type of device feels like a natural erection.

The other type of penile implant is a three-part hydraulic device consisting of a hollow cylinder in the penis, a reservoir of fluid in the lower abdomen, and a valve underneath the skin of the scrotum. When the man wishes to have intercourse, he turns the valve, and fluid moves from the reservoir and fills the cylinder in the penis so that it becomes erect. One of the problems with this type of device is that the penis actually becomes too hard, especially in the tip. It has no give to it, like a normal penis would, and so may feel artificial.

The previous two chapters have concentrated on male pleasure. In the next two chapters we turn our discussion to women, specifically what can help a woman increase her arousal levels and reach orgasm more readily. Men should read them too, because many of the exercises require a partner's participation.

chapter 11

Awakening Your
Full Capacity
for Arousal

A Chapter for Women

by Michael Gesinger

*I*n *this chapter you'll learn arousal techniques that can help you create more excitement with your partner. Back in Chapter 4, I had you explore the nature of your own arousal, on your own, so you* *could come to know about yourself in the most relaxed way. Now it's time to share this aspect of yourself with your partner.*

The exercises that follow are similar to the ones I have asked men to do in Chapters 9 and 10. Each of them can help bring you to very high levels of arousal. Some may even lead to orgasm, but I have a separate chapter for women with exercises specifically for orgasm.

Enhancing Your Arousal

Enhancing your arousal is a useful first step, whether you are currently orgasmic or not. Remember how in the chapter on the sexual-pleasure cycle I described two separate arousal scales for women: a subjective, or psychological, scale and a physical scale? The first four exercises I describe in this chapter work on physical arousal through self-touch, and the remaining exercises work on psychological arousal through partner touch. Self-touch is essential for a woman's arousal. As a first step toward learning to become more aroused, I hope you learned the peaking and plateauing exercises by yourself, as described in Chapter 4. They are absolutely the first stage in your arousal process.

When you do any of the exercises in this chapter or the ones that follow, remember to follow the basic sensate-focus principles:

- As the active partner, touch for your own pleasure

- When you are the passive partner, focus on your sensations

- If your mind drifts, bring it back to the exact point of contact between your skin and your partner's skin

- If your partner does anything that bothers you, let him know

- Keep all of your muscles relaxed

- Remember to breathe

- Try not to expect any particular levels of arousal

The next four exercises show you how to stimulate four different areas that should trigger physical arousal. You could do separate exercises to stimulate each area, or you could do one exercise in which you take turns stimulating all four areas.

✐ Exercise 47. STIMULATING THE CLITORIS

In this first exercise, I'm going to encourage you to explore and stimulate your clitoris with your hand before you explore stimulating it with a vibrator (which we'll discuss in the next chapter). There are many enjoyable ways to touch your clitoris. Do all of this in the context of a sensate-focus exercise so you don't pressure yourself to respond in a particular way.

Use some baby oil or other lubricant and gently start to rub the tip of your clitoris. Feel it start to swell under the pressure from your fingertips. Hold the clitoris between two of your fingers and squeeze it as if it were a small penis. Or take two fingers and rub them along the sides of your clitoris if direct stimulation is too intense for you.

Note your response. Do other areas of your genitals swell up at the same time? Do a peaking exercise with just clitoral stimulation; remember that a level 10 on the physical-arousal scale is maximum clitoral hardness and orgasm. (Refer to Exercise 10 if you need a refresher on how to do a peaking exercise.) As your level of arousal increases, notice how you can rub your clitoris harder because you can handle more stimulation.

One of the best ways I know of to stimulate your clitoris is to use hot water. Buy one of those shower massage devices and install it. Lie in the bathtub, direct the water at your clitoris, and make it as hot as you can stand it without hurting yourself. It's also possible to do this with the jets in a jacuzzi. Alternatively, I've seen a type of round vibrator that you can use underwater. Check it out.

✐ Exercise 48. STIMULATING THE BARTHOLIN'S GLANDS

Bartholin's glands are located under the skin of the inner vaginal lips about halfway between the top and bottom of the vagina, if you're lying on your back. In other words, if you were looking at your vagina at the same angle from which your gynecologist sees it, the glands would be located at about the midline. Bartholin's glands secrete a drop or two of very slippery lubrication when you are aroused. You can stimulate them during a genital caress. Caress yourself as you normally would, focusing on the sensations and remembering to breathe and relax. At some point during the caress, take the first and middle finger of one hand and just lightly press on your inner vaginal lips about halfway between the top and bottom of the vagina. You don't have to rub to stimulate the glands; just lightly pressing or tapping is enough. You won't see the lubrication because it is secreted inside the opening of the vagina.

✐ *Exercise 49.* STIMULATING THE G-SPOT

Remember that the Gräfenberg spot, or G-spot, is a very sensitive area located on the front wall of the vagina behind the pubic bone. It's a little difficult to stimulate it yourself, but some women can do so. Here's how.

Give yourself a sensate-focus genital caress, using plenty of lubrication. Caress all the parts of your vulva—clitoris, inner and outer lips, and vaginal opening. Use a position where you are sitting up with your back against a headboard or wall. Bend your knees and spread your legs apart slightly.

Take your right hand and bend all of your fingers except your middle finger. Stick your middle finger up like you were going to give someone the finger. Bend your wrist and insert your middle finger into your vagina with your palm up. Curl your middle finger back toward the front wall of your vagina and hook it behind your pubic bone, as if you were trying to touch your clitoris from the inside. That's your G-spot. Gently rub the pad of your middle finger on the G-spot and feel it swell and start to pulse. If you have trouble touching your G-spot with your own hand because your arm isn't long enough, show your partner how to do it.

✐ *Exercise 50.* STIMULATING THE
ANTERIOR FORNIX

The anterior fornix erogenous zone, or A-spot, is the whole front wall of the vagina between the G-spot and the cervix. It appears to be the area that's responsible for most of a woman's vaginal lubrication.

To stimulate the A-spot, use the same position you used for G-spot stimulation—sitting with your back against a wall or headboard with your knees bent and your legs slightly spread. Caress your vulva, using plenty of lubrication. When you are ready to stimulate your A-spot, insert your middle finger straight into your vagina. Instead of curving it to find the G-spot, keep it straight and gently rub the front wall of your vagina between the G-spot and the cervix. Gently rubbing this area for ten to fifteen minutes could cause you to lubricate and possibly have an orgasm. Alternate between stroking the A-spot and then stroking the vaginal sponge (the area between the urethral opening and the opening of the vagina). Use long, repeated, in-and-out strokes of the finger along the whole length of the front wall of the vagina. Compare the sensitivity of your A-spot and your G-spot. You could also show your partner this technique when he does a genital caress with you.

The next exercise and the rest of the exercises in the chapter are partner exercises. Before you begin, review the psychological or subjective arousal scale described on pages 39–40. Set aside about an hour for this exercise. Have your favorite lubrication handy. Do focusing caresses, such as back caresses, to get both of you centered.

⚘ Exercise 51. AROUSAL AWARENESS FOR WOMEN

Lie comfortably on your back with your arms and legs slightly spread. Have your partner begin a front caress and gradually move to the genitals. Have him use plenty of lubrication. He will then slowly do a genital caress, along with oral sex if he chooses to, in a very sensuous, slow, sensate-focus manner. Pay attention to what you are feeling as his tongue and/or fingers stroke your vulva and your excitement builds.

Every five minutes or so, your partner will ask you your arousal level. Let your partner know what level you are at on the 1-to-10 arousal scale. Use the subjective scale rather than the physical scale. Keep your focus on your mounting pleasure as he continues with the caress. Notice what feels particularly good.

Have your partner ask you your arousal level four or five times during this exercise. It doesn't matter how high you go or whether your arousal level goes up or down when he asks. The important thing is for you to relax, recognize your levels of arousal no matter what they are, and communicate them to your partner.

The self-awareness you gain from this exercise is useful no matter how aroused you get. If the exercise takes you all the way to orgasm, go ahead and enjoy. Just don't push for it.

✌ *Exercise 52.* PEAKING DURING ORAL
AND MANUAL STIMULATION

The point of this exercise is to learn how to manipulate your psychological arousal level so that it starts to happen in a wave-like, predictable pattern, like you did in the solo peaking exercises in Chapter 4. This will stimulate the release of endorphins, those feel-good brain chemicals. Twenty or twenty-five minutes of peaking will build enough sexual energy to help you familiarize yourself with your different arousal levels.

Before you begin, be sure you have your preferred lubrication handy. With your partner, do short focusing caresses, such as the back caress, to get relaxed and make the transition from the rest of your day.

Lie comfortably on your back with your arms and legs slightly spread. Have your partner begin a front caress and gradually move to the genitals. Have him use plenty of lubrication. He will gently move your legs so that he can see your inner vaginal lips. Your partner can then slowly lick from the bottom of your vaginal opening up the center of your lips with the tip of his tongue. His tongue will glide or flick over your clitoris as if it were a "speed bump." Use all of your attention to follow the path his tongue takes. He should repeat this several times, each more slowly than the last. You may find the sensation quite thrilling.

Your partner can insert the tip of one finger into your vaginal opening and stroke your PC muscle. He can caress your clitoris, your outer and inner lips, your pubic mound, and the area around your urethra. When he moves his finger into your vagina, he can caress your vaginal walls, your G-spot, your anterior fornix, and your cervix.

When you reach an arousal level of 3, tell your partner, "Three." He will stop the caress for a few seconds to let your arousal decrease a couple of levels. Really notice what happens in your body as your arousal level drops. Then your partner will start caressing you again.

This time, see if you can go up to arousal level 4, and if you can, let your partner know. You will be most likely to go up to the next arousal level if you remember to focus on your sensations, breathe, and keep all of your muscles (including your PC muscle) relaxed.

With this continued manual caressing, see if you can peak at levels 5, 6, 7, 8, and 9. After each peak, let your arousal go back down two levels.

If you reach orgasm during this exercise, that's fine. Try to stay as passive as you can during orgasm if it happens. Some amount of involuntary muscle tension usually occurs during orgasm, but the more passive you stay, the more familiar you will become with how your body feels during really high arousal levels and orgasm.

If you do not go up very high the first time you do this peaking exercise, don't worry about it. It sometimes takes practice to be able to reach the higher levels. Recognizing your arousal level and telling your partner will help you go higher the next time. Remember that the sensations associated with the down curve of a sexual peak are as important to recognize as the sensations that accompany the up curve.

There are several other ways you can do this peaking exercise. You could do an exercise in which you only peak at the low levels like 2, 3, 4, and 5. Or you could do an exercise in which you only peak at the high levels like 6, 7, 8, and 9. You could do an exercise in which you experience several peaks at the same level. All of these variations will fine-tune your ability to know your arousal levels.

This peaking exercise uses the psychological, or subjective, arousal scale. In another variation on peaking, you could use the physical arousal scale, in which you tell your partner your arousal level based on how much you perceive you are lubricating and how much your clitoris and vaginal sponge area are swelling.

Exercise 53. PEAKING DURING INTERCOURSE

Practice the following exercise until you are able to easily go up to level 8 during a twenty-minute period. Then you will be ready for the orgasm exercises in Chapter 12. Your lover will be the active partner again in this exercise. The more you focus together while your partner circles his penis slowly inside you, the more sensual this exercise will feel for both of you.

Make sure you have a vaginal lubricant handy. You may actually have to start the exercise by providing your partner with some manual and oral stimulation so that he can become aroused enough to kneel over you and penetrate you. Usually a man can do the active part of this exercise even if his erection is at a fairly low level.

Start with focusing caresses, as you would during any session. Then have your partner begin a front caress with you and move to the genitals.

With manual and oral stimulation, peak up to some comfortable levels like 3, 4, and 5. Now bend your legs and raise them in the air. Bend your knees back toward your chest as far as is comfortable for you. Have your partner kneel between your legs with his genitals against yours. (This is the butterfly position described in Chapter 8.)

Your partner will then slowly rub his penis against your vaginal lips in the same way that he used his tongue during the previous peaking exercise. You will feel your clitoris as a bump that he slowly flicks with his penis. Peak at medium levels (5, 6, or 7) with this type of stimulation. Both of you should remember to focus, breathe, and keep all of your muscles relaxed.

Then your partner will apply lubricant to your vagina and to his penis, before he begins to insert just the head of his penis into your vagina. Do another peak while the head of his penis stimulates your PC muscle. Remember to breathe every time you feel your arousal go up.

Your partner will then insert his penis all the way into your vagina and thrust as slowly as he can. He should move his penis in a circular motion as well as in and out, focusing on his own sensations rather than trying to excite you.

Your partner will continue to slowly caress the inside of your vagina with his penis. Think of his penis as a giant tongue that is licking the inside of your vagina. If your partner's penis has a curve to it, see if you can feel it hitting your G-spot. This may be so pleasurable that it takes your breath away, but try to remember to breathe anyway. See if you are aware of whether your partner comes into contact with any of your other sensitive vaginal areas, like your A-spot, your cervix, or even your cul de sac. With this slow type of penetration, your vagina is even more sensitive than you thought, isn't it? You may find with this type of stimulation that you can peak at levels as high as 8 or 9. If you are able to peak all the way to orgasm, that's great. Just enjoy it (especially if it happens several times!). But be sure to peak at all of the levels on the way up as well.

You can peak with intercourse in any of the intercourse positions. I recommend the butterfly first, but you can also use the missionary position, the female-superior position, or the side-to-side scissors position. It's a little more difficult to peak in the rear-entry position, because rather than actually saying their arousal level out loud, some couples just get into the habit of making eye contact with each other when they have reached a certain arousal level. If you try to peak in the rear-entry position, it will be easier if you say your arousal level out loud.

✍ Exercise 54. VAGINAL PEAKING TO STIMULATE LUBRICATION

Since extra lubrication feels good to both parties, in this exercise your partner will stimulate your A-spot during intercourse to see if you lubricate more. Start with focusing caresses. Caress your partner's penis with your hand or mouth until he has a firm erection. Use the butterfly position for this exercise.

When your partner is kneeling in front of you and is ready to insert his penis, use as little lubrication as you can while still feeling comfortable. Use the lubrication only around the opening of your vagina, not on the inside. When your partner inserts his penis, have him rub it against the upper front wall of your vagina to stimulate your A-spot. He should use long, slow strokes along the whole length of the front wall of your vagina.

Peak up to levels 5, 6, 7, and 8. With your partner's penis inside you, you may be unable to tell whether you are lubricating. As you reach each peak, have your partner pull out and stroke his penis on your clitoris. Use your finger to check whether you are lubricating and how much. After you have peaked up to level 8, finish the exercise however you would like.

✍ Exercise 55. PLATEAUING DURING MANUAL AND ORAL STIMULATION

In this exercise you will learn to plateau—or maintain yourself at particular arousal levels—with manual and oral stimulation from your partner. Remember that breathing, using your PC muscle, moving your pelvis, and switching your focus can all help you maintain a particular arousal level. (To review these techniques, see Chapter 4.)

Another way to maintain a plateau is to ask your partner to stop and start the stimulation. When you reach a point at which you would like to plateau, say, "Stop." When your arousal level starts to dip, say, "Start." Or you can have your partner speed up and slow down the stimulation by saying, "Faster" and "Slower."

Experiment to see how much sexual charge you can sustain. Notice how your body confidence builds as you become better and better at modulating your own arousal, riding the waves until you are ready to climax.

Lie on your back with your arms and legs slightly spread. Your partner will begin a front caress and then move to your genitals. Start by peaking up to level 3 or 4 with some manual and oral stimulation. When you reach level 5, see if you can stay there for a few seconds by changing your breathing patterns. As you reach a level slightly higher than 5, slow your breathing down until you are back below level 5.

Then, to take yourself up above level 5 again, breathe a little faster until you are almost panting. See if you can stay at level 5 for a few seconds or even minutes by just paying attention to your breathing and adjusting it as your partner continues to stimulate you.

Next, try a higher plateau by using your PC muscle to maintain your arousal level. As you reach a point slightly beyond level 6, give your PC muscle a couple of quick squeezes until you are back below level 6.

When you want to go back up to a higher arousal level, relax your PC muscle and let your arousal build. See if you can maintain your arousal level at about level 6 by using just your PC muscle.

Try plateaus at the same levels or higher levels using changes in your hip movements and in your focus, as well as by asking your partner to stop or start or to go faster or slower. Notice which combination of techniques is most effective for you. See if you can combine all of the plateauing techniques and use them at the same time. If you can plateau with manual and oral stimulation for at least a few seconds at level 7 or 8, you are ready to move on to vaginal plateauing.

✒ *Exercise 56.* PLATEAUING DURING INTERCOURSE

Remember the difference between peaking and plateauing? When you peak, you allow your arousal to go up to a certain level and then go back down. When you plateau, you go up to a certain arousal level and let your arousal stay there for a while.

This exercise will help you plateau during intercourse when your partner is active. Learning to plateau can help you have multiple orgasms. To try to have multiple orgasms, after you have a first one, ask your partner to keep thrusting so that your arousal level doesn't fall below a 9. At that point, it may only take a few more strokes to send you over the edge again.

Make sure you have lubricant handy. You may need to caress your partner before penetration so that he can become erect.

Lie on your back with your arms and legs slightly spread. Your partner will begin a front caress and will continue with a genital caress and some oral sex.

Do a couple of comfortable peaks at levels 3, 4, or 5. Then put your legs up into the air to prepare for the butterfly position. Your partner will kneel between your legs and put lubrication on his penis and on your vagina. He will slowly start to caress your genitals with his penis. At first he will caress the outside of your genitals. Then he will slowly insert the head of his penis, and then the shaft until he is caressing the inside of your vagina with his penis.

As your partner starts to stroke against you, see if you can plateau at levels 5, 6, 7, 8, and 9 using the techniques you have practiced so far—slowing down and speeding up your breathing, squeezing and relaxing your PC muscle, moving your hips, and switching your focus. Also, have your partner stop and start, or move slower or faster. Try combining techniques or even using all of them at the same time.

For each plateau, tell your partner at what level you plan to plateau and how you plan to do it so that he, too, will learn about your arousal patterns. With practice, all of these techniques will become automatic and you will no longer need to think about them in order to do them.

Take about twenty to thirty minutes to do the penetration part of this exercise. During the exercise, you can plateau at any levels you like. It is easiest to practice at the lower levels. Doing so will help you enjoy yourself more when you are ready to try plateauing at higher levels. Try to plateau at level 9 for as long as you can. Then just stop everything and let yourself fall over the edge into orgasm.

You can do versions of the plateauing exercise in other intercourse positions as well. The same thing I said earlier about peaking applies here—the female-superior, missionary, and side-to-side positions are easiest for this exercise, while the rear-entry position is a little more difficult due to the lack of face-to-face contact.

Viagra for Women?

Men can take Viagra to improve their erections, which occur at the excitement phase of the sexual-response cycle. Is there an equivalent drug for women that can promote arousal, or can women take Viagra? It seems that if Viagra promotes erections in men, it should also promote the genital swelling and lubrication responses that are the equivalent of erections in women. Although I don't believe that the use of Viagra has been specifically approved for women, I know that some clinicians have prescribed it and that it has produced increased genital blood flow in some women.

In addition to Viagra, there are a couple of nonprescription preparations that appear to help women's sexual enjoyment. One of these is called Zestra. It's a botanical massage oil applied directly to the vulva. In a study reported in *The Journal of Sex and Marital Therapy,* ten women with female sexual-arousal disorder and ten women without it used Zestra. Both groups showed improvements in desire, arousal, genital sensation, ability to have orgasms, and sexual pleasure.

I mentioned Avlimil in the chapter on sexual desire. In addition to boosting desire, it has been found to improve arousal, orgasm, and sexual satisfaction.

Alprostadil (the drug in MUSE) is a powerful, localized vasodilator that has been found to improve erections in men. In women, it has been found to produce vaginal warmth, tingling, and lubrication when applied to the vagina.

Finally, there is a device for women that is similar to the vacuum erection device for men. It's called the *eros clitoral stimulator.* It looks kind of like a little oxygen mask. You strap it over your clitoral area and pump air out of it, creating a vacuum that sucks blood into the clitoris and surrounding areas.

Accessories

Until now I have kept things simple. I wanted you to get to know your own body and your partner's body without the distracting input from senses other than touch. It's important to learn the sensate-focus techniques, for example, without having to deal with the distraction of music playing or the scent of candles. However, if you are a woman who would like to increase her ability to become sexually aroused, especially physically aroused, it's now time to add more sensual elements to the mix.

Many women respond physically (i.e., with vaginal lubrication) to input from all five senses. Some women lubricate when they see their partner naked or when they view sexually explicit material. Other women lubricate when they smell their partner's body odor or hear his voice on the phone, when they hear a particular song, or when they feel sexy lingerie against their breasts and genitals. If any of these things turn you on, or if you believe they would, now's the time to use them. Bring it on!

When a woman is in sex therapy for difficulty becoming aroused, one of the things that most therapists recommend is for her to find some kind of sexually explicit material she likes and to use it while practicing self-touch. It doesn't have to be hard-core porn; it could be romance novels, if that's what works for you. If you've ever noticed in the past that any kind of sexually explicit reading or pictures or videos has caused you to lubricate, get them out again and see if they still have the same effect. You've got nothing to lose.

Men and women differ somewhat in their reactions to sexually explicit material. Both men and women have been conditioned through evolution to respond to naked bodies of the other sex with quick genital arousal. But remember that a man's sexual desire is more under the control of nature and a woman's sexual desire is more shaped by culture. When men watch sexually explicit material, they are likely to admit that they are turned on both physically and psychologically. And there is a lot of research that shows that when women watch sexually explicit material, they may lubricate but claim they are not psychologically aroused because, for example, they find the images on the screen objectionable in some way. Women sometimes aren't aware that they are lubricating, or they may deny that they are turned on because they're embarrassed to admit that they are turned on by some sleazy porn.

If you are at all open to looking at sexually explicit material, please do so at this stage of the program. Touch yourself while viewing or reading sexually explicit material and experiment to see which types of images cause you to lubricate the most.

Another thing most sex therapists recommend for women who are in sex therapy for difficulty becoming aroused is the use of sex toys, including vibrators and dildos. I'll deal with this topic in the next chapter, which discusses female orgasm. (See also the list of resources for adult toys, located at the back of the book.)

chapter 12

Sensate-Focus Techniques for Sensational Orgasms

A Chapter for Women

by Ron Raffaelli

*I*n *Chapter 3, I briefly described female anatomy and orgasm triggers. Here I'll go into a lot more detail about areas in the female body that can trigger orgasms. But first I'll give you a little bit of history and describe some of the controversies that have surrounded female orgasm.*

History Lesson

It's been clear throughout recorded history that women enjoy sex. Many ancient books and works of art depict women in the throes of sexual ecstasy. Centuries ago, before people had a clear understanding of male and female anatomy, it was believed that both the man and the woman had to orgasm for the woman to become pregnant. It was believed that both the man and the woman produced fluids that had to combine to generate a pregnancy.

Flash forward to the Victorian era. During that time, a double standard existed with regard to female orgasm. On the one hand, if a woman was too orgasmic, it was seen as a sign of pathology, the cure for which was removal of the ovaries or, in some cases, of the clitoris. On the other hand, during the Victorian era, many women suffered from a condition that was then called "hysteria." At that time, hysteria was considered to be a combination of depression, anxiety, fatigue, and the sexual "blahs." The cure for hysteria was for a woman's physician to do a pelvic examination, during the course of which he would stimulate her genitals until she had an orgasm. This practice influenced the development of the modern vibrator, because physicians got tired of spending so much time massaging women's genitals.

Sigmund Freud was a product of the Victorian era. Based on the case histories of his female patients, he described two types of orgasms: clitoral and vaginal. Most women reported that they could have an orgasm from stimulation of the vulva, including the clitoris. But some women reported that they had orgasms that felt deeper and seemed to emanate from deep inside the vagina. Freud believed that vaginal orgasms were "better" than clitoral orgasms. The reason he believed this is complicated and has its roots in his theory of psychosexual development. Freud believed that a young immature girl could have clitoral orgasms, but that only a mature woman could have a vaginal orgasm. This value judgment on female orgasms did not sit well with many women, as you can imagine.

When the famous sexologist Alfred Kinsey published *Sexual Behavior in the Human Female* in 1953, knowledge of female sexual anatomy was not very advanced. Based on the anatomical information available to him at the time, Kinsey did not believe that it was physically possible for women to have vaginal orgasms.

In the 1960s, Masters and Johnson studied the physiological sexual responses of hundreds of women under laboratory conditions. They believed that the source of all female orgasms (including those during intercourse) was the clitoris. They believed that the vagina was incapable of feeling the kinds of sensations that could lead to orgasm.

In 1972, two not very well known sex researchers named Singer and Singer published an article on types of female orgasm. Based on anecdotal reports from women, they described three types of female orgasm: vulval, uterine, and blended. A vulval orgasm was the same as a clitoral orgasm and resulted from stimulation of any part of the vulva, including the clitoris and PC muscle. A uterine orgasm was the same as a vaginal orgasm. Singer and Singer believed a uterine orgasm resulted from deep, vigorous penetration that actually moved the internal organs, including the uterus. A blended orgasm could occur if a woman had both types of sensation; for example, if a woman was having intercourse and was stimulating her clitoris with her hand at the same time.

A real milestone in the study of female orgasm occurred in 1982 with the publication of *The G Spot,* by Alice Kahn Ladas, Beverly Whipple, and John D. Perry. The existence of the G-spot proved once and for all that Masters and Johnson were wrong about one thing concerning female orgasm: The vagina contained at least one erogenous zone that was sensitive enough to trigger orgasm.

Whew! If you've ever experienced problems having an orgasm, no wonder! It's complicated. In the next part of this chapter I will provide a guide to the major female genital erogenous zones that can trigger orgasm. We generally divide female genital erogenous zones into two types: external triggers and internal triggers. (Refer back to the illustrations of female genitalia on pages 27 and 28 if you want a visual aid during this discussion.)

External Triggers

The clitoris is an external female genital structure. It is the most common orgasmic trigger for most women (I usually call it "Old Faithful"). The clitoris contains erectile tissue and becomes hard when it is stimulated.

The PC muscle, which surrounds the opening to the vagina, is the next body part we'll consider. Even though it is a muscle and is therefore located beneath the skin, sex therapists group it with the external triggers because it isn't located inside the vagina. You know from earlier chapters that a well-toned PC muscle is important for both pelvic health and sexual pleasure. Toning the muscle makes arousal, penetration, and orgasm more satisfying. This is because strengthening the PC muscle tightens the vagina and builds muscle mass. The greater the muscle mass, the more blood that can collect in the area when you are aroused. Increased blood flow adds to the sensations during arousal and creates a greater sense of release when the PC muscle spasms during orgasm. In fact, stimulating the PC muscle alone can produce an orgasm. I'll explain how later in this chapter.

The urethra is the very small opening of the urinary tract through which you urinate. Research on females of other species indicates that stimulation at the opening of the urethra can trigger orgasm. Anecdotal evidence shows that many women find stimulation of the urethra very arousing, though it can also feel unpleasant. Sometimes this area is called the "U-spot."

The best way to locate the urethra is to push up on the clitoris and spread your vaginal lips with your fingers. If you wish to stimulate the opening of the urethra, do so gently, and make sure your hands are really clean, because the urethra and bladder are very susceptible to irritation and infection. Never put objects in the urethra, because they can get lodged there.

Internal Triggers

In Chapter 3 I discussed the G-spot, which is located on the upper front wall of the vagina about two-thirds of the way in, behind the pubic bone. Have your partner help you find it by inserting his longest finger into your vagina as far as it will go. Then have him hook the finger back toward himself, as though he were trying to touch the clitoris from inside. When he touches a spot that provides an intensely pleasurable feeling for you, he's found it. You can try to find the G-spot yourself, but it is often difficult to do because it is hard to position your wrist just right; still, doing so is possible, and I have described how on page 147.

The G-spot is an area of extreme sensitivity. Stimulating it often produces a very intense orgasmic response, which is sometimes accompanied by a female ejaculation or "gusher." A female ejaculation is the expulsion of a large amount of thin, clear, warm fluid.

Many women have had this ejaculatory experience once and have never had it again. Some of them became afraid because they consulted a medical professional and were told that they had lost bladder control and urinated during intercourse. So they never again allowed themselves to let go and have this intensely pleasurable experience.

Attitudes toward the G-spot have changed greatly in the sex-research community. When *The G Spot* was published in 1982, it was met with some skepticism. Many researchers did not believe that such a spot existed. The consensus now is that every woman has a G-spot that produces some amount of fluid, but sometimes the amount of fluid that is produced is so small that women don't notice it because it's overshadowed by the lubrication produced by the rest of the vagina.

Some women report that when they have a G-spot orgasm, the fluid comes out of their urethra, whereas some women report that it comes out of their vagina. The G-spot fluid has been analyzed. When it comes out of the urethra, it is similar to urine but without the ammonia. When it comes out of the vagina, it is similar to the semen produced by the male prostate gland minus the sperm. This would make sense, because given where the G-spot is located, its closest male equivalent is probably the prostate gland. If you are interested in learning more about female ejaculation, see *Female Ejaculation and the G-Spot,* by Deborah Sundahl (listed in the "Suggested Reading" section).

Most people are familiar with the clitoris and have probably heard of the G-spot by now. But the cul de sac is a new one for most women because of a common misconception about the female anatomy. Most people believe that the vagina ends at the cervix, which opens into the uterus. But this isn't true. When you are not aroused, the uterus rests on top of the vagina about two-thirds of the way back. When you become aroused, the muscles supporting the uterus tighten, and the uterus lifts up, exposing an area of the vagina that is normally behind the cervix. This area is called the *cul de sac.* It opens only when you are highly aroused and allows penetration into the deepest part of your vagina.

The cervix is the knobby structure at the base of the uterus. You may also hear it referred to as the "neck" of the uterus *(cervix* is Latin for neck). In some intercourse positions, the penis stimulates the cervix. Some women experience this as an unpleasant cramping sensation, but for others, stimulation of the cervix can trigger an orgasm. The cervix is sometimes called the "X-spot," with *X* standing for *ecstasy.*

Other Orgasm Triggers

One thing we know about orgasm in general is that women report a more diffuse orgasm ability than men, and men have a more reliable orgasm ability than women. If a man and a woman are having intercourse, on the average the man is more likely to have an orgasm than the woman (all other things being equal). However, most women report that they are able to have an orgasm from stimulation of more different areas of the body than men are. We've described some of those areas in this chapter. In addition, some women experience orgasm with no physical genital stimulation at all; for example, you may awaken from a dream and find that you are having a very intense orgasm. Some women have reported having orgasms from sun exposure without touching their genitals. Others may experience orgasm through the fondling of their breasts, especially the nipples. Some women experience orgasm through stimulation of their mouth when they do oral sex. It appears that the body is just a mass of erogenous zones waiting for some pleasurable stimulation.

Clitoris Versus Vagina, Finally

Can we finally lay to rest the controversy over clitoral versus vaginal orgasms? They're different—that's all. One isn't objectively "better" than the other. Whether a woman prefers one over the other is strictly a matter of individual preference.

It's clear that there are many areas on a woman's body that can trigger orgasm. Plus, we now know enough about female anatomy to know that there is a difference between orgasms produced by the external triggers (vulval or clitoral orgasms) and those produced by the internal triggers (vaginal or uterine orgasms). Researchers now know that the sensations of vulval orgasm travel to the spinal cord via the pudendal nerve, whereas the sensations of vaginal orgasm travel to the spinal cord via the pelvic nerve. What this means is that if you receive stimulation deep in your cul de sac area, and if that stimulation leads to orgasm, the orgasm will include more of the "weak-in-the-knees, close-to-hyperventilation, making-noises-deep-in-your-throat, lights-behind-the-eyeballs" sensations than a clitoral orgasm will.

Changes During Orgasm

Despite the existence of so many areas on a woman's body that can trigger orgasm, some women have never had one. Still others remain confused about what an orgasm actually feels like.

A very mild orgasm can feel like this: You feel your PC muscle twitch and you are aware of your heart pounding. These sensations might be easy to miss, especially if you have a penis inside of you.

In more intense orgasms, the muscles around the uterus spasm so that your abdomen sucks in. Your blood pressure, heart rate, and breathing all reach peaks. Your neck, arms, and legs may spasm involuntarily. You may feel a tingling sensation in your fingers and toes, as well as a sensation of warmth that moves from your genitals up to your face, neck, and chest. Because of this release of energy from the pelvic area, most people also experience a psychological feeling of relief or release.

Orgasms vary in intensity from woman to woman. Some orgasms include only PC muscle spasms, rapid heart rate, and a mild good feeling. Other orgasms may be so strong that they cause your body to contort and arch off the bed (I call these "Exorcist" orgasms—just kidding). I'm telling you all of this so that you can take the pressure off of yourself about expecting orgasm to occur in a particular way. Everyone is unique. What's important is that you open yourself more and more to your orgasmic capacity in whichever ways work best for you.

Before I describe exercises you can do to help yourself become more orgasmic, let's explore some of the reasons that women don't have reliable orgasms.

What's Holding You Back?

Given that women's bodies have so many sites that can act as orgasm triggers, why is it that so many women don't have orgasms at all, don't have reliable orgasms, or don't have orgasms during intercourse?

I have an unusual view of female orgasm. I believe that every woman's body is capable of orgasm, and I believe that almost all women experienced orgasms during childhood, beginning probably between the ages of three and six. This probably occurred while riding a bicycle, playing on playground equipment, or lying in bed waiting to go to sleep. But when you're three or four years old, you don't know what an orgasm is and you don't interpret genital sensations as sexual.

Try to remember: When you were a child, did you ever accidentally touch yourself between your legs and feel an intensely pleasurable sensation, often accompanied by shivering or muscle spasms? Guess what? That was an orgasm—or a child's version of a clitoral orgasm, anyway. You may have been on the right track then, but for whatever reason your body shut itself down at some point.

I believe that many women have difficulty with orgasm as adults because they don't remember or can't connect with those childhood sensations. To get past this block, lie on your back, do some belly breathing, and relax all of your muscles. Drift back in your mind and visualize yourself at five or six years old. Prime your imagination with pictures of yourself at that age if you have any. Slowly begin to touch yourself the way you picture that a child of that age would touch herself. Don't masturbate the way an adult woman would. Try to bring a sense of childlike innocence to touching your clitoris.

Another reason why I believe some women have trouble with orgasm is that they have lost the connection with their unconscious mind that occurs during dream sleep. Many adolescents and adult women experience orgasms during dream sleep. This tends to occur more as women get older. Having an orgasm during dream sleep doesn't depend on the content of the dream. Rather, the orgasm, similar to a man's nocturnal erection or emission, seems to be the body's way of checking out that all systems are "go." Of course, if you have an orgasm during a dream about sex, so much the better.

There are a couple of ways to stimulate sexual dreams and accompanying orgasms. To stimulate sexual dreams, before you go to sleep, do some belly breathing and deep muscle relaxation. As you drift off to sleep, let your mind wander to a detailed, graphic sexual fantasy about making love with a partner whom you really desire and enjoy. Replay a real past experience in your mind if you want to. The combination of the muscle relaxation and the alpha waves your brain produces when you're relaxed will hopefully create a type of self-hypnotic state that will prime you for sexual dreams.

To stimulate orgasms during sleep, before you go to sleep do deep breathing and muscle relaxation. As you are drifting off to sleep, massage your clitoris for up to twenty minutes until you feel that it's engorged. Don't allow yourself to have an orgasm at this point. Just go to sleep. Hopefully, some degree of clitoral engorgement will remain as you enter the dream phase of your first sleep cycle.

A warning: Women often report that the orgasms they have during sleep are very intense, to the point that their PC muscle and leg muscles cramp and they have to get out of bed and walk around. A dream state–induced orgasm will feel like the following: You'll wake up just as your PC muscle goes into intense rhythmic spasms. You'll feel a sensation that there is a train coming toward you and there's nothing you can do to stop it. You'll be breathing very heavily and your heart will pound. If you go back to sleep immediately, you may have another orgasm right away. (And another, and another...)

Another reason that more women don't have orgasms is lack of experience with self-touch and self-exploration. I think (I hope) all sex therapists would agree with me that the biggest factor in a woman's ability to have orgasms is her history of self-touch. Girls who masturbate during adolescence report that they are more consistently orgasmic as adults.

Here's another area where men and women differ in their typical sexual experience. Most men begin a concentrated history of masturbation right around the split second they realize they have a penis. Therefore, by the time they have sexual intercourse with a woman, most boys or men are very well-versed in what it takes for them to have an orgasm and ejaculate. In fact, this tendency sometimes works against men, because they are so good at masturbating to orgasm quickly that they often have trouble lasting as long as they would like to during intercourse.

On the other hand, many women have their first experience with intercourse before they have ever masturbated. Many women don't even start masturbating until they have a history of sexual intimacy with several partners.

From clinical experience, I can tell you that the easiest clients to work with are women who want to learn to have orgasms but have never masturbated. These women do very well in therapy because their orgasm problem is a direct result of a lack of education about their body and its responses. Bonnie's comments to me are typical of women in this situation: "I had no idea what my body was capable of," she said. "I was always taught 'don't touch yourself down there.' The whole area was really the dark continent to me. I would feel things during intercourse but not have any idea what was causing those feelings. Now I know how to ask my partner for stimulation that I know will help me have an orgasm."

If you are having difficulty with orgasm, you owe it to yourself to explore your own body. Use the exercises in Chapter 4 to prime yourself for orgasms with a partner.

Yet another reason why some women have difficulty with orgasm is that their expectations are too high. Remember that an orgasm can be a few spasms of the PC muscle accompanied by rapid heart rate, or it can be a mind-blowing experience with screaming, yelling, muscle tension, and an altered state of consciousness—or it can be anything in between. Some women have PC muscle spasms and a fluttering heart and think, "Is that all there is? That was the Big O? Why bother?"

You have to start somewhere. Paying attention to those less intense orgasms will set the stage for you to add in some voluntary behaviors that will make your orgasms more intense.

Just as high expectations can be a problem, so can low expectations. In our culture, we have what's called an "orgasm gap." Ask yourself this question: "If a man and a woman are having sexual intercourse, all other things being equal, which one of them is more likely to have an orgasm?" In other words, if you were going to bet, who would you bet on? From a statistical point of view, the answer is the man. A lot of times women get sabotaged because they believe that they're less likely than their partner to have an orgasm, so they don't even try. It doesn't help that their partners probably believe this too. Don't let low expectations shut you down. Many women want their partner to do oral sex with them before they have intercourse because women are more likely to have an orgasm during oral sex. Have your partner orally stimulate you to arousal level 8 or 9 before you start intercourse. This will increase your chances of having an orgasm during intercourse.

Remember the discussion of the sexual-pleasure cycle in Chapter 3? Now look at Figure 8. It's a drawing of Masters and Johnson's human sexual-response cycle that indicates how aroused a woman usually is when intercourse starts (Point A), and how aroused a man usually is (Point B). One

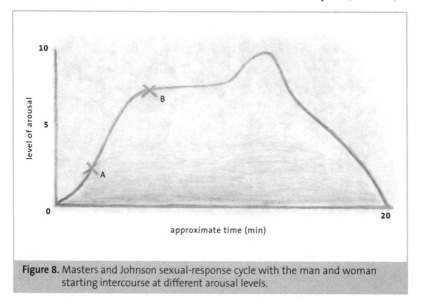

Figure 8. Masters and Johnson sexual-response cycle with the man and woman starting intercourse at different arousal levels.

reason for the existence of the orgasm gap is that many couples start sexual intercourse when the man is at about level 7 or 8 and the woman is still down at level 2 or 3. She's got farther to go to catch up. No wonder he gets there first!

To make it more likely that you will have an orgasm during intercourse, make sure that you receive plenty of the type of foreplay of your choice before you start intercourse. If that means your partner has to wait a little longer for his orgasm, so be it. (He'll learn to live with it.)

Another reason that women sometimes have difficulty with orgasm during intercourse has to do with the PC muscle. Remember that the PC muscle, which surrounds the opening of the vagina, is the muscle that spasms rhythmically when you have an orgasm. If your PC muscle is weak or out of shape, it's especially difficult for it to spasm when there's something (a penis or other object) inside your vagina. Many of the exercises in this chapter have you insert a dildo inside your vagina and purposely tighten and loosen your PC muscle around the dildo. Doing your PC muscle exercises while something is inserted in your vagina will strengthen it to the point where you will be more able to have an orgasm during intercourse. Also, be sure to do the advanced PC muscle exercise in Chapter 4.

During the above discussion I have mostly talked about orgasm from a physical standpoint. Many women have psychological issues regarding orgasm. Perhaps they are afraid of letting go and losing control, or they are afraid they will look funny if they have an orgasm. Some women do not trust their partner enough to allow themselves to be vulnerable enough to have an orgasm. In addition, some women have difficulty with orgasm because of past sexual trauma.

Is your experience of intercourse and other sexual practices that you can reach an arousal level of 8 or even 9, but at that point you shut down, lose your focus, start thinking about something else, and don't make it all the way to orgasm? If so, maybe your body is trying to tell you something. Maybe you don't really know your partner well enough to be this intimate with him. Has your partner betrayed you in ways you haven't acknowledged? Or maybe you are unconsciously reacting to some sexual trauma in your past. Or maybe there's a simpler explanation. Maybe your sensate-focus abilities just need a little more practice at those higher arousal levels. The exercises in this chapter should take care of that. If your issues are more serious, involving an exaggerated sense of control or relationship problems, perhaps professional help is necessary.

Using Sex Toys in
Your Solo Explorations

The solo exercises below will make a big difference in how orgasmic you are when you have intercourse. Take care to pay attention to your responses as you do them. If you have never experimented with sex toys before, you will be surprised at how much they can help. My colleagues and I consistently recommend them to women who would like to learn to become more aroused and more orgasmic. I even hesitate to call them "toys," because they do their job so well.

There are two main types of sex toys to choose from: vibrators and dildos. Dildos are penis-shaped sex toys. Vibrators vibrate and may or may not be shaped like a penis.

Vibrators come in all shapes and sizes. Some are as small as car cigarette lighters, while others can be as large as your forearm. Larger vibrators are not meant to be inserted into the vagina and may have massage uses that are not necessarily sexual. Vibrators also differ in the strength of the stimulation they provide, depending on the battery size. Some contain more than one vibration setting. There are even vibrators that strap onto your hand, allowing you to touch yourself with your hand rather than with a machine.

Dildos do not necessarily vibrate. They also come in all sizes. They are usually meant to be inserted into the vagina. Some are made out of hard plastic, but the newer ones are made out of soft rubber or a gel-like substance that feels more like a real penis. Some are flexible and can be bent into different shapes. Some of the newer ones are made from molds of real penises, so they include details like realistic heads and veins. Some also include suction cups on the base so that they can be freestanding.

Some of the newer vibrators strap onto the pubic area, and the vibration is controlled by a small switch at the end of a cord. Some companies make panties that have a vibrating egg built into them. I have also seen a vibrator shaped like a large tongue that moves in a tongue-like motion.

If you haven't ever shopped for adult toys or haven't done so in a while, it's definitely time to check out the new technology. If you feel embarrassed about buying sex toys in a store, you can always go online and purchase them discreetly. At the end of the book I list several catalog and online sources for adult toys.

If you purchase a dildo or vibrator to do some of the exercises in this chapter, I recommend looking for one with the following features: First, make sure that it is shaped like a realistic penis and is about the size of your partner's penis. This is especially important if you want to learn to become orgasmic with your partner during intercourse. Second, look for a sex toy with a suction base. Third, make sure it is somewhat flexible so that it can be bent into a gooseneck shape to stimulate your G-spot. And fourth, if you can get your full wish list, look for one that vibrates at both a high and low setting. If you can find all of these qualities in one sex toy, that's great. If not, you might need to buy two—for example, one with a gooseneck shape and one without.

✑ *Exercise 57.* USING BEN-WA BALLS TO IMPROVE VAGINAL MUSCLE TONE

Besides dildos and vibrators, there is another type of sex toy called Ben-Wa balls. These are small metal balls about one-half to three-quarters of an inch in diameter. They come in pairs. They look like metal marbles. They are inserted in the vagina and are used to increase vaginal muscle tone.

I wasn't sure whether to put this exercise in the arousal chapter or the orgasm chapter, but I think it's most applicable here, because it prepares your vaginal muscles to form the orgasmic platform and tighten around your partner's penis.

Buy yourself a set of Ben-Wa balls. (You're probably the adult store's best customer by now, aren't you?) To use them, insert one into your vagina and see if you can move it up and down using your vaginal muscles. This will probably take a little bit of trial and error. You can also practice putting one of the balls inside your vagina and using your PC muscle to push it out.

For a more advanced exercise, insert both of the balls into your vagina and see if you can make them click together, or see if you can move your vagina in such a way that you can feel the balls change places with each other.

✑ *Exercise 58.* USING A VIBRATOR ON YOUR CLITORIS

This is the easiest female masturbation exercise for orgasm, so we'll start with it. This exercise uses a vibrator to stimulate your clitoris, urethra, and vaginal lips. You will probably find that your clitoris is your most reliable orgasm trigger.

To use your vibrator most effectively, hold it loosely and gently stimulate yourself. Don't make the mistake, as some women do, of holding the vibrator too tightly and pressing on your clitoris too firmly. If you hold it with the same level of tension you use to hold a pencil, you'll be fine. If you hold it any tighter, the stimulation will be too intense and you will find yourself fighting against it. Keep the stimulation on your clitoris or the area around it, which includes the urethral opening and the outer and inner lips. For this exercise, don't insert the vibrator into your vagina.

I can't stress enough how important it is to pay attention to how you are using the vibrator. I once worked with a female client who was having difficulty with orgasm and who complained to me that her vibrator wasn't helping her at all. I had her demonstrate on her hand to show me how she held the vibrator and how much pressure she used. As we talked, I discovered that she was doing a lot of things that prevented her from having an orgasm.

In addition to pressing the vibrator too hard against her clitoris, she was also using it on too high a setting before she was aroused. She kept her leg muscles very tense and actually tensed up against the stimulation of the vibrator. When she made the changes I suggested, she was able to become aroused enough to orgasm, both with and eventually without a vibrator.

Remember your sexual-pleasure cycle. It's best to become aroused gradually, with gentle stimulation, before you set the vibrator on its highest setting and try to go for orgasm.

Before you begin this exercise, make sure your hands are clean and that your fingernails are clean and trimmed. Lie on your back and start a peaking exercise. Remember to breathe, pay attention to your feelings, and stay relaxed—all of the basic sensate-focus principles. Put some lubrication on your hand and gently start to caress your clitoris and outer and inner lips. Peak up to levels 2, 3, and 4 using just hand stimulation.

Now turn on your vibrator at a low setting and see if you can peak up to levels 5, 6, and 7 by gently massaging your clitoris with the vibrator. Don't forget to allow your arousal level to go down between each peak. If you've never used a vibrator before, allow yourself to be curious about the sensations it creates.

Now set the vibration level up higher. See if you can peak up to levels 8 and 9. At this point, right before orgasm, you'll probably notice that you have an uncontrollable urge to thrust or grind your pelvis against the vibrator and to hold the vibrator more firmly against yourself. Go with it. To maximize your orgasmic response, slowly and sensuously thrust against the vibrator as you use it to stimulate your clitoris. Do pelvic rolls and thrusts without tensing your thigh muscles. Peak yourself up to one orgasm, or more if you would like. Don't hold back. You aren't limited to one. Be sure to adjust your breathing at the high arousal levels so that you are panting as you reach orgasm. Try an orgasm while staying passive and not moving at all. Then add the pelvic movements again.

☞ *Exercise 59.* **VAGINAL BREATHING**

This exercise will help you identify the cul de sac and your uterine muscles. The contractions of your uterine muscles can greatly enhance your experience of orgasm.

The cul de sac is the end of the vagina that normally remains closed off unless you are very aroused. When you become very aroused, muscle tension causes the uterus to lift up, and the cul de sac opens up.

Like any muscles, the ones that support your uterus respond to exercise. The problem is that many women find it difficult to exercise these muscles because they cannot identify them. The way to practice voluntary control of your uterine muscles is to practice sucking air into your vagina and blowing it back out.

Start the exercise by lying on your back and relaxing. Raise your knees, and experiment with tightening various muscles in your lower abdominal area. If tightening any of these muscle groups causes air to be sucked into your vagina, then you are using the correct muscles.

Practice sucking air into and blowing it out of your vagina. Your cul de sac opens and closes every time you do this. After practicing solo, you might find that using these muscles during intercourse has a deliciously pleasurable effect.

If you can't locate the right muscles while lying flat on your back with your knees bent, try an old calisthenics position: the upside-down bicycling position. Do you remember this one from exercise class? You lie flat on your back and lift your lower body up by bracing yourself on your elbows. You don't need to actually "bicycle." The position alone will cause your uterus to settle on top of your vagina. When you return to a lying position, air will blow out of your vagina. Practice alternating the bicycling position with tightening the muscles while lying down until you get a sense of which muscles are at work; then start to tighten them on your own to do the vaginal breathing exercise.

✍ Exercise 60. USING A DILDO IN YOUR CUL DE SAC

Allow about twenty minutes for this exercise. Lie on your back and start a self-caress of your genitals, using plenty of lubrication. Remember your sensate-focus principles. For this exercise you will need a dildo that can fit comfortably into your vagina. Put plenty of lubrication on your dildo and rub your clitoris with it. Peak at low levels like 4, 5, and 6, using the stimulation of the dildo on your clitoris.

Now insert the dildo into your vagina. Bend your legs and slowly thrust with the dildo as if you were having intercourse. At the same time, tighten your uterine muscles as you learned to do in the previous vaginal breathing exercise. If you need to get into the upside-down bicycling position, go ahead. Your cul de sac will open up, and you will be able to insert your dildo into it. If you are very aroused when you do this, the feeling can be quite intense, like plugging a cord into an electric socket.

Now relax your legs and allow the cul de sac to close up with the dildo inside it. Gently tug on the dildo as you try to hold it in your cul de sac. This is great exercise for your uterine muscles. With practice, you will be able to tighten your muscles so that you can tug really hard on the dildo without pulling it out. This can make you very adept at gripping your lover's penis during intercourse, which will delight your partner as much as it does you. Finish the exercise by peaking as high as you can and having an orgasm from the cul de sac stimulation if you are aroused enough to do so.

✍ Exercise 61. USING A DILDO ON YOUR G-SPOT

This is similar to the previous exercise, but instead of exploring the cul de sac, you will explore the G-spot. This exercise will take about twenty minutes. You will need a dildo that is shaped like a gooseneck and is specifically made for G-spot stimulation, or one that you can bend into a gooseneck shape.

Lie on your back and caress your genitals, using plenty of lubrication. Let yourself peak up to levels 4, 5, and 6. Slowly insert the dildo into your vagina. Gently rub the dildo against your G-spot on the front of your vaginal wall. Feel the G-spot start to swell and expand. Hook the dildo gently into the G-spot and gently tug it toward the opening of your vagina. Focus on the sensations this produces. Is it pleasurable, or too intense for you? Use the dildo on your G-spot to peak all the way up to the highest arousal levels and up to orgasm if you can.

✑ *Exercise 62.* USING A DILDO ON YOUR PC MUSCLE

We know that the PC muscle is very important for female sexuality, because it is the muscle that spasms rhythmically when you have an orgasm. Sometimes just teasing your PC muscle with your finger or with a dildo is enough to trigger orgasm.

This exercise will take about twenty minutes. You'll need lubrication and a dildo that fits comfortably into your vagina. Lie on your back and caress your genitals, using plenty of lubrication. Peak up to levels 4, 5, and 6, using just manual stimulation. Now, insert the dildo about one inch into your vagina and move it in and out and in a circular motion in the opening of your vagina. See if you can peak up to level 7 with this stimulation of the PC muscle.

Now take the dildo out of your vagina and use it to stimulate your clitoris until you are very close to orgasm (level 9). Insert the dildo back into your vagina an inch and just hold it there. You'll begin to feel your PC muscle twitch. Now go for it! Start thrusting the dildo all the way into your vagina, and feel your PC muscle go into full-on orgasmic spasms.

✑ *Exercise 63.* USING A DILDO ON YOUR CERVIX

This exercise will take about twenty minutes. You will need a dildo that you can comfortably insert into your vagina. Lie on your back and begin with a sensate-focus caress of your upper and lower body. Caress your genitals, using plenty of lubrication, and see if you can peak up to levels 4, 5, and 6 with manual stimulation. Now insert the dildo into your vagina. To find the cervix, gently move the dildo around the deepest part of the upper front wall of your vagina until you feel it rub against a knobby surface that yields a slight cramping sensation. That is your cervix. You may recognize the sensation as similar to what you feel when your gynecologist takes a Pap smear. Of course you can't insert the dildo into your cervix; the opening is much too small. Just use the dildo to move all the way around your cervix in a circular motion to see which area of the cervix or which area around it feels the best.

This will usually be the rear area of the cervix. Use the dildo to thrust against your cervix to peak at higher levels or use one of your other internal trigger sites if you want to go all the way to orgasm.

☉ *Exercise 64.* USING A DILDO
WITH A BASE

The next two exercises will prepare you to enjoy intercourse with your partner. If you can explore peaking and plateauing with a dildo, imagine how satisfying it will feel with your lover inside of you.

For this exercise you will need a dildo with a suction base so that it can stand upright. As you did in the previous few exercises, you will use it to explore the internal orgasm trigger sites such as the G-spot, the cervix, and the cul de sac, but you'll use a different position.

To begin, lie on your back. Caress your upper and lower body using the sensate-focus approach. Peak yourself up to arousal levels 4, 5, and 6 with your hand, using plenty of lubrication.

Now take the dildo and place its suction base on a flat surface like the floor. Slowly kneel or squat on top of the dildo, as if you were doing the female-superior intercourse position. Lower yourself so that you can feel the dildo on your G-spot. You may need to curve the head of the dildo to do this. See if you can penetrate far enough with the dildo to stimulate your cervix. Suck in your abdominal muscles and see if the cul de sac will open enough so that you can penetrate into it and fit the whole dildo into your vagina. Recognize that it is more difficult to tighten your uterine muscles when you are kneeling or squatting than it is when you are lying on your back, so you may need extra practice to do this.

The first time you do this exercise, just use the dildo to explore the sensations that arise when you've touched one of your orgasm triggers. Don't pressure yourself to peak or plateau up to high levels, because doing so will distract you from discovering what feels best. Then, when you are familiar with how these different areas respond to contact, thrust up and down on the dildo and do whatever peaks and plateaus you feel like.

☉ *Exercise 65.* HAVE A GUSHER ORGASM

This exercise is the best way I know to have a female ejaculation or "gusher" orgasm, which many women would like to experience but aren't sure how to achieve. You'll need about twenty minutes, plenty of lubrication, and a dildo with a base. The dildo should also have a gooseneck shape.

Lie on your back and give yourself a sensate-focus caress on whatever part of your body you feel like. Then caress your genitals with lubrication and peak up to levels 4, 5, and 6. Place the suction area of your dildo on a flat surface. Kneel or squat on top of your dildo and insert it so that you are stimulating your G-spot. Gradually increase the pressure until you can feel your G-spot start to swell and you become aroused up to about a level 8.

Now adjust your position so that you hook the curve of the dildo into your G-spot. Thrust so that the dildo feels like a hook gently tugging at your G-spot. Remember to breathe deeply and evenly to enhance your arousal.

Continue thrusting to level 9, and then orgasm. At the moment of orgasm, climb off the dildo. You may experience a gushing of fluid down your legs. At the very least you will experience a lot of lubrication—much more than normal. Keep practicing until you can have a gusher.

Partner Exercises for Orgasm

In the next section, we move to the partner exercises. You have already practiced a bit with toys, and maybe you've done some peaking, using intercourse with your partner active. Let's switch control of the exercise to you.

The peaking and plateauing processes can both be used to increase your chances of having an orgasm. You'll find these exercises similar to the ones in Chapter 9, but this time you are the active partner. With these exercises, you can enjoy not only the physical but also the psychological excitement of being the active lover.

Exercise 66. **PEAKING WITH INTERCOURSE FOR ORGASM**

When women do a peaking exercise, they have an advantage over men, because they can peak to level 10—orgasm—several times. Try for several really high peaks, each one focusing on a different orgasm trigger. For example, try one whole set of peaks in one position while you focus on the G-spot. Then try another set of peaks using your PC muscle as the focus of stimulation, then another using your cul de sac.

Begin by lying next to your lover and exchanging focusing caresses. Then pleasure him with a front, genital, or oral caress.

When your partner has an erection, slowly kneel on top of him and start to caress your genitals with his penis. Run his penis all over your clitoris and inner and outer lips. Use it like you did the dildo in the above exercises. Your partner should remain passive and relaxed.

Allow yourself to peak up to low and medium arousal levels (3, 4, 5, and 6) by caressing your vaginal lips and clitoris with his penis. Use his penis to pleasure yourself. Explore sensuously and spontaneously with different kinds of strokes. When you are ready to move on, insert just the head of his penis and allow it to stimulate your PC muscle. See if you can peak up to level 7 doing this.

Remember to focus on your sensations, breathe, and keep your muscles as relaxed as possible even though you are kneeling. When you are ready, slowly lower yourself and insert your partner's whole penis inside you. Move up and down on it as slowly as you can. Use your partner's penis to explore your vagina the way you used your dildo. See if you can do a couple of peaks around level 8.

While you're at it, experiment with different ways to thrust. You can kneel so that you move straight up and down on your lover's penis. Use long thrusts and allow his penis to go all the way in and all the way out. Or, if you have strong leg muscles, you can squat over your partner. You may have practiced this with your suction-base dildo. You can rest part of your weight on the palms of your hands and use your arm strength to move yourself up and down on his penis.

Now really start to thrust deeper and see if you can peak at level 9. Don't allow that peak to go down. Focus on whatever internal orgasm trigger you are using and feel yourself fall over into orgasm.

One of the most sensuous ways to do this exercise is to change your position slightly so that while you are still on top, you are thrusting back and forth on your partner's penis instead of up and down. To do this, kneel over him and lie against his chest. Support yourself on your elbows, and keep your buttocks as high in the air as possible while still keeping his penis inside you. This will probably put his penis in contact with your G-spot. You will be able to feel your partner's penis rubbing against your G-spot as you slowly thrust back and forth. You may even have a gusher in this position.

Or you could try this exercise in conjunction with the pelvic thrusts you learned in Chapter 4. Think of yourself as thrusting up along the penis rather than down on it. Move your hips in a circular motion and slowly thrust your lover's penis all the way in and almost all the way out. Focus on every centimeter of his penis as it goes in and out. Go as slowly as possible, thinking of your vagina as a mouth sucking on his penis.

Peak to levels 7, 8, and 9 this way or do several peaks at level 9. At the moment before orgasm, open your eyes, take a deep breath, and stop thrusting. Passively experience your orgasm—just allow it to happen. Focus all of your attention on your PC muscle and feel it spasm around the shaft of your partner's penis. You will experience your orgasm as a shivering or spasming which may include not only your PC muscle, but your arms, legs, and facial muscles.

I suggest you experience at least one session of vaginal peaking with you on top and your partner completely passive until you have reached orgasm. After that, you can experiment with him becoming more active, and you can do the peaking exercise for your orgasm in any of the other intercourse positions.

Hint for men: When your partner is peaking to orgasm in the butterfly position, have her signal you when she's about to have an orgasm. At that point, stop your thrusting and focus on your penis so that you can feel her PC muscle spasms.

✐ Exercise 67. PLATEAUING WITH INTERCOURSE FOR ORGASM

Once you have learned to peak using your partner's penis, you can use the same positions and strokes to plateau at high arousal levels for long periods of time. Start with focusing caresses. Then pleasure your partner with a non-demand manual or oral genital caress. When he gets an erection, climb on top of him as you did in the previous exercise. Do a couple of low-level peaks (4 or 5) to get used to the position.

Now try kneeling, squatting, or lying flat on your partner, as you call your plateauing skills into play. Remember that these include squeezing your PC muscle, adjusting your breathing, changing your hip movements, and switching your focus. Practice plateauing with each orgasm trigger site using the techniques separately at first and then combine them until you can use all of them at the same time. Try to maintain yourself at higher and higher arousal levels for longer and longer periods of time.

Practice as much of this as you can while your partner remains passive. If he is focusing on the point of contact as you are, his arousal levels will probably rise as yours do. As you get better at this, your partner can start to move. If you have practiced plateauing at high levels with your partner passive, you will still be able to do it without being distracted by his movements.

Look at each other as you thrust. You can make this more exciting if you both focus together on your thrusting. This is even more important than how fast you thrust.

The best way to have an orgasm after a series of high plateaus is to plateau at level 9-plus using heavy breathing, intense pelvic thrusting, and PC muscle contractions. Then when you want to have an orgasm, stop everything you're doing. Just slam it to a halt—you will feel your body fall over into the orgasmic spasms involuntarily.

✑ Exercise 68. ORGASM AT THE MOMENT OF PENETRATION

Women have been taught that it can take from seven minutes to several hours to have an orgasm during intercourse. Actually, if you are not aroused, you won't have an orgasm no matter how long intercourse lasts. But if you are very aroused before intercourse starts, you can have an orgasm immediately upon penetration. This really is possible. This exercise will show you how.

The real secret to this exercise is peaking, not the penetration itself. You may need to spend fifteen to twenty minutes pleasuring yourself with your partner's penis. While you do this, it is important to remember the sensate-focus principles and stay in the here and now. If you anticipate the orgasm or work at it or worry about it, it won't happen. Your ability to concentrate, peak yourself up to level 9, and completely focus on that high level of arousal is what will produce the orgasm at the point of penetration.

Start with focusing caresses. Then have your partner lie on his back and lovingly stimulate him with a nondemand front and genital caress. As you do so, remember to focus on your sensations, touch for your own pleasure, breathe, and keep your muscles relaxed. Your partner should also focus on his sensations so he can fully enjoy the caress.

Start a nondemand oral genital caress. As your partner gets an erection, slowly stimulate yourself by rubbing his penis against your clitoris and vaginal lips, but don't insert his penis.

Peak up to levels 7 and 8 with this stimulation. In between your peaks, do oral sex with your partner so that he maintains high arousal levels. Peak up to level 9 by slowly rubbing his penis on your clitoris and your PC muscle.

Keep your leg muscles and PC muscle as relaxed as possible. Keep your eyes closed and start breathing faster. Then, when you are at the brink of orgasm, open your eyes, take a deep breath, and thrust yourself all the way down on your partner's penis. You will likely have an orgasm, if not on the first stroke, then within about five strokes. Keep practicing this exercise until you can have an orgasm on the first stroke. If you peak yourself to level 9 several times before penetration, rather than only once, this will also increase your likelihood of having an immediate orgasm.

The most difficult thing about this exercise is the timing. As you feel your PC muscle about to go into its orgasmic spasms, you have to have enough hand-eye-vagina coordination to climb onto your partner's penis really fast. If you're not fast enough, that's okay. Climb on anyway and see if you can have another orgasm from your partner's thrusting.

In another variation of this exercise, you can use your PC muscle to help you have an orgasm on the first stroke. Do the exercise as described above, but when you sit on your partner's penis, in addition to opening your eyes and taking a deep breath, slam your PC muscle shut around the shaft of his penis. This will often trigger an instant orgasm.

✐ *Exercise 69.* THE CAT POSITION

This is a wonderful alternative to the missionary style of intercourse, which frankly is the position least likely to bring a woman to climax. In the missionary position, the woman lies with her legs straight out and the man lies on top of her. In this position, it is difficult, if not impossible, for the woman to move her pelvis enough to get the stimulation she needs to have an orgasm. The only way she can thrust is to tense her leg muscles, but the tension reduces her arousal.

There is a subtle adjustment you can make during missionary-position intercourse that provides more direct stimulation to the clitoris and greatly increases your chances of having an orgasm. This position is called the *coital alignment technique,* or *CAT*. I have seen it increase a woman's arousal from a level 5 to a level 9.

Much of the research on this position was done by Edward Eichel and his colleagues. His research and the resulting techniques are described in his book *The Perfect Fit,* cowritten with Phillip Nobile.

Exchange focusing caresses. Pleasure your partner with a manual or oral genital caress. Stimulate him until he has an erection. When your partner has an erection, lie on your back. Your partner will lie flat on top of you and insert his penis as he normally would to have intercourse in the missionary position. Then—and this is the important adjustment you need to make to enjoy the CAT—have your partner hold onto your shoulders and move his entire body up toward your head about two inches so that he is in the intercourse position we used to call "riding high" when I was in high school. Your partner's pubic bone will rest on top of yours so that the base of his penis presses on your clitoris. He will be moving his penis up and down in your vagina rather than in and out.

The type of thrusting you do with the CAT is different from the thrusting you may be used to. In normal thrusting, many couples move in opposite directions and actually slam their genitals together as thrusting becomes more vigorous. In the CAT position both partners move together, and the actual range of movement is very small. It is as if your genitals are locked together and the clitoris and the base of the penis rub up against each other. Your pelvises will move, but the rest of your bodies won't.

The use of this position has many benefits. It will provide continuous stimulation of your clitoris during intercourse. And, since your bodies don't move that much, you are less likely to become fatigued. You can use the CAT position to do any peaking or plateauing exercise.

Exercise 70. IMITATING ORGASM

If you are having difficulty experiencing orgasm even with the above exercises, try this unusual twist: Learn how to fake your body into thinking you are having an orgasm. Doing so can actually trigger a real orgasm. This exercise is a solo exercise. It is most likely to help you reach orgasm if you are able to peak up to level 9 but can't quite seem to go over the edge.

Remember that the orgasmic response is a full-body response, not something that only occurs in your genitals. At the moment of orgasm, your face contorts; your arms, legs, and neck spasm; and your PC muscle contracts. The PC muscle spasms are involuntary. The other muscular responses are part reflex and part under your control. Enhancing these responses can help trigger orgasm.

You will need about twenty minutes for this exercise. Have plenty of lubrication handy. You can do the exercise with either your hand, a dildo, or a vibrator, or you can alternate using all three forms of stimulation.

Start caressing your genitals, using plenty of lubrication. Peak yourself through all of the arousal levels using your most reliable orgasm trigger. For many women, this will probably be the clitoris. Stimulate yourself until you reach an arousal level of 9-plus. Then take a deep breath, suck in your lower abdomen, hunch your shoulders into the bed, thrust your pelvis up, open your eyes wide, and relax your PC muscle. This may trigger an orgasm, which you will experience as a fluttering or spasming of the PC muscle.

I admit that it's hard to remember to do all of these things at the same time. Practice each of them separately at higher and higher peaks until you can do all of them together.

You can also do this exercise by acting the way you think highly orgasmic women act. Many of us believe that other women are wildly orgasmic in bed, but that we ourselves are repressed. You may think that other women respond sexually with screaming, moaning, and contortions. The next time you are at the brink of orgasm, let yourself go and really overdo it. Believe it or not, acting out a huge orgasm can often trigger a real one. This is because expressing the orgasm actually makes you enjoy it more. (This is true of all emotions, not just orgasm.)

Another option is to wait until you are at the very brink of orgasm, and instead of relaxing your PC muscle, slam it shut. This often triggers the involuntary PC muscle spasms.

Use these orgasm techniques not as ends in themselves, but as ways to accustom yourself to having orgasms. As with any skill that involves learning complex patterns of behavior and combining them, the first few tries may seem artificial. After you practice faking for a while, your body will learn what it feels like to orgasm, and eventually just staying focused and relaxed at level 9 will trigger orgasm.

Exercise 71. THE BRIDGE MANEUVER

I believe that the exercises in this chapter can help any woman develop her ability to have powerful orgasms, whether she has had them before or not.

But what if you have tried every exercise three times and you still have not been able to have an orgasm during intercourse? Please don't give up—I have another suggestion: Manually stimulate your clitoris during intercourse.

The reason you may have been unable to have an orgasm during intercourse is that your internal orgasm triggers (the G-spot, cervix, and cul de sac) don't work for you yet. Until they do, your clitoris is your most reliable orgasm trigger. The problem is that many intercourse positions don't stimulate the clitoris enough for you to have an orgasm. If you or your partner manually stimulate your clitoris during intercourse, your chances of having an orgasm will greatly increase.

Sex therapists call this a "bridge maneuver." In behavioral psychology, a bridge maneuver is an activity that connects two behaviors that you already know how to do to form a new behavior. Here, the two behaviors you already know how to do are having intercourse and having an orgasm by touching your clitoris.

Begin a session with focusing caresses and then have your partner lie on his back. Do a genital caress and have oral sex with your partner until he gets an erection.

Climb on top of your partner and begin peaking and plateauing, using his penis to pleasure yourself. As you reach high peaks and plateaus (levels 7, 8, and 9), stimulate your clitoris with your fingers and focus on how it feels.

Masturbate to orgasm by stimulating your clitoris and allowing your partner's penis to stroke you. Notice the added sensations of simultaneous masturbation and intercourse. With some practice, you will need less and less direct clitoral stimulation with your fingers, and your ability to have an orgasm will transfer to the stimulation of intercourse.

There are two other variations of this exercise. They both work best when you are on top. Ask your partner to stimulate your clitoris with his hand instead of doing it yourself. Or either one of you can use a vibrator or dildo to stimulate your clitoris once you have reached a high level of arousal.

✑ Exercise 72. SHALLOW PENETRATION

This exercise will stimulate your PC muscle and increase the chances that it will spasm. Begin the exercise with focusing caresses. Then give your partner a manual and oral genital caress until he has an erection. Get into the butterfly intercourse position. Using lots of lubrication, have your partner insert his penis. With your partner doing deep thrusts into your vagina, peak up to arousal levels 6, 7, and 8. When you reach an arousal level beyond 8, signal your partner. At that point, he will adjust his position so that he is only thrusting an inch into your vagina at most. He should slow down his thrusting so that he is barely moving, and he should use the head of his penis to tease your PC muscle by moving both in and out and in a circular motion. You will probably feel your PC muscle start to twitch with some preorgasmic spasms. When you are on the brink of orgasm, signal your partner again and have him resume normal thrusting, which should send you over into orgasm.

✐ Exercise 73. DRAW YOUR ORGASM

This is a visualization exercise that stems from an article I was interviewed for in *Marie Claire* magazine. The writer of the article asked five women to draw visual representations of their orgasms. This is a projective technique that helps you get in touch with your unconscious feelings about orgasm. I was then supposed to analyze the pictures.

If you would like to try this exercise, do it now before you read any further. Relax and think about what your orgasm feels like. There's no right or wrong way to do this. Gather some materials. You'll need paper and either paints, markers, crayons, or colored pencils—whatever artistic implements you think will help you represent your orgasm.

When you have finished your drawing, consider the following questions to help you analyze it:

> Is your drawing simple or complicated?
> Does it show vibrant colors or is it monochromatic?
> Does it show only female symbolism, or does it include male symbolism also?
> Is the drawing large or small?

These are just a few areas you might explore. You will be the best analyst of your particular drawing, just as you are the best analyst of your dreams. One of the things I noted was that most women viewed their orgasm as a solitary experience. Only one woman's drawing indicated that a penis was somehow involved.

For an extension of this exercise, have your partner draw his orgasm, and compare the two drawings. Note any areas of ambivalence or contradiction. Think about how you could change your experience of orgasm so that the next time you draw one it will look more dynamic.

✑ *Exercise 74.* **FEMALE MULTIPLE ORGASM**

One of the great things about being a woman is that we are more likely than men to be able to experience multiple orgasms. A typical female multiple-orgasm pattern is illustrated in Figure 9, which shows a typical response to masturbation or intercourse. Most women who experience multiple orgasm do so in this pattern: They have an excitement and plateau phase and then a quick series of orgasms without dropping below level 8 in between. Other women have a multiple-orgasm pattern in which their first orgasm is really strong and the subsequent orgasms are less strong.

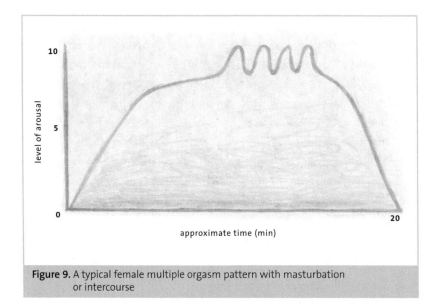

Figure 9. A typical female multiple orgasm pattern with masturbation or intercourse

Another typical pattern is illustrated in Figure 10. This is a pattern in which the man does oral sex on the woman, during which she has a series of orgasms, and then the woman does oral sex on the man, and then they have intercourse, during which she has another orgasm.

The best way that I know for you to experience multiple orgasms is to make sure that the stimulation doesn't stop after you have the first orgasm. And the best way that I know to do that is while masturbating with a vibrator. Do a peaking exercise with your vibrator on low-level vibration. After you have your first orgasm, switch the vibrator to high and keep going with the stimulation on your clitoris. You'll experience either one long, stretched-out orgasm or two discrete ones.

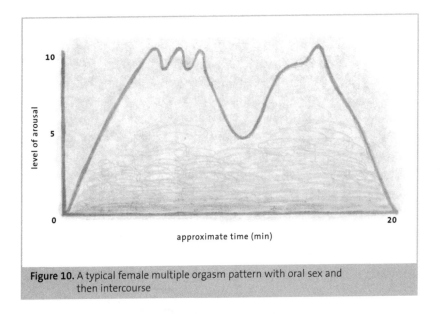

Figure 10. A typical female multiple orgasm pattern with oral sex and then intercourse

It's more difficult to have multiple orgasms with partner stimulation, because your partner does not have the staying power of a vibrator. The stimulation he gives you during oral sex will probably be more reliable initially than the stimulation you get from intercourse.

If you're trying to learn to reach orgasm more reliably, it's essential that you use the peaking process to help you. Awareness of your arousal level up and down the scale makes it much more likely that you will be able to reach orgasm in any given session of sex, and it also makes your eventual orgasms stronger.

Have your partner do oral sex with you. Peak or plateau up to levels 6, 7, 8, and 9. After you have your first orgasm, before your arousal level drops below 8, hold your partner's head and thrust your clitoris against his tongue. Again, you may experience one long, extended orgasm or two discrete ones.

There are several techniques you can use during intercourse to have multiple orgasms. One technique is to try to have orgasms using two different triggers, one external and one internal. For example, use the butterfly position. Have your partner alternate thrusting inside of you and pulling out and rubbing his penis on your clitoris until you come. Or you could rub your clitoris with your hand while he's thrusting inside you.

After your first orgasm, don't allow your arousal level to go down past 8. Have your partner immediately start to do deep thrusts into your cul de sac, which should be open by now since you've just had an orgasm. See if you can have a vaginal/uterine orgasm with this cul de sac thrusting.

This also works in reverse. In fact, it works better in reverse. Before you have intercourse, stimulate your partner so that he has a really firm erection. For this version of the exercise, use as little lubrication as you can while still staying comfortable. When you first get into the butterfly position, have your partner thrust as hard as he can into the cul de sac to bring you to orgasm. Then have your partner rub your clitoris with either his hand or his penis to bring you to a second orgasm.

I don't know why this version of the exercise works so well, but it does. Technically, it shouldn't work that well, because after you've had a short-term cul de sac orgasm, there's no reason your clitoris should be hard, but it will be.

See if you can have one of those blended (splendid?) orgasms that Singer and Singer described. To do this, get into a position in which your partner's penis is hitting an internal trigger such as the G-spot, the cervix, or the cul de sac. Reach down and stimulate your clitoris with your hand or your vibrator while you have intercourse. Switch your focus back and forth between your clitoris and the internal trigger you're using. See if you can simultaneously peak with both triggers so that you reach level 10 with both of them at the same time. It's kind of like having simultaneous orgasms with yourself.

The next chapter is once again addressed primarily to men, with advice and exercises for enhancing a man's experience of ejaculation and orgasm.

chapter 13

Ejaculation and Orgasm: From Ordinary to Extraordinary

A Chapter for Men

by Charlotte Morrison

*M*en, *if you enjoy ejaculation and orgasm now (and I'm betting you do), there are ways to make them even stronger and more powerful. Read through this chapter and see which techniques you would like to try first. The advanced orgasm and ejaculation exercises at the end of the chapter can have particularly potent effects.*

It is not uncommon for adult men, over time, to begin to require intense stimulation of the penis before they can experience any sexual sensations at all. In sex therapy, the name for this condition is *penile insensitivity*. Over a period of time, if nothing is done about it, it can greatly interfere with a man's ability to have satisfying ejaculations when he is making love. Fortunately, penile sensitivity can be restored. My client Joseph's experience is typical: "After years of having 'normal sex,' I found myself having difficulty ejaculating. Through these exercises, I learned to slow down, pay attention to how aroused I am, and relax my pelvic muscles so I could really enjoy ejaculation again."

Joseph identified three common reasons why men sometimes lose sensitivity in their penis:

1. They have sex too fast. They rush through the act and don't pay attention to their feelings.

2. They are worried about premature ejaculation, and so they unconsciously squeeze their PC muscle almost the whole time they are having sex. This can make the penis feel numb after a while.

3. They have what I call "brain-dead sex." They just go through the motions and think about something else during sex.

Others lose penis sensitivity because

1. they masturbate in a way that decreases their sensations

2. they go so long without having sex with a partner that they become unaccustomed to the delicate sensations of being inside a vagina

3. they practice the withdrawal method of birth control when younger and thus go for long periods of time without ejaculating during intercourse

Increasing Penile Sensitivity

One of the most common causes of decreased penile sensitivity is a man's masturbation style. It is possible to masturbate in a way that actually decreases your sensations. This happens if you habitually use a masturbation stroke that is either too fast or applies too much pressure. After you have spent many years masturbating with a firm, hard stroke, you may be unable to feel stimulated by or respond to the lighter, more sensitive touch of your lover.

Some men "forget" how to enjoy the feeling of caressing the inside of a vagina with their penis or how to experience its different sensations. So they find it difficult to ejaculate with just the stimulation of intercourse.

I've included these next few exercises for men who would like to change their masturbation habits to increase their sensitivity. All of these are exercises for you do to alone, and you should practice them two to three times a week. You may feel your sensitivity sharpen significantly in as little as a week, but it will probably take a month or so before you notice substantial changes.

✍ *Exercise 75.* DECREASING MASTURBATION TIME

How long do you usually take when you masturbate? Research indicates that some men masturbate to ejaculation in a few seconds, while others may spend several hours stimulating themselves before they allow themselves to ejaculate.

There is no "right" amount of time to spend before ejaculation. However, other sex therapists and I have found that clients who have the most penile sensitivity tend to spend about ten to fifteen minutes masturbating before they ejaculate.

If you currently like to masturbate for half an hour or more, there is nothing wrong with doing so. But keep in mind that this habit may cause your penis to be less sensitive than it could be. By reducing your masturbation time by half, you can increase your sensitivity a great deal.

The easiest way to do this is to simply keep track of how long you masturbate. You may be surprised to look at the clock and find you've gone on much longer than you thought. For two weeks, keep a chart of your masturbation time without trying to change anything. During week three, try to take five minutes off your time. Each successive week, try to take two minutes off your time until you can easily masturbate to orgasm and ejaculation within ten minutes or so. This "tapering-off" process will be much easier (and certainly more enjoyable) than trying to change your masturbation habits overnight or going cold turkey.

✐ Exercise 76. DECREASING MASTURBATION FREQUENCY

Frequent masturbation also contributes to lowered penile sensitivity. There is no moral or health rule that says how much masturbation is too much. However, if you masturbate a lot, cutting down on the frequency of masturbation can increase your sensitivity.

Again, try keeping a two-week log to see how often you masturbate. Then cut down the frequency by about 10 percent each week until you begin to feel a noticeable increase in your penile sensitivity and a greater ease at and enjoyment of your ejaculations.

Some men find that they can make changes in their masturbation stroke (see below), their frequency, and the amount of time they spend during the same week or weeks. Other men find it easier to do all this in stages. For example, first they may decrease frequency, then the following week do an exercise to change their stroke (as described in the next exercise), then the week after that decrease masturbation time. Most of my clients have found that they reached their maximum sensitivity when they could easily masturbate to ejaculation within ten minutes by using a mostly slow, caressing stroke.

✐ Exercise 77. CHANGING YOUR STROKE

Using an extremely firm, fast, high-pressure masturbation stroke is probably the most common cause of lowered penile sensitivity. It is difficult for me to describe what is too fast compared with a slow stroke, but this exercise will help you slow your stroke down and awaken the sensitivity in your penis. Set aside fifteen to twenty minutes for this exercise.

Begin masturbating with whatever type of lubrication and stroke you usually use. Now slow down so that you are stroking only about half as fast as you did before. After another minute, cut your speed in half again. Continue this slowing down process until you are giving yourself a genital caress rather than masturbating.

Another way to change your stroke is to use your open palm or your fingertips and to caress your penis rather than using a closed fist to manipulate it. See if you can go slowly enough and use a light enough touch to feel which parts of your penis are more sensitive and which parts are less so. This caress should be similar to the genital caress you learned in Chapter 4. If you find it difficult to stay aroused with such a slow touch, alternate the old, firm stroke with the new, slower stroke.

Over a number of sessions your goal should be to spend most of your masturbation time with a slow, sensuous stroke. One way to do this is to keep track of, and gradually modify, the percentage of fast stroking and slow stroking you use each time you masturbate. You will increase your sensitivity if you can masturbate at least 80 percent of the time using a slow stroke. In any of these exercises where you are attempting to get used to a new, slower, stroke, if you feel like ejaculating at the end of fifteen or twenty minutes, go ahead.

Exercise 78. SIMULATING THE VAGINA

Some men find that their penis feels sensitive during masturbation but less sensitive during intercourse. If you are used to always masturbating with a very hard, firm, fast stroke, you may be unable to duplicate these sensations during intercourse and it may take you longer to ejaculate. One way to change your masturbation habits is to find a way to masturbate that feels more like intercourse. Men have tried many creative ways to do this.

As I mentioned before, some men are not fully satisfied by intercourse because they are not used to being inside a vagina. To simulate the feeling of a vagina, some men simply masturbate with one hand over the head of their penis and a lot of lubrication. Others masturbate into a reusable lambskin condom filled with a water-based lubricant. Still others use an empty banana peel heated up with hot water and filled with lubricant. One of the more creative suggestions I've heard is to use an old sock warmed up in the clothes dryer and filled with lubricant. Adult stores sell artificial vaginas, called "penis sleeves," that could also be used.

You can use anything you can think of that simulates the sensations of a vagina. Use your imagination and have fun. Decide on something that is well-lubricated, warm, and that can contain your penis. Whatever you decide to use, you can heat up your oil or other lubricant by placing it in a dish next to a candle for a few minutes.

Practice giving yourself a genital caress using your vagina simulator for fifteen or twenty minutes. Use the same slow, sensuous strokes you practiced in the previous exercise.

✐ Exercise 79. **PROLONGING YOUR ORGASM**

If you would like to enhance your orgasmic potential in addition to increasing your penile sensitivity, try the following exercises. Remember how in Chapter 3 I discussed the difference between ejaculation and orgasm and described the two distinct phases of ejaculation? Learning to pay attention to these differences can result in prolonged and exquisite pleasure. Also, simply paying attention to your pelvic area at the moment of orgasm and ejaculation can result in a sense that your orgasmic response is longer. This exercise will also help you recognize the two phases of ejaculation: emission and expulsion. The exercise involves the peaking process you learned in Chapter 4. It will take about twenty to twenty-five minutes. Do the exercise either lying on your back or sitting comfortably in a chair.

Start a slow, sensuous genital caress, using plenty of lubrication. Remember to breathe, focus on your sensations, and keep all of your muscles, including your PC muscle, completely relaxed. Let yourself peak up to the middle levels, such as 4, 5, and 6. Pay attention to the downsides as well as the upsides of the peaks. Let your arousal decrease two levels between peaks. Let each peak last three to five minutes. Now peak up to levels 7 and 8, and then come down to 5 or 6.

Now peak up to level 9. When you reach the point of inevitability, stop thrusting, hold perfectly still, close your eyes, and take a deep breath. Focus all of your attention on your pelvic sensations. Feel the semen start to move from your testicle area into your urethra. This is the emission phase. Feel the contractions of accessory organs such as your prostate and then notice how a few seconds later your PC muscle starts to pulse rhythmically. This is the expulsion phase. Now breathe deeply again, open your eyes wide, and focus all of your attention on the base of your penis. You will distinctly feel each spurt of semen as you ejaculate, and you will experience a sense that your orgasm lasts longer than usual. Repeat this exercise until you are able to recognize all of these distinct sensations.

Once you are able to recognize all of the different sensations of orgasm, this process will become automatic for you. Every time you have an orgasm, you'll get a sense that it takes longer than it used to.

ℰ *Exercise 80.* USING THE PC MUSCLE TO STRENGTHEN YOUR EJACULATION

As soon as you are able to recognize the sensations of emission and expulsion, you can make your ejaculation stronger by squeezing your PC muscle at a particular point during your arousal cycle. Usually, squeezing your PC muscle at any peak during your sexual-pleasure cycle will cause your arousal to either maintain or go down a level, but there is an exception to that. You can use your PC muscle voluntarily when you reach the point of inevitability to give your ejaculation a kind of a turbo charge.

Do Exercise 79, "Prolonging Your Orgasm." When you reach the point of inevitability, close your eyes, stop your movement, and feel your emission phase. Now, just before the first involuntary PC muscle contraction of the expulsion phase hits, take a deep breath, open your eyes, and squeeze your PC muscle really hard! You will magnify your first PC muscle contraction so that your ejaculation will feel as if it is exploding out of you. This can create an extremely intense orgasmic experience for both you and your partner when you learn to use it during intercourse. The more strongly your PC muscle spasms when you have an ejaculation, the more likely your partner is to feel it. Many women find it a turn-on to feel their partner ejaculate inside of them.

The toughest part about this exercise is the timing. You need to practice the "Prolonging Your Orgasm" exercise several times so that you can predict exactly when that first contraction is going to hit and anticipate it for maximum pleasure.

ℰ *Exercise 81.* PEAKING TO ENHANCE ORGASM AND EJACULATION

In Chapter 9, "Making the Pleasure Last and Last: A Chapter for Men," I described some detailed peaking exercises a man could do with his partner to learn to last longer during intercourse. The peaking process can also be used to enhance ejaculation and orgasm.

To use the peaking process to enhance ejaculation and orgasm, you can do the partner peaking exercises described in Chapter 9, with a couple of differences. The difference between peaking to last longer and peaking to ejaculate and orgasm more easily is this: The man who is peaking in order to learn to last longer needs to overpractice the lower arousal levels (4, 5, and

6), whereas the man who is peaking in order to enhance ejaculation and orgasm needs to overpractice the higher arousal levels (7, 8, and 9). So, however you want to do a peaking exercise (with manual or oral stimulation or intercourse), you want to make sure that you do at least one exercise with repeated peaking at levels 7, 8, and 9. You can also do an exercise in which you practice repeated peaks at level 8 and repeated peaks at level 9.

There's another technique that's different from what you would do if you were learning to last longer. Squeezing the PC muscle at high arousal levels is a good technique for lasting longer. However, if you are peaking to enhance ejaculation and orgasm, you must make sure not to squeeze your PC muscle, especially when you are at high arousal levels. In fact, the reason why you might feel that your ejaculation and orgasm need enhancing is probably because you've gotten into a habit of unconsciously tightening your PC muscle at high arousal levels. The first few times you do peaking exercises at high arousal levels, you will probably really have to monitor yourself to make sure that your PC muscle isn't tense. As you reach each peak, stop your movement, take a deep breath, and consciously relax your PC muscle.

A third thing you'll need to watch out for is tension in muscles other than the PC muscle. As you peak at high arousal levels, be sure to relax the muscles in your inner thighs and buttocks.

Remember that the peaking process accomplishes several things. It allows for the optimal release of endorphins, those pleasure-inducing brain chemicals. If you allow your arousal to increase in a peaking pattern rather than in the pattern associated with the classic Masters and Johnson sexual-response cycle (see Figure 4 on page 30), you increase your chances of having an orgasm. You are also more likely to be able to have multiple orgasms, and the orgasms you have are likely to be more intense than the ones you would have as the result of proceeding normally through the excitement and plateau phases of the sexual-response cycle.

ℰ Exercise 82. PLATEAUING TO ENHANCE EJACULATION AND ORGASM

The same comments that apply to the peaking process also apply to the plateauing process, described in Chapter 9. You can plateau with manual or oral stimulation or intercourse in any position. You can remain at a certain level by changing your breathing, changing your thrusting, or switching your focus. If a man is trying to learn to last longer, he can squeeze his PC muscle to keep himself from going beyond a certain arousal level. However, if you are plateauing to enhance ejaculation and orgasm, you should not squeeze your PC muscle in order to plateau. Instead, at any plateau level, you should relax your PC muscle in order to let yourself go to a higher level.

The guidelines suggested in the previous exercise also apply here: You should mostly practice plateauing at high levels rather than low levels. Make sure that the muscles in your thighs and buttocks stay relaxed, especially at the highest arousal levels.

Sometimes a visualization technique helps men who are trying to learn to sensitize their penis and enhance ejaculation and orgasm. Instead of trying to ejaculate or working at it, as you are peaking or plateauing, picture yourself floating in the ocean. Some of the swells that lift you up are peaks and some are plateaus. As you reach higher and higher levels of arousal, picture yourself plateauing on a wave that's level 9. When you reach orgasm, visualize yourself plunging down into orgasm rather than trying to climb up the face of a wave into orgasm.

Once you feel comfortable with the last few solo masturbation exercises, you can move on to working with a partner. The exercises that follow are partner exercises that should help men who are trying to further increase their sensitivity or enhance the quality of their orgasms.

✌ *Exercise 83.* EJACULATING NEAR THE VAGINA

Some men are able to ejaculate easily with masturbation or even with their partner's manual or oral stimulation, but they experience a little bit of difficulty ejaculating during intercourse. Here's a progression of exercises that can help you with this.

You and your partner should start with focusing caresses. Then lie next to each other on your backs on the bed. Each of you should begin to do a peaking exercise by yourself. Try not to get distracted by what your partner is doing. Do a combination of peaking and your favorite masturbation stroke, remembering to keep your PC muscle relaxed. When you reach the point of ejaculatory inevitability, signal your partner and turn toward each other, and then ejaculate either between your partner's thighs or at the entrance to her vagina.

Repeat this exercise, entering your partner's vagina a little earlier each time, until you are confident that you can start intercourse at arousal level 8 and ejaculate inside your partner. Variations of this exercise include having your partner stimulate you manually and orally to the different peaks, or doing the peaks using all of the different intercourse positions.

✐ Exercise 84. ALTERNATING MANUAL, ORAL, AND INTERCOURSE PEAKS

This is similar to the previous exercise, but with more time spent inside your partner's vagina. Begin the exercise with focusing caresses. Give your partner a manual or oral genital caress. Then have her stimulate you manually or orally so that you reach arousal levels 4, 5, and 6 and have a fairly firm erection.

Now get into the butterfly position. Using lots of lubrication, use your hand to peak yourself up to level 7. At that point, remember to stop your movement, take a deep breath, and relax your PC muscle and other muscles to allow your arousal level to go down a couple of levels.

Insert your penis into your partner's vagina and peak up to level 7 again. Let your arousal go back down a couple of levels, and this time have your partner give you oral sex until you are again at level 7. Continue alternating peaks with your hand, your partner's vagina, and your partner's mouth. Peak up to levels 8 and 9 this way. When you are ready to ejaculate, try to ejaculate in your partner's vagina or as physically close to it as possible.

✐ Exercise 85. USING A VIBRATOR TO ENHANCE ORGASM AND EJACULATION

Think vibrators are just for women? Think again. A lot of men like them too, and using a vibrator on your thighs, scrotum, or the base of your penis can often provide the needed stimulation to push you over the edge to orgasm.

Men can use a penis-shaped vibrator of any size on their penis, scrotum, and thighs. Many men prefer to use the type of vibrator that straps onto the back of the hand, so that the hand and not the vibrator touches their body.

If you want to use a vibrator to enhance orgasm and ejaculation, do a peaking exercise by yourself. Use the kind of stimulation you read about earlier in this chapter—in other words, don't use a hard, fast, firm masturbation stroke; instead, peak using a sensate-focus genital caress. When you are at level 8 or 9, apply the vibrator, on a low setting, gently to your genitals to help you have an orgasm. Focus, breathe, and relax all of your muscles.

Here's what I would recommend for men who have a tendency toward delayed ejaculation. Don't overuse a vibrator. You don't want to become dependent on it for orgasm and ejaculation. Use it for special occasions when you want to have some extra stimulation. Remember to keep your PC muscle and thigh and buttocks muscles relaxed when you use a vibrator. Don't set the vibrator setting so high or push with it so hard that you find yourself fighting against the stimulation. Keep it relaxed and fun.

⚖ *Exercise 86.* INTRODUCTION TO MALE MULTIPLE ORGASM

I mentioned in Chapter 3 that male orgasm and ejaculation are not exactly the same thing, although they usually occur together. Orgasm is the full-body response that includes rapid heart rate, muscle tension, and psychological release. Ejaculation is the localized genital response that occurs when the PC muscle spasms reflexively and forces semen out through the urethral opening.

Because orgasm and ejaculation aren't the same thing, it's possible for a man to have an orgasm without ejaculating and vice versa. Some men (probably between 5 and 10 percent) naturally have the ability to enjoy more than one orgasm in a row without ejaculating. This ability can be learned.

A full discussion of male multiple-orgasm techniques is beyond the scope of this book (if you are interested in reading a full treatment of the topic, try my book *How to Make Love All Night*). However, I can give you some information about the theory and practice of male multiple orgasm here.

I am aware of three patterns of male multiple orgasm: nonejaculatory orgasm (NEO), multiejaculation, and what I call female-style.

In *NEO*, a man reaches the brink of orgasm and squeezes his PC muscle really hard right before the point of inevitability. Since full-body orgasm is a reflex and he can't stop it, his body will go over into orgasm, but he won't ejaculate. That means he'll stay hard and be able to continue having inter-course. At the next orgasmic peak he can choose to ejaculate or not.

Multiejaculation is a style in which a man has several orgasms in a row, each with a partial ejaculation. I believe one way a man can learn to do this is to squeeze his PC muscle right between the emission and expulsion phases of ejaculation. Most men who have this ability seem to do it naturally.

In *female-style multiple orgasm,* a man has a strong orgasm with a full ejaculation, and then by continuing to move and by changing his breathing he immediately has a series of smaller orgasms, or "aftershocks." These are orgasms, but they are usually unaccompanied by ejaculation.

There are several benefits for men who learn to become multiply orgasmic. The techniques help you last longer during intercourse and make it easier to have orgasms. Being multiply orgasmic helps you understand your partner's responses better. Men who are multiply orgasmic secrete more oxytocin, the bonding hormone that can increase feelings of intimacy in your relationship. Plus, with multiple orgasm, you double (or triple) your pleasure.

Research and observation indicate that there are several keys to becoming multiply orgasmic:

1. Male multiple orgasm is more likely to occur in a committed monogamous relationship with an interested partner.

2. Multiple orgasm is more likely to occur in conjunction with the peaking and plateauing processes.

3. A man needs to have a really good ability to focus on sensations for male multiple orgasm to happen.

4. Men over forty are more likely to be able to learn the process.

5. Men who have a tendency to ejaculate quickly are more likely to be able to learn it.

6. It's more likely to occur in the butterfly intercourse position.

Choose one of the types of male multiple orgasm and try it in the context of a sensate-focus exercise that includes focusing caresses, manual and oral peaking, and peaking with intercourse in the butterfly position. Don't try to do too much in one exercise. Try the following progression:

> Do the exercise in this chapter on prolonging your orgasm.

> Then do an exercise in which you squeeze your PC muscle really hard and open your eyes wide right before the point of inevitability.

> Next, do an exercise in which you squeeze your PC muscle between the emission and expulsion phases, and have your partner press with both her hands on your lower back when you come.

> Do an exercise in which you experiment with changing your breathing at the point of inevitability to try to experience female-style multiple orgasm. The type of breathing to use for this exercise is very heavy breathing, like panting.

We've covered a lot of territory so far and have learned many exercises for enhancing sexual pleasure. As I mentioned in the Introduction, following the program in this order builds a foundation for the mutuality and intimacy skills presented in the book's final two chapters. Let's turn now to the topics of bonding, intimacy, and love.

chapter 14

Pleasure Bonds:
Enhancing Mutuality
and Intimacy

by Steven Baratz

*This chapter contains exercises that can bring you and your part-
ner closer together. The exercises range from simple pleasures like
kissing and spooning to more complicated exercises that can help
you explore and push the boundaries of your sexuality.*

✑ Exercise 87. SENSUAL KISSING

In all of this discussion of sexual pleasure, you may think I have ignored the
simplest and easiest pleasure of all—a kiss. Well, I haven't. A kiss may be
the most intimate erotic caress you share with your lover. Some of our most
sensitive nerve endings are in our lips, so it is no wonder they can feel and

communicate with exquisite precision. No wonder romance often begins with a kiss.

Kissing as part of a romantic attraction or connection is highly valued and romanticized in Western cultures. However, it is not a cultural universal—there are many cultures in which kissing on the lips is not considered romantic or is even considered objectionable in some way.

When you're kissing sensually, you kiss as you do any other sensate-focus caress: Kiss for your own pleasure, stay in the here and now, and focus on the exact point of contact—that velvety contact of your lips and tongues. Notice everything about your lover's kiss—the taste of her mouth, the feel of his tongue, the softness of your lips as they meet. When you kiss, keep your lips, tongue, neck, and chin as relaxed as possible. That way you won't get sore muscles.

Gaze into each other's eyes and feel your connection. Focus, breathe, and relax, slowly licking your lover's mouth. You might graze your lover's lips or tongue with your teeth—whatever gives you different sensations. The idea is not to leave each other's mouths sore, but rather to kiss as softly, sensuously, and intimately as possible. Don't kiss too fast or too hard, and don't begin to think of where your kissing might lead. Just enjoy the moment.

Sensual kissing is a wonderful pleasure you and your partner can share in a leisurely way or steal at a moment's notice. While it is a wonderful prelude to making love, it is important that you share it often outside of other sexual contact. I suggest that each partner give each other a kissing caress for at least five to ten minutes. Kissing can be the cornerstone of your sensual and intimate connection. Don't stop with just kissing each other on the mouth. Use your lips and tongue to explore your partner's neck, ears, eyelids, and nipples.

✑ *Exercise 88.* NONSEXUAL BONDING

To "bond" is to form an emotional attachment with another person. The term *bonding* typically refers to the emotional attachment that develops between a child and its primary caregiver, especially during the first few months of life. But adults also need to bond with their partners in both sexual and nonsexual ways. Bonding brings depth and richness to our relationships and creates intimacy. Bonding makes us feel more secure and allows us to experience closeness in a pressure-free way. Nuzzling is especially nice, particularly when you appreciate your partner's natural body scents or favorite colognes.

In the first nonsexual bonding exercise, you and your partner simply hold each other. I suggest you lie on your sides, face-to-face. Get comfortable, put your arms around each other, and gaze into each other's eyes. Sometimes it's difficult to gaze into both of your partner's eyes at the same time. If this is the case, gaze into one of your partner's eyes. Gaze into the eye that corresponds with your partner's nondominant hand. In other words, if your partner is right-handed, gaze into their left eye. Don't talk. Many times talking enhances intimacy, but it can also create discord or distraction. We all need to spend some time with our partner in which our bodies learn to know and trust each other on a physical and nonverbal level. Do this for about fifteen minutes—or longer if you like.

Another position for nonsexual bonding is the "spoon" position. In this position, one person lies with their chest against their partner's back, and holds the other close by draping an arm over the other person's belly. This is not as intimate as the face-to-face position, but it is very relaxing because you can pay attention to each other's breathing. When you use this position, you will notice that your breathing tends to synchronize with your partner's breathing.

There are three other positions you can use for nonsexual bonding. In the nurturing position, lie on your sides, again facing each other. The partner in need of nurturing should slide down just low enough to burrow his or her face into the other's chest.

In the lap reclining position, one of you sits up in bed or on the couch, or even on the floor. Hold your lover as he or she reclines in your lap. This is the same position you used for the face caress in Chapter 6. This position really helps you reconnect with each other, especially after a long day or a period of separation.

In a final position, one person sits on the couch. The other person lies perpendicular to him and wraps her arms around his waist and buries her head in his abdomen. This is a nice position in which the sitting person can caress their partner's hair.

I recommend at least five minutes of bonding a day. You can do it before you go to sleep at night or in the morning when you both wake up. Choose your bonding position for each day based on how you feel. For example, if one of you had a bad day and needs to be nurtured, use the nurturing position. If you both need to relax, use the spoon position. If you feel pretty good and want to just be close, use the face-to-face eye-gaze position.

ⵣ *Exercise 89.* **SEXUAL BONDING**

I believe that adults need to bond with their partners sexually as well as nonsexually. This happens naturally if you lie together, insert the penis into the vagina, wrap your arms around each other, and gaze into each other's eyes. Don't talk. Just look, appreciate, and feel the sensations of containment in the vagina without pressuring yourself to perform. Being physically close and connected at the genitals, without moving and without expectation, lets energy build between the two of you. Couples have reported feeling "bathed" in this energy, which would otherwise be discharged by the movements of intercourse.

Try bonding in this way for about fifteen minutes and notice your experience. What does it feel like to just be inside her? How does it feel to have him so quietly inside of you? It doesn't matter if the man has an erection. If he does, fine. If his erection goes up and down, that's okay too. If the man doesn't have an erection, he can lie on his side facing his partner. She can put lubrication on his penis and her vagina and then lie on her back and interweave her legs with his. In this position, she'll find it easy to insert the penis from the base first, as described in the earlier chapter on erections.

Sexual bonding does not have to lead to intercourse. If after fifteen minutes of sexual bonding you feel like moving into intercourse, go ahead. But don't feel pressured. Some people like to fall asleep connected in this way, and others like to stay bonded sexually even after the man's erection goes down after intercourse.

I recommend that you bond sexually with each other every day for ten or fifteen minutes. This process is very powerful. Sexual and nonsexual bonding, as well as sensual kissing, will create strong feelings of closeness between you. Few people take the time to do this, but it can really pay off in terms of enhanced intimacy.

Sharing Private Sexual Experiences

The following few exercises involve sharing sexual experiences like masturbation, which we normally think of as private. I need to give you a caveat here. Not every couple has reached a level of intimacy that will allow them to do these exercises. Only you know enough about the nature of your intimate relationship to know whether these exercises would be good for the two of you.

✍ *Exercise 90.* **MUTUAL MASTURBATION**

Masturbation is one of the most intimate things we do with ourselves. Many of us feel so private about it that we hesitate to share the experience with a partner. It's unbelievable how many couples who have been together for years don't know what the other person does for self-pleasure.

There are two ways to do a mutual masturbation exercise. The first is for both of you to masturbate at the same time. Lie together on the bed and stimulate yourself the same way you would if you were alone. Pay attention to your own arousal. If you want to, look at each other as you become more and more aroused while touching yourselves.

Or you can take turns masturbating while the other watches. It is very intimate to share your most private activity with another person. After one person has masturbated for a few minutes, the other will take a turn. Try not to be self-conscious that your partner is watching you. Relax, close your eyes, and pleasure yourself the way you most like to. Take yourself as high on the arousal scale as you wish.

The mutual masturbation exercises will help each of you learn how your partner likes to be touched. If you want to, you can combine them with a sexual bonding exercise in which the partner cradles the person who is masturbating.

After you have done one of these exercises together, talk about it. If it made you nervous or embarrassed in any way, share those feelings too. Telling each other the truth can only make you more intimately connected. Share what you've learned about yourselves and from each other by doing the exercise.

✍ *Exercise 91.* **SHARING FANTASIES**

Sharing your sexual fantasies as you masturbate together can deepen your intimacy. Decide who will go first. The active partner describes a fantasy while one or both of you masturbate.

If you're hesitant to share a fantasy because it's too revealing for your comfort, then create one for the moment about something you'd like to do with your present partner or would like to have done to you by your partner. Be lavish with the details. Tell how the fantasy unfolds, how you feel, how your body responds. As you get more comfortable with this activity, you and your partner can share fantasies about other activities that you might consider to be forbidden.

When you hear your partner's fantasy, try not to feel threatened. Accept that you and your partner both have sexual desires that differ, and realize that your partner is trying to be accepting of your fantasies as well. Allow yourself to relax while you're listening and to appreciate the openness that your partner feels toward you to be sharing something so deeply personal.

✍ Exercise 92. SWITCHING FOCUS

This exercise can be lots of fun. It calls upon all of your powers of focus and your ability to connect harmoniously with your partner. It will help you fine-tune your sensate-focus abilities, so you can take in even more sensation, and it will increase your feelings of mutuality.

The exercise is an extension of the plateauing process I described in Chapter 4. There I showed you how to maintain yourself at certain levels of arousal by switching your focus from the way your hand felt on your genitals to the way your genitals felt being touched by your hand. I also showed you how to switch your focus from a part of your body that was being touched to a body part you were not currently touching. When you add a second person to the exercise, the possibilities become much more interesting.

For example, when you are having sexual intercourse, there is a lot more going on than just the sensations in your genitals. You could focus on your own genitals or on your partner's. You could focus on sensations in other parts of your body. There are also sights, sounds, and smells you could focus on. You are not limited to focusing just on your genitals. Remember the analogy about the symphony orchestra? An experienced musician can listen to an orchestra and pick out the sounds of the individual instruments. The more sexual experience you have, the finer the sensations you will be able to focus on. Let's start with the simplest version of this exercise first.

Begin the exercise with focusing caresses and then lie in a comfortable side-by-side position in which you can touch each other's genitals with one hand. Caress each other's genitals simultaneously throughout the rest of the exercise. When you begin this mutual caress, both of you should focus on how the penis feels. Then, after several minutes, both of you switch your focus to the woman's genitals. For the next switch, you both concentrate on the man's hand. Switch again and focus on the woman's hand. Remember to breathe and stay relaxed.

The exercise is not easy at first! It really takes intense concentration to be able to switch your focus to different aspects of your experience. The simplest way to do the exercise is to put one person in charge of deciding when to make the switch. That person should say, "Now we'll both focus on your penis" or, "Now we'll both focus on my hand."

After you have practiced switching your focus back and forth among single items, try focusing on more than one source of sensations at once. For example, practice focusing on both the woman's hand and the man's penis. Or practice focusing on both of your hands at the same time. Then try to focus on the combined sensations. Again, you may find the process easier if one partner takes charge of deciding what to focus on and for how long. You can take turns being the deciding partner if you like.

Switching focus is a skill that can definitely increase your feelings of mutuality, since you know that both you and your partner are concentrating on the same sensations at the same time. You can use switch-focus skills in any sexual activity—oral sex, intercourse, and especially mutual oral sex, the classic "69" position.

Once you know how to do the basic switch-focus technique, you can practice different versions of the exercise. Try one version in which one partner is active with oral sex. The active partner should practice switching back and forth between how the mouth feels and how the genitals feel in the mouth. This can literally double your enjoyment of oral sex. The passive partner can switch focus between his or her own genitals and how the partner's mouth feels on the genitals. Then trade roles, so you both get practice with all aspects of the exercise. In an exercise like this, it would probably be best for each partner to be in charge of when he or she switches focus, as each will be focusing on different things.

You can also practice switching focus during intercourse. Practice switching back and forth between focusing on the penis and focusing on the vagina. Try this with the woman on her back and the man kneeling between her legs. In this version of the exercise, one person can decide when you will both switch, because you will both focus on the same thing at the same time.

As I mentioned above, this exercise makes mutual oral sex even better. A lot of people enjoy mutual oral sex, but some find it frustrating. Sometimes, just as you get aroused from your partner's oral caresses, you all of a sudden lose your focus because you're caressing too—and then your arousal level decreases! Practicing the switch-focus techniques will help you control what you focus on and will help you stay with it long enough to remain aroused.

✐ *Exercise 93.* MUTUAL ORGASM

Timing your orgasm so that you both come at the same moment, while you gaze into each other's eyes, requires an openness and an ability to be at one with each other as you make love. Some people call mutual orgasm "simultaneous orgasm." I prefer the phrase *mutual orgasm* because to me the word *simultaneous* conveys only that two things occurred at the same time, not that they were connected. To me the phrase *mutual orgasm* conveys that the orgasms not only happened at the same time, but that the partners shared in the experience of the other's orgasm. Also, the term *simultaneous orgasm* got kind of a bad name several years ago because it was thought to convey pressure on the woman to somehow speed up her orgasmic response to match her partner's. This left many women feeling inadequate if they typically did not have an orgasm with intercourse as fast as their partner did.

When you practice these mutual-orgasm techniques, practice them with a sense of celebration of all that you've learned since you experienced your first sensate-focus session. This exercise takes you back to the basics: focusing, breathing, and relaxing. It allows you to combine things that you like about your previous style of lovemaking with the sensate-focus techniques you have learned in this book. Notice how sensate focus changes your lovemaking.

Start with some unstructured foreplay—anything you and your partner like to do to prepare for intercourse. Decide in advance on a position for intercourse and use any position where you and your lover are face-to-face.

The partner who is on top controls the speed of the thrusting and should start as slowly as possible. The other partner should follow at the same speed. Both should focus on the sensations arising out of the contact between the penis and the vagina. Breathe and relax.

Men, think of yourself as caressing the inside of your lover's vagina with your penis. Women, think of yourself as caressing your lover's penis with the walls of your vagina.

Look at each other as you move. Keep your muscles as relaxed as possible and remember to breathe. If you've done the many peaking exercises outlined earlier in the book, your awareness of your arousal levels is probably automatic. You probably also have a good idea of how aroused your partner is. The best cues for that are heart rate and breathing. See if you can both mutually plateau at level 8 and then 9.

When the person on top reaches the beginning of orgasm, the partner should thrust harder and follow. As you reach orgasm, take a deep breath, relax your body, open your eyes wide, and look deep into your partner's eyes.

Here's a hint for women for this exercise: Do this mutual-orgasm exercise in the butterfly position, in which you tilt your pelvis back. When your partner is about to ejaculate, just at the split second before his first PC muscle spasm, put both your hands flat on his lower back right above his buttocks and pull him farther into you. This will intensify his orgasm. (I don't know why this works, but it does.)

Mutual orgasm is an amazing feeling, and once you've had the experience together, you may think that this is as good as sex gets. Believe it or not, there are levels of sexual experience that go beyond even this. I call them healing and ecstasy, and I discuss them in the next chapter.

Drawing Close Through Better Communication

The next few exercises are a little different from most of the material in this book. They all involve learning to communicate better verbally with your partner during sex. Good communication is as essential to intimacy as trust. Until now, you have been developing your ability to communicate through touch. With few exceptions, the sensate-focus exercises I have had you do were nonverbal. There was a reason for this. I wanted you to feel as free from pressure as possible while you were learning the basics. Getting you to stop talking also encourages you to feel more.

When you progressed to the peaking and plateauing exercises, you and your partner shared some very specific information with each other about your arousal levels. My intention there was to lay down a foundation for helpful communication, so you could overcome any negative communication habits you may have had. Many people think that they are good at sexual communication, when in fact they come off to their partners as either whiny or demanding.

The way you communicate can even get in the way, as my client Jack discovered. "I never realized before how my wife and I would say things during sex, and the other person would take it the wrong way," he told me. "It seemed like if you said it during sex, even the most innocent comment would take on this huge meaning. These techniques showed me how to recognize what I was feeling and say it immediately. We are not reading as much negative stuff into simple comments anymore, so we have a lot more energy to devote to pleasure."

⟂ *Exercise 94.* GENITAL CARESS WITH VERBAL SHARING

Let's begin with a genital caress. In this version, after the touching stops, you give specific feedback about what you like. This will be much like any other nondemand genital caress, wherein one partner is active and the other is passive. As with any sensate-focus exercise, exchange focusing caresses before you begin the main exercise.

If you are the active partner, pleasure your partner with a front and genital caress for about fifteen minutes. You can use both your hand and mouth to do the genital caress. When you've finished, say so. If you are the passive partner, experience the sensations, without speaking, unless something is hurting or bothering you. When your partner has finished with the caress, you can ask for a repeat of something you liked.

You can ask your partner for a particular type of caress that he or she already did. For example, say, "I really liked when you licked just under the head of my penis. I'd like you to do that again" or, "I liked when you ran your finger slowly up my lips and over my clitoris. Please do that again."

Notice that each verbal communication includes something about what you like and a straightforward request to repeat it. This teaches you to use personal "I" statements when talking about sexual matters, and it teaches you to be clear and assertive about asking for what you want.

If you are the active partner and you are unclear about exactly what it is that your partner is asking for, ask, "Do you mean like this or like this?" If you're agreeable, spend a few minutes touching your partner in the specific way that he or she requested.

If you are the passive partner and your partner starts to repeat something that is not exactly what you asked for, communicate this. For example, say, "I want you to do it slower," or faster, or whatever. Don't settle for something that is not what you asked for.

Then continue the exercise by asking for something your partner hasn't done yet as part of the genital caress. Guide him or her until you receive the exact type of touch that you want.

Each of you should realize that you are always free to say no if you find the request unappealing or objectionable. You can discuss the reasons why later. Be aware that saying no does not mean "No, not now, not ever, never." It simply means "I don't feel like doing that right now."

As you can surmise, there are other ways to ask for sex that are less effective. For example, some people don't feel comfortable asserting themselves and so they hedge it by saying, "It would be nice if you touched my penis" or even, "You wouldn't want to touch my penis, would you?" That type of communication does not work. If you want to receive something from your partner, you need to ask for it in an assertive way: "I would like this" or, "I want you to do this." You also need to be very specific about the exact type of caress that you want. For example, say, "Please put your finger into my vagina slowly and move it slowly in and out" rather than, "Put your finger inside me."

Here are some pointers for the passive partner. There are a couple of pitfalls you can encounter when doing this exercise. One is to spend so much time worrying about what you are going to ask for that you don't enjoy the genital caress while it is happening. Trust me, you will remember something your partner did that you liked. Try to keep an open mind while receiving the caress and focus on your sensations the way you normally would during any caress. You will also be able to think of something your partner didn't do that you would like to try.

Also, when you are receiving the caress and you ask for something, take some time to allow yourself to enjoy it. Don't decide in two seconds, "Oh, I changed my mind—that is not really what I wanted." Give yourself a chance to enjoy it. On the other hand, you might make a snap decision to ask for some other kind of caress a few seconds after the first, and that's okay too. You are free to ask for whatever you want. Your partner won't think it's strange if you change your mind, plus your partner is free to refuse a request if he or she really has an objection to a particular practice.

Here are some pointers for the active partner. There are more and less effective ways to hear what your partner says to you. Let's say your partner asks you to repeat a particular type of touch by saying, "I liked it when you caressed my scrotum. Please do that again for a few minutes." The less effective way to interpret this would be, "Of all the things I did, that was the only thing he liked?" or, "Are you sure you want that? Why not something else?" If you can help it, try not to read too much into a simple request or second-guess your partner.

It also doesn't help if you wonder, "Why didn't I think of that?" Instead, realize that your partner is sharing with you by telling you about what he or she wants or likes at the moment.

One more caution—because you know your partner wants something and has asked for it, you may forget to do the caressing for your own pleasure and fall back into trying to please your partner. This is probably the toughest thing about adding verbal communication to the nonverbal exercises you have done before. You have to develop a mindset in which you can touch for your own pleasure, even though you know that your partner is enjoying it too. If you are able to strike this balance between pleasing yourself and being consciously aware that you are pleasing your partner, you have reached the state we call *mutuality*—a sense that you and your partner are sharing a deeply pleasurable experience and feeling the same things at the same time.

⟁ *Exercise 95.* OBSERVE, REFLECT, ASK

This is a basic communication exercise that can be adapted for use during sexual activity. It is especially helpful for individuals who have a difficult time saying anything during sex. Many people who are uncommunicative during sex are that way because they are shy or self-conscious, not because they are withdrawn or antisocial. If your partner often complains, "I never know what you like," then this is the exercise for you. You may even find it stimulating to learn to ask for what you want sexually.

Start with focusing caresses. Decide who will be the active partner first. If you are the active partner, pleasure your partner with a front caress, genital caress, and oral sex. Enjoy this sensual loving for about twenty minutes.

If you are the passive partner, in this exercise you won't wait until the end to say what you like and what you don't like. Instead, stop your partner at some point in the exercise when he or she is doing something you really like. First, think to yourself, "My partner is stroking my penis in a way I particularly like." This is the "observe" phase. Then repeat the same sentence to your partner using an "I" statement: "I like the way you are caressing my penis right now." This is the "reflect" phase. Then ask your partner to continue the caress: "Please caress my penis this way for a few more minutes." This is the "ask" phase. Repeat the process several times during a twenty-minute exercise and then switch roles if you want to.

✐ *Exercise 96.* ASK FOR WHAT YOU WANT

This exercise brings together all of the communication and mutuality skills you have learned in this chapter. It will give you practice at recognizing what you want, asking for it, enjoying it, and switching focus.

The exercise begins the minute you enter the room; you do not do focusing caresses to prepare for it. One person will be active for the first half hour, and the other person will be active for the second half hour.

The partner who is active first begins by asking for anything that he or she wants. Let's assume that the woman is active first. Nothing can happen until she requests it. If she wants her partner to remove his clothes, she must say, "Please take off your clothes."

When you are active, you need to tell your partner everything you want him or her to do. You may ask for anything you can think of that you would like your partner to do, but you need to be specific (as you learned to do in Exercise 94, when you first gave verbal feedback).

If what he does is not exactly what you want, give him further directions until he is doing exactly what you want. Feel free to enjoy, for as long as you want, whatever you have asked your partner to do.

When active, you may also do whatever you like, as long as you tell your partner what you are going to do. For example, if you would like to be the initiator for a while, you could say, "I want you to lie on your stomach so I can caress your back for a while."

When you are the passive partner, do as your partner asks, unless your partner asks you to do something unpleasant. If this is the case, say, "I don't want to do that right now." There is no need to get into a heavy discussion about why you may not feel like doing a particular activity; you can discuss it later. Your partner will move on and ask for something else.

When you are the passive partner, see if you can do what your partner asks you to. Just remember to approach it in a sensate-focus way so that you do it for your own pleasure. See if you can reach that state of mutuality in which you are doing a caress so that it feels good to you, but you are aware that your partner is enjoying it too.

When you are in the active role, try not to second-guess your partner. Ask for something you want, rather than what you think your partner wants to do.

A secret to success with this exercise is to take a minute to think about what you want, based on your feelings at that moment. Do you feel like doing something to your partner's body, or are you so stressed out that you want your partner to take care of you in some way? Do you feel like relaxing and doing sensual activities, or do you feel like you want something sexual right away?

Whether you are active or passive with this exercise, remember to focus on your feelings, breathe, and relax. When you are asked to touch your partner in a certain way, touch for your own pleasure and practice switching your focus back and forth between how your body feels when it is touching and how your partner's body feels as you touch it.

This is one of the most complicated exercises you can do, in the sense that if you are the passive partner, you practice focusing even though you don't know what your partner will ask for next. But it can be very rewarding.

Talking Dirty and Talking Sexy

Many people find talking during sex to be very erotic and pleasurable, but it's an individual thing. Some people get turned on by the use of what we would consider to be four-letter words. Other people are repulsed by the use of four-letter words during sex. Still others like to have romantic phrases whispered to them during sex. All of us have certain words or phrases that turn us on for inexplicable reasons. (Mine happen to be "Dom Perignon" and "American Express," but there's no accounting for taste.)

Whether your thing is "I love you, sweetheart" or "You dirty, little whore" or anything in between, most of us appreciate a little aural sex. Rule of thumb: When you hear about a particular sexual practice at a moment when you're not aroused, the idea of it might seem negative or even repellent. However, if you were really sexually turned on, the same practice might sound like a huge turn-on. Here's an example: If you weren't turned on and your partner said to you, "I'd like to come all over your tits," you would probably say, "Ew, gross!" But if you were at a level-9 arousal and your partner said the same thing, you might say, "Go for it!" I'll give you an anecdote that illustrates my point.

I was recently driving to work and listening to Howard Stern. I had had some really great sex the night before, and I was still kind of aroused. A woman called in and said that she'd never had an orgasm. Howard instructed her to lie down in bed naked and touch herself. He told the woman that he would talk her through an orgasm. He dropped his voice down really low and started saying things to her like "Call me your master, you dirty, little whore." I started feeling really funny while I was listening, and I asked myself why, and I realized to my eternal shame that I was actually getting aroused by his voice. I don't think under most circumstances I would like someone calling me a whore, but for some reason, because I was already aroused, I found his voice to be a turn-on.

I'm not going to provide specific exercises in this chapter to teach you how to talk sexy. I've already written a book on that topic. It's called *Talk Sexy to the One You Love (and Drive Each Other Wild in Bed)*. Instead, I'll summarize some of the ideas from that book for the shy or tongue-tied.

If there are certain sexual words or phrases you would like to say but are too embarrassed, practice saying these words or phrases out loud in front of a mirror until you can say them with a straight face. Or masturbate and practice saying the words or phrases when you get to high levels of arousal. Or, make a tape of yourself saying these words or phrases when you are at high levels of arousal and notice how much it turns you on to listen to the recording. Or practice writing the words or phrases.

Don't walk your partner to bed; instead, talk your partner to bed. If your partner says, "Let's have sex" or, "Let's make love," reply, "Talk me into it. Tell me exactly what it is that you are going to do to me." Then listen while your partner does just that.

Give yourself permission. It's okay to talk sexy or even use four-letter words if it turns you on. And it's okay to get turned on by sexy or even sleazy language. You're an adult. Don't apologize for liking to hear adult language.

Make lists of things you would like to hear your partner say to you or that you would like to say to your partner. Share the list with your partner.

Go to a movie with a romantic or sexy theme. When one of the characters says something you find sexy, whisper to your partner, "I think it's really sexy that he said that" or, "If you said something like that to me, it would really excite me."

Keep a sense of humor about it. Mild sexual humor can not only turn you on, it can also defuse potential arguments or negative interactions.

Read erotica that you find sexy. Read enough of it, whether it's bodice rippers or *Lady Chatterley's Lover,* and you'll get so used to sexy language that the phrases will pop right out of your mouth before you realize it.

Make up names for your private parts. Don't be too serious about it. I had one boyfriend who referred to my vagina as "the Holy City" and another who called it the "Bermuda Triangle." (Guess which one was better at oral sex?) Make lists of all of the slang terms you can think of for genitals and practice using them. If you need some help getting started, Yvonne Fulbright's *The Hot Guide to Safer Sex* and my book *Talk Sexy to the One You Love (and Drive Each Other Wild in Bed)* contain lists of words to get the wheels in your brain turning.

Have phone sex (not on company time). Describe to your partner what you're doing to yourself.

If you are embarrassed to say certain words or phrases, wait until you're having intercourse and then whisper them into your partner's ear, especially when one or both of you is about to come. Watch your voice tone. Our voices naturally get lower when we're turned on. When you say sexy things to your partner, pitch your voice a little lower.

If you really can't think of anything to say, here are a few tried-and-true phrases:

"I can't believe how beautiful you are."

"I can't wait to feel you inside me."

"You are the most beautiful woman I've ever held in my arms."

"I can't believe how good I feel with your arms around me."

"I love the way your penis feels inside me."

"I love the way my penis feels inside you."

"I can't believe how hard you are."

"I can't believe how wet you are."

If you're really tongue-tied, don't forget the basics you have already learned in this chapter: Observe, reflect, and ask for what you want.

Vulnerability Explorations

The next few exercises may seem a little extreme. What they all have in common is that they involve the risk that you will become more vulnerable in your relationship with your partner. Only do these exercises if you are willing to take that risk and you know that your relationship is intimate enough that you both can handle the added vulnerability. The potential payoff is the experience of even deeper levels of intimacy.

᠀ Exercise 97. TOWEL OVER THE FACE

This exercise may sound very unintimate at first, but it can truly build trust and banish performance pressure for both of you. Bobbie's experience was typical. "The first time I tried this exercise, it really freaked me out," she said. "I had so much going on mentally that I wasn't even aware of what my partner was doing. But then I let myself relax. It was great to have no responsibility."

In this exercise, you place a light towel or piece of clothing over your lover's face. Then you pretend that your lover's body is a toy, and you play with it for twenty minutes to an hour. You can use any part of your partner's body to give you pleasure. Your partner will also take a turn doing the same.

For this exercise, I recommend that the woman go (be the active partner) first so that she is lubricated and ready when her partner takes his turn. It's also a good idea to have lubrication on hand in case you need it.

Here are some pointers for women: When you're the active partner, slowly rub yourself all over your partner's body. Lick his body. Masturbate with his penis. If he has an erection, climb on top of his penis and slowly thrust in and out. Masturbate by rubbing your clitoris on your partner's knees or hips. Thrill yourself and moan appreciatively. Remind yourself that sex is an animal activity. Feel free to grunt, groan, bare your teeth, lightly nibble on your partner, or growl.

Here are some pointers for men: When you are active, pretend that your partner is a doll that you can play with for the next few minutes. Have you ever had a fantasy about having sex with a sleeping woman? Now is the time to indulge that fantasy. Rub yourself against her, rub your penis all over her, insert your penis into her vagina. She will try her best to remain passive.

When you are passive, adjust the towel on your face so that you can breathe but can't see. Try not to move or respond in any way, unless your partner is doing something that hurts or bothers you. If so, tell him or her.

It will be a little scary not to know what your lover is going to do next. You may feel yourself tense up, but remind yourself to relax. Explore what it feels like to have no responsibility for what happens and what it feels like to be in your partner's fantasy. It's your lover's responsibility to make sure he or she has fun, not yours. If you have an erection, an orgasm, or an ejaculation, just take a deep breath and enjoy yourself.

This exercise will help you trust that your partner is not going to do anything to hurt you. If you've done this exercise and found that it increased your mutual trust, you may be ready for the next exercise, which will really help you explore the limits of your trust with your partner.

ℰ *Exercise 98.* BONDAGE

In this exercise, you'll let your partner gently tie up some part of your body or restrain you. Velcro or fur-lined restraints are available at adult stores or through catalogs. You can also use stockings or scarves or other items you have around the house. Other than that, do this exercise just as you did the last one. Allow each partner a twenty- or thirty-minute turn.

When you are active, tie up your partner. Then use your partner's body to pleasure yourself. When you are passive, tell your partner if he or she is doing anything that hurts or bothers you. If not, stay passive. As the passive partner, remember to remain aware that you have no responsibility at all in this situation. Relax as much as you can and focus on your sensations.

Many people are aroused by being tied up because it feels kinky and a little bit dangerous. You and your partner will become much more intimate doing this together, and you will learn that you can really trust one another. "I was a little hesitant to try this, but I was curious too," said my client Susan. "As I started to trust my partner, I could feel myself relax and stop fighting the feelings. The big difference between doing the exercise this way and doing it as part of S and M is that the turn-on in S and M is the fear in the tied-up partner as he or she fights against the bonds. That's not what happens here."

ℰ *Exercise 99.* STREAM OF CONSCIOUSNESS, SOLO

What does a literary technique have to do with your sex life? You can use a stream-of-consciousness or free-association technique to help you loosen up your way of communicating with your partner sexually.

Some people feel inhibited about communicating during sex. They censor their thoughts so much that they are no longer capable of purely spontaneous communication. This exercise can help you feel comfortable with free and spontaneous sexual communication.

Do a genital caress by yourself. As you caress yourself, say whatever comes to your mind. Say it out loud, without censoring anything. Because this is uncensored, there is no way to predict what you will say. Your stream could consist of random thoughts, grunts, moans, descriptions of what you are feeling or what is happening, or descriptions of fantasies. You may latch onto one thought and stick with it, or jump from one meaningless phrase to another.

The first time you do this exercise, you will be very self-conscious. If you spend fifteen minutes at it, you may be lucky to produce twenty seconds of truly uncensored speech. Try to keep talking constantly throughout the exercise, even if what you say sounds silly or doesn't make sense. That's the whole point. If you are having difficulty, you can always fall back on describing what you are doing or what you are feeling. This is a way of communicating that is most likely to be uncensored. If you do this exercise by yourself a few times, it can loosen you up so that it will be easier to engage in spontaneous communication when you are with your lover.

✑ Exercise 100. STREAM OF CONSCIOUSNESS, TOGETHER

Now I'd like you to use the stream-of-consciousness technique to develop trust between you and your lover. Lie on your back and have your partner caress your genitals. As your partner caresses you, say whatever comes to your mind without censoring or editing. Just the experience of receiving a genital caress should help bring spontaneous sexual thoughts to the surface. This is unconscious material and may include emotional, nonverbal communication such as moaning or crying.

If you are caressing your partner during this exercise, concentrate on caressing in the way that feels best to you. Don't even pay attention to what your partner is saying. If the verbal stream stops, just gently remind your partner to keep talking. The caressing partner could even wear earphones at first to make the verbal partner less self-conscious. This exercise can help you share an intimate, emotional experience with your partner as you bring up a lot of unconscious material.

When you've finished, find a mutually agreeable way to bring the exercise to a close. You may need to talk with each other about what came up, or you may feel so sexually charged that you choose to make love. If you need comforting after this exercise, use one of the bonding positions described earlier in the chapter. Do whatever feels natural.

Anal Sex

I've taught different versions of human-sexuality classes at the university level for well over ten years. The class I currently teach is a junior-level survey class that covers all aspects of sexual attitudes and behaviors. When I first began teaching human sexuality, many textbooks did not even include sections on anal sex. Anal-sex practices were somewhat stigmatized in the minds of most people due to the association they have with antisodomy laws or prison populations. But recent research shows that between 20 and 40 percent of heterosexual couples have experimented with some form of anal sexual contact and that anal sex is one of the fastest-growing mainstream sources of sexual pleasure.

The anus is a source of eroticism for many people. There are both physical and psychological reasons for this. From a physical standpoint, the anus is located near the genitals and receives some secondary stimulation during many forms of sex play. During orgasm, the anal sphincters contract along with all of the other pelvic muscles, creating pleasurable sensations. The anus is also an erogenous zone in itself, because it contains many sensitive nerve endings.

Anal sex can include masturbating while touching your own anus, fingering your partner's anus, licking the anus (anilingus), or inserting a finger or the penis into the anus. For many people, the thought of any kind of anal contact is very negative. Others are curious about it and would like to try it. I include only one introductory anal-sex exercise in this book, but if you and your partner are both curious and receptive to the idea, you could design your own anal-sex exercises using sensate-focus techniques.

The best resource I can recommend on anal sex is *Anal Pleasure and Health,* by Jack Morin, Ph.D. The book is in its third edition. This is not a sleazy book; it is very mainstream and responsible, and it is sold in most bookstores and by most online book retailers.

Dr. Morin makes a few suggestions I will pass on to you. The anus has a different muscle structure than the vagina. The vaginal opening is surrounded by the PC muscle, which is not a true sphincter muscle and usually opens very easily. In contrast, the anus has not only one but two sphincter muscles—one internal and one external. This means that if you are going to insert anything into the anus, you need to thoroughly massage those muscles and make sure they are completely relaxed before any insertion takes place. You will also need to use a lot of lubrication—much more than you would use for vaginal intercourse.

If you believe that anal-sex practices would be pleasurable for you, Dr. Morin recommends that you explore your anal area yourself with your hand before you allow your partner to stimulate it. This will allow you to find out what kind of touch it takes for you to relax. If you are the receptive partner in anal intercourse, take an enema before you begin. Always use a condom for anal intercourse even if you are in a monogamous relationship, because the anus and rectum contain E. coli bacteria that should never be transferred to the vagina. If you engage in oral-anal contact, make sure your partner is free of hepatitis. Finally, and most important, never do anything that causes you pain. If anal sex hurts, you're not relaxed enough.

I interviewed Jack Morin when I hosted a radio show on sexuality at a university station several years ago. I asked him the question, "Given that vaginal intercourse is such a no-brainer, why would anyone go to the trouble to have anal sex?" (The trouble being extra time to relax, extra lubrication, extra care.)

In his reply he mentioned that although many people see anal sex as erotic, there are also other physical and psychological motivations for having anal sex. Some people have anal sex because they are afraid of getting pregnant. Anal sex feels different than vaginal sex because the anal sphincters are tighter than the PC muscle. We were all taught as children that the anal area is kind of a forbidden area for us to look at or touch, and that "taboo" adds an extra aura of excitement for some people. Finally, many people are turned on by the idea of anal sex because they see it as the ultimate dominant-submissive sex act.

Some anal-sex practices involve toys. A warning is in order here: Don't use a vibrator or dildo intended for the vagina in the anus. The vaginal canal has an end to it. The anus and rectum do not. People have lost sex toys in their partner's rectum, resulting in a trip to the emergency room. There are special dildos—called "butt plugs"—made for anal contact. They have a base or handle on them so they can't get lost in the rectum.

Other people like to use anal beads. These are beads about three-quarters of an inch in diameter that are strung about two inches apart on a string. You push each bead into the anus (using lubrication, of course) and then slowly pull out the string. You can accomplish the same thing with a silk scarf. Take a long scarf and smear it with lubricant. Bunch it up and gently stuff it inch by inch into your partner's anus. Then slowly pull out the scarf, inch by inch. The beads or the scarf can be used either during intercourse or on their own.

Exercise 101. **INTRODUCTION TO ANAL PLEASURE**

Here's a nonthreatening exercise that can be used as an introduction to anal play. The woman should lie flat on her stomach. The man should take some massage oil or body oil and massage her buttocks. Then he should pour a lot of the oil into the crack of her buttocks. From here, there are two ways to proceed. The male partner could give the female partner a caress in the crack of her buttocks with his hand, lightly stroking the area around the sides of the anus but not penetrating it with his fingers. Or, he could run his penis up and down the crack of her buttocks, again gently stimulating the area around the opening of her anus but not penetrating it. Then he could slide down and begin to caress her vaginal opening with his penis. Alternate slipping your penis inside the vagina for a few strokes, and taking your penis out and rubbing it along the crack of your partner's buttocks. This exercise is a way to experience anal eroticism without actual penetration.

Of course, you could do the exercise in reverse too. The man could lie flat on his stomach, and the woman could massage his buttocks, pour oil in the crack, and stimulate the area around his anus with her fingers.

Remembering to Play

If some of the above exercises sound a little heavy for you, relief is on the way. See if the following suggestions don't bring a sense of youthful exuberance to your physical relationship.

Most of the sensate-focus exercises you have done so far have been fairly structured. It's a good idea to let loose every once in a while and just play. In that spirit, I'd like to offer you some playful sensual activities you can enjoy together. Allow them to inspire you to create your own ways to play together. The spontaneity of play makes sex all the more fresh.

Exercise 102. **THE FOOT CARESS**

The foot caress includes a foot bath, and it is very relaxing. Since it only involves the ankles and feet, you can even do it clothed, if you like. I usually bathe each foot for about five minutes and caress each foot with lotion for about five minutes. This exercise can stimulate sexual desire because it is so relaxing. Use it if your partner has had a bad day and needs some deep relaxation to feel ready for sex. Before you begin, gather two towels, a basin large enough for a person's feet, liquid soap, lotion, hot water, and a comfortable chair for the person whose feet are being washed.

When you are the active partner, fill the basin with warm water and place your partner's feet in the water. Add the liquid soap and slowly caress your partner's feet in the water. Caress as you would for any other sensate-focus exercise, touching for your own pleasure. Don't massage the feet, but rather keep the touch slow and light. Bathe one foot at a time.

When you are done bathing both feet, lift one foot at a time, dry the feet, and wrap them in separate towels. Then take each foot from its towel in turn and caress it, using lotion.

When you are the passive partner, the only thing you need to do is relax and enjoy. Allow yourself to feel pampered. Relax your feet and legs. You don't even have to lift your feet to put them in the basin—your partner will do it.

Exercise 103. THE SENSUOUS SHOWER

The sensuous shower is a whole-body caress that takes place in the shower. The purpose is not to soap up and get clean, but to enjoy your body and your lover's body along with the added sensation of water.

There are a number of ways to do this. Just taking a shower together is a good bonding exercise for some couples. You can also practice any of the sensate-focus exercises, with each of you taking a turn being the active partner. Or simply make the caress mutual. Use liquid soap and caress any part of your partner's body that feels good. Remember to caress for your own pleasure when you are the active partner.

If you become aroused during the sensuous shower, just enjoy the feelings of your partner caressing you and the water beating down on your skin. If you have an erection, an orgasm, or an ejaculation, just enjoy it. Some people like to have intercourse while standing up in the shower. Be careful, though, because some kinds of soap can irritate the penis and the vagina.

Exercise 104. THE TOM JONES DINNER

Sensuality includes all five senses, not just touch. In the Tom Jones dinner, named for the sensuous eating scene from the movie *Tom Jones,* you prepare several foods that can be eaten with your hands. There are three rules: no feeding yourself, no talking, and no utensils. This exercise will help you get into the purely sensuous aspects of eating, free from the restraints of table manners.

First, choose appropriate foods. Some suggestions include fruit (especially juicy ones such as oranges and peaches), hors d'oeuvres such as cheese and crackers, any meat that can be pulled off a bone, and anything messy that can be licked off fingers or elsewhere. Things that are creamy or juicy feel especially good in your mouth. For beverages, use wine or champagne if you drink alcohol, or sparkling water or fruit juice if you don't.

Arrange the food on an old sheet to protect your carpeting and furniture. Take off your clothes. Relax, caress each other if you need a transition, then start feeding each other. Eat with the goal of feeling every sensation as the food passes through your lips and moves in your mouth.

Watch your partner eat. Put food on your partner's body and slowly lick it off. If you want a drink, your partner can take the drink and transfer it to your mouth while you're kissing.

For fun, arrange the food into the shapes of genitals, breasts, and buttocks, and watch your partner lick and eat them. Feel free to belch and make lip-smacking noises and all of those other things you're not supposed to do in polite society. If you spill some food on yourself, don't worry about it. You can lick it off, or better yet, your partner can lick it off. Finish the Tom Jones dinner by washing each other off with warm, wet towels or by taking a sensuous shower.

✐ *Exercise 105.* **EXCITING THE FIVE SENSES**

This exercise allows you to combine a sensate-focus caress with other sensual pleasures that you know your partner likes. It requires a little forethought. You'll need to gather together just the right combination of elements to engage all five of your partner's senses. Each of you can take turns being the bearer of delights.

Here are some ideas: When it's your turn to prepare the room, you might choose to light a jasmine-scented candle to appeal to your lover's sense of smell, wear something sexy that's pleasing to the eyes, and play some soulful music on the stereo. Then you might uncork your lover's favorite wine to stimulate the taste buds, and use your fingertips or palms to caress his or her skin.

When it's your turn to be passive, allow yourself to focus on each of the different senses. One stimulus for each sense is plenty. If there are too many things going on in the room, it can be distracting.

✐ *Exercise 106.* BODY DECORATION

Body paints can give you hours of fun. Some are even edible. You can buy them at an adult store or through a catalog. Temporary tattoos are also good for this purpose.

Try this exercise in the bathtub or shower, or in some private area outside. If you decide to paint each other indoors, protect your furniture and carpets with plastic.

Be outlandish with your designs. The more primitive, the better. Use the activity as a gateway into the more animal, primal aspect of sexuality. Moan, growl, and lightly chew on your partner. Make love while still decorated. If the paints are edible, you can lick them off each other. Try playing some tribal music to help you get into the spirit.

More about Play

Some of the best mutual experiences that bring people closer together are unstructured. They're spontaneous or "just happen." Most of the best mutual experiences involve some degree of innocence or childlike fun. It's hard to plan that kind of thing. It's more of a mindset than it is any particular activity. The mindset I'm talking about involves deciding, as a way of life, to seek out and enjoy the basic pleasures of life, which haven't really changed much since Homer's day. They include sex, eating, drinking, dancing, watching the sunset, reading, playing music, creating something, swimming, and enjoying nature. (And did I mention sex? Oh, yeah—first.)

I don't have to be encouraged to play, because I'm the world's biggest kid. In my household (which consists only of adults), we have soap bubbles, pool toys, hula hoops, frisbees, and paddle balls, among other toys. What do these toys have to do with your sex life? To quote Jimmy Buffett, "Therapy is extremely expensive; popping bubble wrap is radically cheap." Getting silly with each other can help your sex life because it helps you recapture those years of childlike innocence before you had adult responsibilities. (Plus, all of the toys I mentioned above can be used while naked.)

I've been fortunate enough to have been sexually involved with many men who made me laugh. My ex-husband (who was an engineer, not exactly known for being a lighthearted profession) used to do things like spell out my name in pancake batter and draw faces on inside-out grapefruit rinds to make me laugh. I had another boyfriend who would wear my clothes to make me laugh. He'd put on my leopard-print bathrobe and high-heeled bedroom slippers to go across the hall to the bathroom. I'd wear his boxer shorts to do the same. Another friend of mine (also an engineer) built a tree house for himself in his front yard when he was sixty-five. He and his wife go up there to have a couple of drinks, watch the sunset, and get away from it all.

Here are some of the things you and your partner can do together to increase your chances of becoming closer. Figure out how to have a "peak experience." A peak experience is one of those times when you are just awestruck by something and, as a result, feel a sense of connectedness with something greater than yourself. Peak experiences happen to individuals, but if two people who are intimately connected experience something awesome at the same time and share the experience, it's even better.

You can't really plan peak experiences because you don't know how you're going to feel at any given moment, but you can set the stage for them by traveling to unusual locales or by performing unusual or challenging activities. The elements of risk and novelty (which we talked about in Chapter 5 on sexual desire) will enhance your chances of sharing a peak experience with your partner.

I mentioned travel for a reason. One of the recommendations made by sex therapists so often that it has become a cliché is this: "If your sex life has become boring, or if you've lost your desire for each other, take a weekend off, leave the kids with the babysitter, go to a hotel, and do nothing but have sex all weekend." It may be a cliché, but it's not bad advice. (In fact, it's sounding pretty good to me right this minute.) The hotel doesn't have to be the Ritz-Carlton. It could be Motel 6—just as long as it's a change of scenery. The important thing is that you are taking a temporary break from your life, which is just the thing to get your sex life jump-started. (This is an especially good idea if you're like me and you have a cheap-motel fetish. The minute I walk into a cheap motel room with a man, I get horny.)

Leave reality behind. Pretend to be whoever you want to be, if that's what excites you sexually. A lot of couples wear costumes and role-play. I always find Halloween to be a particularly sexy holiday, because wearing a costume disinhibits you and you become less self-conscious. An older friend of mine said to me recently, "If I had a lot of money, I would wear a tuxedo to dinner every night and sit at a long table with candles all over it." I asked him, "Why don't you just do it? It wouldn't take a lot of money! I mean, a tuxedo and a few candles, what's that going to cost? Plus, you'd save on your electricity bill!"

Enjoy nature. Whether your thing is the beach, the desert, the forest, the mountains, or whatever, there's something about being together in nature that's profoundly rewarding. This is especially true of being with your lover in or near water, whether it's a lake, waterfall, river, or the ocean. My best times on vacations are always when I'm sitting on some water-front, eating and maybe drinking some champagne. Swimming in the ocean always makes me feel sexy.

Finally, get away from it all—together. Remember when you were a kid and you and maybe a friend built a secret hiding place? Maybe you made it in the garage by hanging old sheets from the rafters, or maybe you cleared out an area under the front porch, or maybe you set up a tent or tepee in your backyard and slept out there in the summer. That's the idea, but now you should do this on an adult scale. Build a private retreat for the two of you. It could be a tree house like my friend built. If you're pressed for space, it could be a small balcony, patio, or hot tub area. The only requirement is that it be private. It could be a covered open-air meditation room decorated with statues and wall hangings. It could be a private patio where you hang tapestries and lie around on cushions, eating and having sex and just generally pretending that you're king and queen for a day. It could be a luxury bathroom for two. It could be a massage room with a sauna and spa equipment. (Take advantage of that "woman having sex with her masseur" fantasy.) The only limit is your imagination.

chapter 15

Beyond Sensate Focus: Love, Healing, and Ecstasy

by Charlotte Morrison

This is a book about how to fall in love—together—with the pleasures of the body. But what about the feeling of loving your partner or being in love with your partner? Where do these fit in?

It's clear that you can have great sex with someone without being in love, and you could love someone and never have sex with him or her. But it's also clear that love and sex are tied up with each other. When you ask most people what it means to be in love or to love their partner, you will find that a huge component of a couple's definition of their love relationship has to do with sexual desire. Most people feel that a relationship is not a love relationship unless it includes an element of desiring to have sex with the other person.

James Giles made this point in a 1995 article titled "A Theory of Love and Sexual Desire" that appeared in *The Journal for the Theory of Social Behaviour*. Giles believes that the experience of being in love involves a longing for both a psychological and a sexual union with the other. He also says that being in love involves the desire to be physically in the presence of the other and to care for and physically caress the other. For Giles, the most important aspect of both love and sexual desire is the element of vulnerability—the desire to be emotionally vulnerable by baring our souls and the desire to be physically vulnerable by baring our bodies.

It's clear that you can have great, pleasurable sex without emotional vulnerability, but I believe sex is better when you're in love with your partner. That's why in this chapter I present several of the most influential psychological theories of love. After I've explained each theory, I'll offer some conclusions about how to use the information from the theories to make sex more pleasurable.

There are five major psychological theories of love. They are Sternberg's Triangular Theory, John Lee's Lovestyles approach, attachment theory, misattribution theory, and, for lack of a better name, what I'll call hormone theory. All of these theories have a main idea. Translate them to your own relationship. Get some insights. Becoming familiar with these theories can be an eye-opener, because you will find out if you and your partner view love in the same way.

Sternberg's Triangular Theory

Robert Sternberg of Yale University believes that love has three components: passion, intimacy, and commitment. The main idea of this theory is that you could have a love relationship that includes only one of these components or two of the three, but if your relationship includes all three components, you have what Sternberg calls "consummate love," in other words, the best of all possible worlds.

Passion is the component of love that includes sexual desire or romantic or erotic love. Some people might call it *chemistry*. If your relationship has passion but no intimacy or commitment, you would have what Sternberg calls *infatuation*.

Intimacy is the component of love that includes respect, similarity, closeness, and mutual sharing of emotions. If your relationship has intimacy but no passion or commitment, it would probably be characterized as liking or friendship.

In Sternberg's scheme, commitment can mean a couple of different things. I believe that Sternberg use the word *commitment* to mean the desire to stay in the relationship. But I also see commitment as keeping promises to your partner, no matter how large or small the promises are. If you have commitment in your relationship but no passion or intimacy, you probably have what Sternberg calls "empty love." This would be comparable to an arranged-marriage situation in which the participants initially don't even know each other.

If the love in your relationship has passion and intimacy but no commitment, it is characteristic of an intense but temporary romantic relationship that doesn't really have any staying power. If you have passion and commitment but no intimacy, your relationship is characteristic of couples who wed on the spur of the moment without really knowing each other. Sternberg calls this "fatuous love." If your relationship has intimacy and commitment but no passion, it is characteristic of many love relationships after the sexual spark has gone out. This is what Sternberg calls "companionate love," and it characterizes the relationships of a lot of couples who have been together for many years.

If you are reading this book because the passion has kind of gone out of your relationship, you may be slipping into the stage of companionate love. This doesn't have to happen. Please use the exercises in this book to rekindle the spark of passion so you can get back to that feeling of "as good as it gets."

Lovestyles

The main idea of this theory of love, which comes from sociologist John Alan Lee, is that different people mean different things when they talk about love. When I say "I love you" to my partner, I may mean something totally different than my partner means when he says "I love you" to me.

In Lee's typology, there are six lovestyles. They are called eros, storge, ludus, pragma, mania, and agape. People have a primary lovestyle and maybe one or two secondary ones that characterize their love relationships.

Eros is romantic love or sexual desire. It corresponds to Sternberg's passion component. Eros-style lovers do not believe they are in love unless they have these tumultuous, earth-shattering feelings.

Storge is friendship love. It corresponds to Sternberg's intimacy component. Some people do not believe they have true love unless they and their partner are best friends as well as sexual partners.

Ludus is game-playing love. The person whose primary lovestyle is ludus constantly tests the partner's affection, plays hard to get, flirts with other people, and generally tries to keep the partner on his or her toes.

Pragma is practical love, often called "shopping list" love. Pragmatic lovers make lists of qualities they look for in a partner, and when they find a person with all of those qualities, they decide, "This is it. This is the person I'm in love with." The pragmatic lover would seem to be the person who might be most comfortable meeting someone through singles clubs or personal ads or on the Internet.

Mania is an obsessive form of love in which the person is totally absorbed with thoughts of the partner, often calling him or her several times a day and requiring constant reassurances of fidelity. Manic love can degenerate into stalking or other inappropriate behavior.

Finally, *agape* is the form of love that is selfless and self-sacrificing. The word *agape* is usually used in the spiritual or religious sense. Often it refers to the unconditional love that a parent has for a child. Interestingly, in surveys about love, agape does not seem to be an overwhelming part of what most people say they get out of their love relationship with a sexual partner.

The problem, from the lovestyles perspective, develops when two partners differ widely in their definition of what love is. For example, if one partner is an eros-type lover and the other is a pragma-type lover, they are bound to differ on what kinds of behaviors and activities define their love. One of them will want romantic gestures, and the other will want practical demonstrations of everyday caring.

If you believe that you and your partner have disparate views of love, start a discussion on the topic. The first step toward rekindling your passionate relationship will be to understand that things your partner sees as demonstrating love may not seem to do so to you, and vice versa. Make lists of the different things you and your partner do to show your love to each other so you can figure out what your lovestyles are and hopefully help them mesh.

Attachment

Attachment is a technical term for the emotional bond that forms between a newborn and the primary caregiver, who is often the mother. The mother forms the attachment bond with the infant by hugging, holding, eye gazing, cooing, and general non-goal-oriented playing with the child. The main idea of attachment theory is that the nature of your emotional bond in childhood with your primary caregiver will be reflected in your adult intimate relationships.

A child whose bond with the primary caregiver is secure is the child who has the right balance between adventurousness and dependence. This is the person who will probably grow up to be comfortable and confident in intimate adult relationships.

Some children grow up with caregivers who do not foster an intimate bond with them. These children form what's called an *avoidant attachment*. They grow up to be extremely independent and are somewhat uncomfortable in adult intimate relationships. They are the people we describe as having a "fear of commitment." It's not that they're bad people; it's just that their childhood did not adequately prepare them to be close to another person.

Other children grow up with caregivers who are alternately rejecting and clinging—in other words, they are unpredictable. The child may act in a certain way and get punished, and may later act in the same way again and be ignored. This child forms what is called an *anxious attachment*. Unfortunately, children who grow up with this kind of upbringing in turn learn to be alternately clinging and/or rejecting. This is the type of person who will say to a partner (and mean it), "I hate you—don't leave me. I don't know what I'd do without you."

To help with your sex life, analyze your own upbringing and that of your partner for potential problems with attachment. They can be overcome. I've known people from the worst family backgrounds who were bound and determined to have a good relationship in adulthood and not force their kids to go through what they went through. This can be done, but it takes a serious commitment.

Reinforcement and Misattribution

Reinforcement is a very simple idea when it comes to relationships. We like people who provide rewards for us. The rewards could be tangible, like gifts, or intangible, like affection or the pleasure of one's company. When applied to love, the idea is that if we like people who provide some rewards for us, we will love people who provide a lot of rewards for us.

Misattribution theory is an attempt to explain love using more-or-less the opposite of reinforcement theory. Misattribution theory is based on the two-component emotion theory formulated by two psychologists, Stanley Schachter and Jerome Singer. According to Schachter and Singer, emotions have two parts: a feeling of physiological arousal and the cognitive label we give that arousal. Think back to Chapter 1 when I described the activity of the sympathetic nervous system. When your sympathetic nervous system is aroused, your heart beats faster and blood instantaneously flows to your limbs so that you can fight or run away.

Let's say you were crossing a street and a car almost ran over you. You would react before you even had a chance to think about it, and then you would probably think to yourself, "Wow! I was really scared there!" After the fact, you correctly labeled the emotion you felt as fear.

Schachter and Singer's point is that many emotional states, such as fear, happiness, anxiety, anticipation, and sexual desire, involve the same kind of physiological arousal, mostly characterized by a rapid heart rate. Usually it is very clear to us what is causing our emotional state. We see the car that almost ran over us, and we correctly label the emotion as fear, or we see a test in front of us that we haven't studied for, and we correctly label our emotion as anxiety.

But sometimes we feel physiological arousal and we don't have a clear or complete explanation for it. When this happens, we're likely to look to the current context or situation to give us some clues as to what we're feeling. If we feel unexplained arousal and look around and see a person who could be an appropriate love object, we may attribute at least part of our arousal to love or sexual desire for that person. (*Attribution* is a technical term that refers to our interpretation of the causes of our own and other people's behavior.) Misattribution means that we have incorrectly attributed our arousal to love for this other person.

This might sound like kind of a stretch—the idea that we could fall in love with someone because we are excited and don't know why. But misattribution does occur, and it probably explains why people fall in love under unusual circumstances. People who survive disasters together often fall in love with each other. Patients who have been diagnosed with serious illnesses often fall in love with their doctors. You would think that people in these situations would be very clear about what is causing their emotional state, but that's the point—they are clear, but they have so much physiological arousal that some of it spills over onto the perceived love object.

Why are horror movies and amusement parks such popular venues for dating? Because we will attribute at least part of our arousal to the presence of the other person. Think of the typical places where couples are likely to meet: dance clubs or bars. These venues usually involve loud, fast music and the use of alcohol or other drugs that can create a buzz. In this type of situation, people are more likely to be attracted to each other and fall in love.

Misattribution theory is the opposite of reinforcement theory in the sense that reinforcement theory would predict that adversity would drive a couple apart, because if a relationship becomes punishing instead of rewarding, theoretically we should leave the relationship. But misattribution theory would predict that certain types of adversity (for example, serious illnesses or problems with children) should bring couples closer together, and this is clearly the case.

My point here is that you should analyze your relationship and think back to how and when you fell in love with your partner. If the situation involved misattribution, your relationship may be vulnerable to a downturn when that state of high physiological arousal is no longer there. Some of the things that you can do to get back that feeling are the play activities I suggested in the previous chapter. Doing something physically exciting together or sharing an intense emotional experience together will help bring back some of that spark.

A Hormonal Theory of Love

The hormone testosterone is responsible for sex drive. The brain chemical dopamine (discussed in Chapter 5) and the hormone adrenalin (also called *epinephrine*) are responsible for sexual desire and attraction. These chemicals often influence our sex drive to focus on a particular person.

Dopamine has the following effects: It causes you to pay attention to the positive qualities of your partner and to remember trivial specifics about your partner. The person who is high on dopamine is absorbed by thoughts of the partner and feels exhilaration, euphoria, sleeplessness, loss of appetite, rapid heart rate, anticipation, and that walking-on-air feeling. What does that sound like? That's somebody who's in love. Unfortunately, this chemically based state of intense physiological arousal can often include some negatives, like mood swings, insecurity, anxiety, possessiveness, jealousy, and fear of rejection.

The point here about love is that the intense, passionate, romantic feelings influenced by the combination of dopamine and adrenalin can't last. The lifespan of these feelings is six to eighteen months maximum if you and your partner are together often. If you are kept apart by circumstances, the feelings may last longer. But our bodies can't generally handle an intense arousal of the sympathetic nervous system for very long.

The third hormone system is based on oxytocin, which men and women release at orgasm and which women release while breastfeeding. This is the hormone that influences security, intimacy, and attachment, which are necessary for successful parenting.

So don't beat yourself up if you don't feel the same degree of lust for your partner that you used to. Instead, get some regular physical exercise to boost your dopamine and try the exercises for orgasm in this book to boost your endorphins and your sexual desire for your partner.

Conclusions about Love

How can these theories about love affect your sex life? They can help you analyze your relationship by asking some questions. Maybe one of the reasons your sex life with your partner isn't everything that it could be is that you and your partner are lacking some major dimension of love, or you and your partner don't share the same view of love. Go through the theories one by one. Make up some questions for yourself based on each theory. It might be a good idea to jot down your thoughts in a journal.

Do you feel romantic passion for your partner or did you in the past? Do you and your partner share the same intimacy that friends have? Are you truly committed to staying in your relationship and to honoring your promises to each other?

Does your relationship have all three components—passion, intimacy, and commitment? If so, lucky you. Or are you still at the stage where you are merely infatuated with your partner? Are you friends but don't really feel anything sexual for each other? Are you afraid to be totally vulnerable sexually with your partner because you feel unsure about the level of commitment you both have to the relationship?

These and many other questions arise from a study of Sternberg's Triangular Theory of love. Asking yourself these questions and others like them and being able to answer them honestly may provide a real eye-opener for you.

Questions are suggested by the other theories as well. For example, when you and your partner say "I love you" to each other, are you talking about the same thing? What's your primary lovestyle and what do you believe is your partner's primary lovestyle?

How do you believe your childhood upbringing affected the way you view sexual relationships as an adult? Would you characterize your earliest relationship with a caregiver as a secure attachment, an anxious attachment, or an avoidant attachment?

Think back to how and when you fell in love with your partner. Was it love at first sight or were you friends first? Did you fall in love in an unusual setting—what in the movies they would call a "cute meet"? If your current sexual relationship is lacking some of the spark it had in the beginning, it might be because you originally fell in love in a setting where emotions were running very high and misattribution was at work.

Is your current sex life with your partner characterized primarily by lust, elation, or intimacy? It could be that you are at a stage of your relationship where child-raising pressures are high and so the need for emotional intimacy and trust is paramount. Recognize that lust and elation might return if you give them a chance by injecting an element of risk or uncertainty into your relationship.

What can you do with this information? You can start a dialogue with your partner about these topics after you have both written down your thoughts. You and your partner may be surprised to find that you have very different views on the subject, and sharing those views could bring you closer together and perhaps highlight how you might alter your views to make your sex life better.

Another thing you could do in the context of journaling is to write your own love story. Write the story of how you and your partner met and fell in love with each other. Be sure to include how you felt (or didn't feel). A great guide to help you with this task is a book called *Love Is a Story,* by Robert Sternberg (of the Triangular Theory). (It is listed in the "Suggested Reading" section.) Sternberg believes that the kind of relationship we create depends on the unconscious love stories we have carried within us since childhood. This is a great book that I have found very helpful for people who are trying to get insight into their relationships.

Sexual Healing

Sex is good for you. I'll bet a funny thing happens on the road to making love better and better: You wake up one morning and you notice that your skin is glowing and that you and your beloved are radiating well-being. Regular practice of the sensate-focus techniques can do this and much more.

As you've no doubt experienced, sensate focus is very relaxing. If you are able to set aside time for one to three sessions per week, you may even notice that you become conditioned to this level of relaxation and more resistant to physical and psychological stress.

The sensate-focus program provides you with regular exposure to the healing power of touch. Back in Chapter 2 I talked about how essential touch is to good health. In addition, the exercises in this book provide your brain with the stimulation of learning something new—which can return a rejuvenating freshness to the rest of your life.

And, of course, sensate-focus exercises provide you with ample doses of life-affirming physical pleasure. You may find that you feel more at home in your body than ever.

The sensate-focus exercises also help you and your partner strengthen your love for each other, as you learn to communicate better, build trust, and become more and more intimate. Research shows that a loving relationship with a committed partner is perhaps the single strongest psychological predictor of resistance to illness and increased longevity. Clearly, the time you spend practicing these exercises brings benefits above and beyond becoming better lovers. From watching my clients, I know that the gains spill over into other areas of life.

Did you know, for instance, that this kind of pressure-free sexual activity is one of the best treatments for stress, anxiety, and depression? A healthy, satisfying sexual relationship can also increase your confidence and build your self-esteem. I have seen clients' lives transformed as they became more comfortable about their sexuality and more confident about themselves. The sexual energy that our bodies can create is so basic it enlivens everything about us when given the space for full expression.

Making love is just as regenerative for the body as it is for the psyche. Research has shown that it can help boost immunity, improve cardiovascular fitness, lessen premenstrual syndrome, and dissolve aches and pains. This is because sexual activity helps you release endorphins, the body's natural painkillers.

Learning the sensate-focus exercises together can even help heal a troubled relationship. You simply can't do them well unless you learn to temporarily shut out the world and also concentrate totally on each other. Gradually, you get into the habit of setting aside time to be with one another in a pleasurable way and to communicate honestly about your needs and feelings. Research shows that people who know how to communicate their feelings in both verbal and nonverbal ways are healthier—both mentally and physically.

You can learn to intensify the healing power of sex by consciously focusing on it when you and your partner make love. Some esoteric Eastern traditions even prescribe certain positions and sexual exercises to heal specific organs. While that topic is beyond the scope of this book, I would like to teach you a simple way to experience the healing power of sex.

There is little that can do more to boost your sense of well-being than knowing that your partner cares for you and desires you sexually. One way to express this to each other is to take turns making love to each other. Do it in a way that allows you to give yourself 100 percent to the experience.

Have your partner lie back and relax. Lovingly lock your gaze on your partner's eyes as you psychologically draw your partner in and compel him or her to focus on what you are doing. The more you enjoy what you're doing and the more intently you focus, the more effective this will be.

Caress your partner's body with your hands. Bend over and place your ear on top of your partner's chest so you can hear his or her heartbeat. Maintain as much body contact as you can. As you start to caress your partner's genitals, keep your ear or a hand on his or her heart. Or keep your face up against your partner's face. Maintain this contact as you begin to have gentle, focused intercourse with your partner.

As you make love, concentrate all of your mental energy toward healing and nurturing your partner psychologically. This is very different from worrying about whether your partner likes what you are doing. Here, you are directing all of your positive sexual energy toward making your lover feel good rather than trying to make your lover feel good about you because you are using the "right" technique or touching in the "right" place.

If you both make love with the intention to focus your innate healing abilities on each other, it can be very powerful. You might even feel the healing energy that you have created together as an intensified current between you. This type of union is intensely fulfilling. Yet you can have an even deeper experience of sexual communion. It's called ecstasy.

Ecstasy

Ecstatic sex is a level of sexual experience beyond arousal, beyond the intense pleasure of orgasm, and even beyond mutuality and intimacy. It comes unexpectedly during intercourse, and most typically, just at the point of orgasm. There is no mistaking it when it happens.

You and your partner may feel yourselves becoming so close that you merge into one, transcending the limits of your bodies. Or you alone may feel the bliss shooting up your spine and catapulting you into a dimension of experience you can only describe as cosmic. I have experienced this myself, and it's hard to put into words.

I've found it most like the Buddhist descriptions of the state of being totally free from desire. It is a state of pleasure so intense that although it may be accompanied by orgasm, you really don't know whether you're having an orgasm or not. And you both turn to each other and say, "Did you feel that? What was that?"

Spiritual experiences are so highly personal that I cannot describe a typical ecstatic moment. But here are ways my clients have described it:

"While my husband and I were making love, I had several orgasms in a row, and then I just seemed to stay in this orgasmic state. I felt like I was there for several minutes, although it couldn't have been more than a few seconds. My husband told me my eyes glazed over. It was like being in an altered state of consciousness."

"I saw God, Buddha, and Allah." (Yes, he was being metaphorical.)

"When I got close to orgasm, I felt this white-hot light start at my tailbone and slowly move up my spine. When it got to my head, I had the orgasm. It was one of the strangest things I've ever felt. I asked my wife if she felt anything strange, and she said she felt almost like both of us lifted about six inches off the bed."

Some people have said they see intense colors or images. Others hear music. Some feel an overwhelming sense of connection with creation. These experiences are probably due in part to the release of endorphins, because besides killing pain, endorphins can cause intensely pleasurable states.

Ecstatic sex is not something you can make happen. Every time I've experienced it, it has been unplanned. It seems to require a certain level of both physical and emotional intimacy. Yet I do know that the sensate-focus approach is much more likely to lead to ecstatic sex than a perform-ance-oriented approach. This is because the state of mind that is a prerequisite for ecstatic sex requires that you be in the here and now and 100 percent focused on your sensations.

The ecstasy associated with intense sexual experiences is the focus of a form of yoga known as *tantra*. Tantric yoga emphasizes reuniting the basic male and female principles in the cosmos through specific practices and postures. Sexual energy is harnessed in a way that can lead practitioners to transcendence and ecstasy. Tantra can be practiced by both couples and individuals. After you have completed the exercises in this book, you may wish to learn more about tantric yoga or tantric sex in order to go further in your exploration of your sexual selves. Margo Anand's book *The Art of Sexual Ecstasy: The Path of Sacred Sexuality for Western Lovers* (listed in the "Suggested Reading" section) is a worthwhile book on the subject.

Going Forward from Here

Through the exercises in this book you have learned to enjoy touching and being touched. You have learned to let go, to relax and enjoy your own sex-ual response, and to savor your desire for your partner. Through the peak-ing and plateauing exercises you have also learned to make the most of your arousal and orgasm patterns. And through it all, you have learned to communicate with your partner and become deeply intimate. Where do you go from here?

I recommend that you continue the breathing, PC muscle, and bond-ing exercises daily for the rest of your life. They will keep your senses, your body, and your passion alive and afire.

Return to the other exercises as you need or desire to. Remember that you can always count on the focusing caresses to relax you. Since you have learned peaking and plateauing, your body has been conditioned and will naturally respond in this way. This gives you infinite options for ways to make love, based on what you have learned about your sexual-pleasure cycle and its possibilities.

Sexual expression can have an overwhelmingly positive effect on your life. It frees you, enriches you, and opens up new dimensions of your humanity. I hope the sensual and sexual activities you have learned in this book will help you enjoy the many healthy and empowering aspects of sexuality: desire, arousal, orgasm, intimacy, and, of course, pleasure.

Suggested Reading

Margo Anand, *The Art of Sexual Ecstasy: The Path of Sacred Sexuality for Western Lovers* (New York: Tarcher, 1989).

——, *The Art of Sexual Magic* (New York: Putnam, 1995).

Roy Baumeister and Dianne Tice, *The Social Dimension of Sex* (Needham Heights, MA: Allyn and Bacon, 2001).

Mantak Chia and Douglas Abrams Arava, *The Multi-Orgasmic Man* (San Francisco, CA: HarperCollins, 1996).

Edward Eichel and Phillip Nobile, *The Perfect Fit: How to Achieve Mutual Fulfillment and Monogamous Passion Through the New Intercourse* (New York: Donald J. Fine, 1992).

Carol Ellison, *Women's Sexualities* (Oakland, CA: New Harbinger, 2000).

Beverly Engel, *Sensual Sex* (Alameda, CA: Hunter House, 1999).

Yvonne K. Fulbright, *The Hot Guide to Safer Sex* (Alameda, CA: Hunter House, 2003).

Paul Joannides, *Guide to Getting It On!* (Waldport, OR: Goofy Foot Press, 2000).

Barbara Keesling, *How to Make Love All Night (and Drive a Woman Wild)* (New York: HarperCollins, 1994).

——, *Talk Sexy to the One You Love (and Drive Each Other Wild in Bed)* (New York: HarperCollins, 1996).

Jack Morin, *Anal Pleasure and Health* (San Francisco, CA: Down There Press, 1998).

Lou Paget, *How to Give Her Absolute Pleasure* (New York: Broadway Books, 2000).

Christa Schulte, *Tantric Sex for Women* (Alameda, CA: Hunter House, 2005).

Robert Sternberg, *Love Is a Story* (New York: Oxford University Press, 1998).

Deborah Sundahl, *Female Ejaculation and the G-Spot* (Alameda, CA: Hunter House, 2003).

Debbie Tideman, *The X-Spot Orgasm* (Chicago, IL: Jetex Publishing Company, 1998).

Leonore Tiefer, *Sex Is Not a Natural Act* (Boulder, CO: Westview Press, 1995).

Sources for
Sex Toys

I don't endorse any specific company. I've listed the larger companies that have websites in case you are too shy to purchase adult products in person. If you're not too shy, you can probably find an adult store in your area.

Good Vibrations
(800) 289-8423
Website: www.goodvibes.com

Lady Calston
1051 Clinton St. #204
Buffalo NY 14206
(800) 690-5239
Fax: (416) 398-0407
Website: www.calston.com

Intimate Treasures
(415) 863-5002
Website: www.intimatetreasures.com

Xandria Collection
Department C 1096
P.O. Box 31039
San Francisco CA 94131-9988
Website: www.xandria.com

Adam and Eve
P.O. Box 900
Department C S 357
Carrboro NC 27510
(800) 274-0333
Website: www.adameve.com

Index

ORDER FORM

10% DISCOUNT on orders of $50 or more —
20% DISCOUNT on orders of $150 or more —
30% DISCOUNT on orders of $500 or more —
On cost of books for fully prepaid orders

NAME

ADDRESS

CITY/STATE   ZIP/POSTCODE

PHONE   COUNTRY (outside of U.S.)

TITLE	QTY	PRICE	TOTAL
Sexual Pleasure 2nd ed. (paper)		@ $ 14.95	
*Pocket Sexuality Library *special offer**		@ $ 25.00	

Prices subject to change without notice

Please list other titles below:

		@ $	
		@ $	
		@ $	
		@ $	
		@ $	
		@ $	
		@ $	

Check here to receive our book catalog ☐   *FREE*

Shipping Costs

By Priority Mail: first book $4.50, each additional book $1.00
By UPS and to Canada: first book $5.50, each additional book $1.50
For rush orders and other countries call us at (510) 865-5282

TOTAL
Less discount @_____%   (   )
TOTAL COST OF BOOKS
Calif. residents add sales tax
Shipping & handling
TOTAL ENCLOSED

Please pay in U.S. funds only

☐ Check   ☐ Visa   ☐ MasterCard   ☐ Discover

Card #_____ Exp. date_____

Signature_____

Complete and mail to:
Hunter House Inc., Publishers
PO Box 2914, Alameda CA 94501-0914
Website: www.hunterhouse.com
Orders: (800) 266-5592 or email: ordering@hunterhouse.com
Phone (510) 865-5282   Fax (510) 865-4295

SXP2-12/2004